FIONA .... :005.
She was first a concert violinist, then studied at the Universities of
Oxford, where she won the Newdigate Prize, and Nijmegen,
where she received a PhD in the philosophy of language. This
research arose from her pioneering residencies in health care, for
which she is recognised internationally. She has published fifteen
books, of which the most recent are: *Common Prayer* (Carcanet
2007, shortlisted for the T.S. Eliot Prize, poem shortlisted for a
Forward Prize), and *On Listening* (essays, 2007). She was the
founding editor of *Orient Express*, a journal of contemporary
writing from the former Soviet bloc, and has co-edited an
anthology of younger Central European poets. Her other transla-
tions include Jaan Kaplinski's *Evening Brings Everything Back*. She
has herself been widely translated, with ten books in translation,
most recently *Distanchijta Meshdy Nas* (Balkani, 2009) and *Zweimal
sieben Gedichte* (Weiser Verlag, 2009). She was AHRC Research
Fellow at Oxford Brookes University 2002–5 and CAPITAL Fellow
in Creativity at the University of Warwick in 2007–8. She
contributes regularly to *The Guardian*, *The Irish Times* and other
periodicals. In 2009, she received a Cholmondeley Award.

A century of great poetry from Carcanet Press

Carcanet Press publishes the most comprehensive and diverse list of modern poetry from the last hundred years. Carcanet authors include:

Chinua Achebe	Hugh MacDiarmid
John Ashbery	Sorley MacLean
Sujata Bhatt	Bill Manhire
Eavan Boland	Charlotte Mew
Joseph Brodsky	Christopher Middleton
Paul Celan	Czesław Miłosz
Inger Christensen	Robert Minhinnick
Gillian Clarke	Edwin Morgan
Donald Davie	Sinead Morrissey
Hilda Doolittle (H.D.)	Les Murray
Thomas Kinsella	Frank O'Hara
Iain Crichton Smith	Cesare Pavese
Elaine Feinstein	Octavio Paz
Louise Glück	Laura Riding
Jorie Graham	Rainer Maria Rilke
W.S. Graham	Lynette Roberts
Robert Graves	Fiona Sampson
Ivor Gurney	C.H. Sisson
Marilyn Hacker	Muriel Spark
Sophie Hannah	Edward Thomas
John Heath-Stubbs	Charles Tomlinson
Elizabeth Jennings	Marina Tsvetaeva
Brigit Pegeen Kelly	Sylvia Townsend Warner
Mimi Khalvati	William Carlos Williams
R.F. Langley	Nikolai Zabolotsky

Visit **www.carcanet.co.uk** for a full catalogue of titles, news, reviews, author interviews and audio material. Order any title online and receive a 10% discount and free UK postage and packaging.

For regular poetry news and a poem of the week, sign up to the Carcanet e-letter by emailing **info@carcanet.co.uk**.

A Century of
Poetry Review

Edited with an introduction by
Fiona Sampson

CARCANET

POETRY REVIEW

First published in Great Britain in 2009 by
Carcanet Press Limited
Alliance House
Cross Street
Manchester M2 7AQ

in association with
Poetry Review
The Poetry Society
22 Betterton Street
London WC2H 9BX

A CIP catalogue record for this book is available from the British Library
ISBN 978 1 84777 016 5

The publisher acknowledges financial assistance from Arts Council England

Supported by
ARTS COUNCIL
ENGLAND

Typeset in Monotype Dante by XL Publishing Services, Tiverton
Printed and bound in England by SRP Ltd, Exeter

Contents

Introduction
For God's Sake, Do Something!

It was going to be easy: I would simply cherry-pick one hundred highlights from the *Poetry Review* archive. After all, a centenary anthology is essentially celebratory. It has a licence to echo the curatorial practice of great travelling exhibitions, like the Treasures of Tutankhamun or, more recently, Treasures of the Winter Palace. Presenting important pieces out of context isn't just Cook's-touring for the MP3 generation, I thought: it can also bring these things to an audience which doesn't have access to them in their original setting.

Very few libraries hold a complete archive of *Poetry Review*. The Poetry Society's own holdings are no longer quite complete: one can't help wondering how much this has to do with its public access remit. The British Library holds a set, but other copyright libraries do not. The holdings of private collectors remain private.

Even with unlimited access, reading one hundred years of *Poetry Review* is a sizeable, and not always particularly digestible, task. In part, this is because there's simply so much of the magazine. It was originally published monthly, then from 1915 to 1951 bi-monthly – although in a format smaller than today's – and didn't become quarterly until 1952. But this indigestibility also comes from a peculiar unevenness of quality. When editorial control has been taken in-house, either through direct editing by the Chair of the Society (during the long reign of Galloway Kyle, from 1916 to 1947) or by a house editorial board (as under the chairmanship of Thomas Moult, 1952–62), the magazine ceases to be a literary review and becomes an organisational mouthpiece. Yet where it is edited by a serious poet or critic, whatever their poetic orientation, it has contributed to literary history, transcending passing organisational concerns to rehearse contemporary attitudes to poetry itself.

Sometimes fussy, by turns cantankerous and charming, the *Review*, read over its lifetime, emerges as a fascinating, infuriating institution, conscious of its responsibility to be what Michael Schmidt has called the 'magazine of record'. Its public role leads it to comment on everything from the appointments of Laureates and Professors of Poetry to the responsibilities of editors;[1] to publish literary memoirs of purely specialist interest as well as of literary celebrity,[2] and to print newly discovered posthumous work, whether by Scott or Sorley.

The *Review* was founded, as *The Poetical Gazette*, in 1909. (Issue title pages carried the legend 'First published as the *Poetical Gazette*, May, 1909' until the 1930s.) It was, and has for a hundred years continued to be, published by the Poetry Society of Great Britain – originally the Poetry Recital Society – whose centenary it shares.

Early issues of the *Gazette* made it clear that this was a members' newsletter. In 1911, however, the Society invited the poet Harold Monro to co-publish – and edit – the magazine. Monro had been living in Italy and fretting over the state of British poetry when Maurice Hewlett told him, in what has become the magazine's founding myth, 'If you feel like that, for God's sake go back to England and do something about it.' Monro's response was a proposal for 'an independent monthly such as the Society required, which might prove of direct benefit to its members, though not its actual property'. *Poetry Review* was launched (with the *Gazette* as a supplement) in January 1912. That year was to prove extraordinary and dynamic. Monro engaged the major literary talents of his day – the first issue alone included essays by Edmund Gosse, Ford Madox Hueffer, John Masefield and Ezra Pound – as well as supporting the young poets of the Georgian movement. When Ezra Pound introduced early work by William Carlos Williams, he commented in so doing that 'Having said recently that no man now living in America writes anything that is of interest to the serious artist, [...] considering the tolerance accorded in England to such authors as Mr Noyes, Mr Abercrombie and Mr Figgis, I think there are a number of American works which might with safety be

offered to the island market.' This provoked a furious response
from Rupert Brooke: 'Lascelles Abercrombie [...] is a poet, alive,
and that is more than can be said of most of us. [...] The "toler-
ance" one accords to [such writing] is the tolerance thirsty men
give to wine, or flowers to sunlight.'³ It's certainly not easy to hear
grounds for this trans-Atlantic complacency in the opening stanza,
characteristic for Pound's selection, of 'The Fool's Song', which
hardly foreshadows the later Williams's 'No ideas but in things':

> I tried to put a bird in a cage,
>   O fool that I am!
>   For the bird was truth.
> Sing merrily Truth; I tried to put
>   Truth in a cage!⁴

According to T.S. Eliot, Monro assumed:

> [...] a role of importance and value during the period of several
> years up to 1914. He cared passionately though not always quite
> discriminatingly about poetry and was one of the few poets of
> whom it can be said that they cared more for poetry in general
> than for their own work. He not only helped in giving publicity
> to what have been called the 'Georgian Poets' but to the work
> of poets of a more advanced type. People like Pound, Flint,
> Aldington and the other 'Imagists' [...]. Flint's chronicles and
> reviews of contemporary French poetry which were published
> in Monro's magazine did a great deal [...] to arouse an interest
> in French poetry in this country [...] anyone whose poetry he
> liked was sure of his support.⁵

However, after just twelve months, in which 'I practically sold
myself to the Society [...] I consented to defray expenses for one
year [...]'⁶ Monro was ousted by the Poetry Society. At their
suggestion, he had signed no formal contract, and their decision
was only revealed to him when he saw its announcement in the
proofs of the *Gazette*'s December issue. Not surprisingly, the
rupture was permanent, and Monro appended to that announce-
ment the news that he would instead found the quarterly *Poetry
and Drama*. Nevertheless, plans for the subsequently-famous

Poetry Bookshop at 35, Devonshire Street in London WC1 – a lease Monro had signed in the *Review*'s name – continued.[7] The shop, which was originally intended to 'sell [...] what we have recommended' in the *Review*'s pages, included office space for the magazine, and a hall in which, during 1912, '*Poetry Review* Lectures' were given by, among others, T.E. Hulme and the Irish Republican Darrell Figgis.

In a move which continues to pose questions about intellectual copyright for editorial 'brands', the Poetry Society replaced Monro with Stephen Phillips: a kind of compromise candidate. Undoubtedly an independent literary editor, he was nevertheless sufficiently in tune with the Society's sensibilities to stay the course for three years. The magazine took shape accordingly. As well as publishing such poets as Laurence Binyon, John Redwood-Anderson and Irving Tree, Philips committed a substantial proportion of his war-time issues to verse by Forces personnel.

The literary knockabout of its first four years perfectly demonstrates the pitfalls of picking a *Review* 'Top Hundred'. British poetry of the last hundred years hasn't been characterised by consensus. The general reader might expect to view a gallery of the most famous names to appear in the magazine. But *PR* didn't, of course, necessarily publish their finest work. What to make, for example, of a somewhat derivative, if sincere, poem on 'Ypres' by Arthur Conan Doyle? Forgotten contexts, though eminently researchable, place other pieces in parentheses. Aleister Crowley's version of 'Villon's Apology' is occasioned by 'On Reading Stevenson's Essay', and G.K. Chesterton's 'Ballade of Cheerful Boredom' tells us, among other things:

> Let Gallup gallop, bloody spurred,
> Till Bacon owns to *Peter Pan*;
> Let Archer 'spell' till every word
> Looks like a curse from Hindustan;
> Let Robertson, pride of his clan,
> Abolish God – and Tacitus;
> Let Nordau – be a charlatan;
> But these things will not do for us.

…How very true. Meanwhile, specialist readers may hope to find their own tastes particularly catered for: with more work from the *Review*'s radical American canon, for example, by Denise Levertov, Alice Notley, George Oppen, Muriel Rukeyser or eco-Beat Gary Snyder. And then there are the glaring omissions by editors of the time: no Dylan Thomas, no Samuel Beckett except a posthumous fragment; modernism seems (*pace* Pound) a million miles away from the poetic worlds of Brooke or Chesterton.[8]

So this anthology represents not necessarily the most important British poetry of the last hundred years, but rather *what has been seen as* most important. *Poetry Review*'s back-list offers something more than a record of the century's writing. Arranging its highlights broadly in order of publication, and contextualising them with some of the best of the critical 'chatter' of their day, records the *reception* of that writing – by a particular characteristic, and characterising, British readership. This volume is a history of that jockeying between poetries and their reception which is called a mainstream. *Poetry Review*'s position at the heart of British poetry makes it something of a litmus paper for changing tastes and attitudes. Yet there's a bifurcation in the magazine's identity. Although an independent literary publication, it has historically been responsive to the tastes of an organisation with a membership including hobby, or emerging, as well as established, professional writers: at times it must have been a bit like curating Tate Modern with the Cheltenham Watercolour Society in mind. *PR*'s tastes, such as the early resistance to modernism, can appear conservative in retrospect.

And yet the *Review* also charts how the Hardy-Thomas-Larkin succession, with its mastery of pastoral and elegy, continues to provide the tactful 'blue note' in British poetry. It's to this tradition that Britain's Favourite Poets – the Betjemans and Fanthorpes – so intelligently refer, and which today's English elegists (such as Alan Jenkins, Andrew Motion and to some extent John Fuller) sustain. Meanwhile, the demotic, narrative verse of Kipling or Chesterton arguably finds its posterity in the 'anecdotage' of some of the New Generation poets particularly advocated by the *Review* of the 1990s. As art forms tried to adapt themselves to an accelerating complexity of social experience, twentieth-century culture found itself split between mirroring that complexity on one hand, and increasingly deliberate 'accessibility' on the other. The *Review*'s own bifurcated identity, as an independent literary magazine and Society publication, makes it a unique mirror of British poetic taste and practice.

Stephen Phillips was succeeded by Galloway Kyle, who was simultaneously the Society's Chair. For three decades, until 1947, he built the Poetry Society into what claimed to be the largest in the world, with an editorial office in the United States. During his editorship the *Review* masthead incorporated approval from the *Literary Digest*: 'The leading poetry magazine of the world... of international eminence.' Kyle engaged as his American editor Alice Hunt Bartlett, whose surveys of 'Dynamics of American Poetry' appeared from Volume 14 until her death in 1949. He also led a series of initiatives concerned with the history of poetry, such as appeals for a Tennyson Memorial Room in Lincoln Library or to maintain Edgar Allen Poe's cottage in Fordham. However, he was less interested in developments in contemporary British verse. Under his editorship the magazine reviewed, but did not much publish, work by established poets; instead largely printing the work of members, aspirant writers and competition winners. It's arguable that this closer relationship between magazine and Society was what enabled publication to continue, despite paper shortages, through two world wars – or, as a glorious editorial circumlocution from *PR* 5:3 has it, 'The dislocation of peaceful interests.'[9]

Kyle was responsible for at least one conspicuous editorial strength. Among the historical essays, anti-modernist polemic and accounts of Poetry Society dinners and branch meetings, were a number of extended surveys of international poetry. Simos Menardos contributed a lengthy series on Greek verse; Cranmer-Byng wrote on Chinese poetry; Federico Olivero on poetics; Sturge Moore returned to the topic of verse-drama. There were also explorations of poetry from Japan and India which it would be easy to suspect as reductively colonialist, since the actual verse was mediated in each case by a Western essayist, were it not that this was the approach the magazine adopted to *all* international writing.

The *Review* was ahead of its time in another way, too. Long before the 1960s, when poets like Ted Hughes were to advocate working with schoolchildren – even before the 1944 'Butler' Education Act, which opened up education to young people regardless of gender or class, and produced such exemplary arts educationalists as Robin Tanner or Richard Hoggart – the *Review* was pioneering the writing of poetry in schools. In 1914, George Ayles told readers 'How London School Boys Find Expression in Verse'.[10] Soon, children started entering the magazine's Premium Prize competitions. By the 1940s, Mary Holliday was arguing that 'It has been recognised by Professor Cizek in Vienna that there is such a thing as Child Art as distinct from adult art. [...] This creative impulse is for them an essential means of self-expression: its results are not to be judged according to adult standards or conventional rules of merit. Children have been allowed for many years to indulge their creative desires in paint. [...] Yet language is used before paint by most children.'[11]

By the 1940s, a group of repeatedly published poets had come to supply much of the journal's tenor. In Kyle's earliest years, he had included several Noh plays by the Japanese proto-modernist Yone Noguchi. Later regulars included Phoebe Hesketh, Ruth Pitter, Henry Treece, Vernon Watkins and Laurence Whistler. The indefatigable Marie Stopes contributed poems and wrote on Lord Alfred Douglas. Reviews were produced by the editorial team, rather than commissioned from a field of critics and free-lancers. The results were undeniably homogenous, but issues from this time can also read as suffocating and over-determined.

All magazines have a house style, of course. Some – Harold Monro's *Poetry and Drama,* Ian Hamilton's *The Review* (1962–72) and its successor *The New Review* (1974–9), or, today, Michael Schmidt's *PN Review* (founded 1973 as *Poetry Nation*) and *Agenda,* founded by William Cookson and Ezra Pound in 1959 – have as their very *raison d'être* their founding editors' vision of what poetry is. Each delineates its own personal 'for God's sake... do something!' To read the hundred years of *Poetry Review is* to trace lines of influence – and sometimes, succession – both creative and critical. To take an example almost at random: George Barker's 'Letter to the Corpse of Eliot' ends 'I hear you. I hear / you. I hear you'; his nephew John Fairfax asks that we 'Listen' to the younger poets he in turn reviews; while in 1967 the critic John Lehmann returns us to Barker. Groups – almost movements – of poets periodically combine to articulate a new English- or Scottishness: Norman MacCaig's 1966 'Poetry in Scotland' feature is a bench-mark, and that nationhood is in turn refigured by Robert Crawford, W.N. Herbert, Kathleen Jamie and others in the late 1990s. A couple of years earlier, it's fascinating to compare Sean O'Brien[12] and Don Paterson[13] as each squares up to review a figure O'Brien calls 'The Totalizer', Ted Hughes. No less interesting is a 2001 review in which Peter Porter contextualises Sean O'Brien's work with his own earlier suggestion 'that a new school of poetry was emerging which would take up the baton from Auden's thirties generation and bring back intellectualism and populism [...]'.[14] It's as revealing to read E.A. Markham reviewing Stewart Brown's reception of Derek Walcott[15] – tracing a line of intellectual succession – as it is to read Walcott himself.

At the same time, *PR*'s particular remit is to address no one clique or movement, but rather a national audience. It canon-forms by being often almost the only contemporary material available to many with an interest in poetry *and* by working with the best writing. Just as poets may write towards an Ideal Reader, so this readership is a *de facto* check and balance which helps its editor prevent the magazine from talking to itself, or to an in-crowd of initiates.

If Galloway Kyle's response to the readership was to make the magazine the mouthpiece of aspiring writers, one who developed rapidly under this policy was Muriel Spark. She made her first appearance in spring 1946 with the Premium Prize-winning poem, 'On Seeing the Picasso-Matisse Exhibition, London, December, 1945'.[16] Thereafter she became a regular contributor. She also started to review. Still, it must have been a surprise when she became Kyle's successor as editor. Naturally, Spark understood the link between critical and creative practice. In an editorial on 'Criticism, Effect and Morals', she argues that the critic tends to compensate for his 'anxiety' about contemporary verse by over-analysis, 'as if he were to examine a tear-drop under a microscope in an endeavour to analyse grief'.[17]

Spark also initiated the payment of fees for published work. At a stroke, this professionalised the *Review*. According to some accounts, it was also what caused Spark to be replaced by John Gawsworth in 1949. As her *alter ego* in *Loitering with Intent*, read as a *roman à clef* of her time at the *Review*, says, 'The wages [...] offered were of 1936 vintage, and this was 1949, modern times. But I pushed up the starting price a little, and took the job for its promise of a totally new experience.'[18] Her 1992 memoir, *Curriculum Vitae*, reports that Spark had to resign in order to be paid. The magazine was not to appoint another woman as editor for over half a century.[19]

Gawsworth, who early acknowledged Monro as his 'mentor', was, like Spark, a serious editor. Volumes 39–42 see the first appearances in the magazine of Dannie Abse, Frances Cornford, Lawrence Durrell, Robert Graves, John Heath-Stubbs, Vernon Scannell and, perhaps surprisingly, Hugh MacDiarmid. Gawsworth was succeeded by an editorial committee chaired by Thomas Moult. A decade later, in 1962, John Smith took over, and the magazine sprang back to life. In 1966, Smith was in turn succeeded by Derek Parker, who dropped the definite article from the *Review*'s title. This was a high middle period of British twentieth-century poetry – then widely affected by the Movement and inflected by the BBC, where George Macbeth was in charge of poetry programming from 1955 to 1976 – and *PR* was publishing Jack Clemo, Veronica Forrest, Elizabeth Jennings, George MacBeth (alas, for this anthology, chiefly in a series of verse-novellas), Rosemary Tonks, and Jon Silkin, alongside critical writing by Robert Graecen, Philip Hobsbaum and David Holbrook.

As if to demonstrate that the 1970s were a transitional passage in British poetry, 1971 (Adrian Henri, Martin Booth, Anthony Rudolf and Eric Mottram) and 1978 (Edwin Brock, Harry Chambers, Douglas Dunn and Roger Garfitt) were years of guest editors. Each also identified a future editor. Under Mottram (1972–7), the *Review* was at the centre of the radical poetics of the Anglo-American 'Poetry Revival'. Mottram published Ginsberg, Levertov, Snyder, Ferlinghetti and Rukeyser. From 1975 to 1977

he adopted an A4-format, whose cover doodles and internal use of
typescript suggested a notebook, work-in-progress shared among
friends. However, his tenure also crystalised frictions which
existed within the Society, and within British poetry, between
radical and more organically tradition-led poetics.[20] In many ways,
these frictions were more dangerous for the *Review* than those
which had been played out between modernism and its detractors.
What had happened before the Second World War had sometimes
caused literary writers and critics to be opposed to the amateur
writer and reader. Now, however, the profession itself was split
between remarkably evenly-balanced forces: both of them repre-
sented among the *Review*'s contributors and readers and within the
Poetry Society's staff and Board.

Strangely responding to a thirty-year cycle, this struggle for the
control of the poetry mainstream has been echoed a third time in
the final decade of the *Review*'s maiden century. The rise of
performance poetry has largely excluded a second generation of
poets drawing on oral traditions – the successors to figures like
Linton Kwesi Johnson, Grace Nichols or Benjamin Zephaniah:
particularly, but not exclusively, Black British young poets – from
what it dismissively calls 'page poetry'. While the *Review* records
this shift too, it must often do so by omissions and silences.

The savagery of the wars which marred Mottram's tenure
wasn't repeated under the custodianship of Roger Garfitt, who
inaugurated a succession of poet-editors in the 1980s. Garfitt was
succeeded by Andrew Motion (1982–3), Mick Imlah (1984–6) and
Peter Forbes, who came to the role as a poet but whose lengthy
editorial tenure (1986–2002) came to define not only the tastes of
a poetic generation but his own professional identity. Motion and
Imlah passed brilliantly through, on their way to becoming succes-
sive poetry editors at Chatto and Windus – and later, in Imlah's
case, the *Times Literary Supplement*. With the discreet, firm hand of
intelligence, each managed to publish the poets who mattered
then and who still matter more than two decades on. They
achieved this in slightly different ways. Motion was perhaps the
shade more conservative force, commissioning surviving greats:
he published Philip Larkin's notorious review of Sylvia Plath,

'Horror Poet', and commissioned 'A Birthday Tribute' for Larkin's sixtieth from Harold Pinter, Gavin Ewart, A.N. Wilson and others. Imlah was very much the bright young man, identifying certain ideas, such as Englishness – as well as writing by peers such as Alan Hollinghurst – as particularly interesting. His *Review* is gossipy, editorial and vigorous in its assumption of high standards. An article titled 'Woman Wins', for example, opens: 'The National Poetry Society Competition has again (see last year) failed to unearth convincing winners from a total of 12,000 submissions.'[21]

Under Peter Forbes, the *Review* experienced perhaps its greatest period of editorial transparency. This is not to say that it was more generous than usual to poetics which differed from editorial taste, but rather that it perfectly reflected a zeitgeist. The mid-1980s saw some Central European poetries, which had first been advocated by Ted Hughes and Daniel Weissbort, move into the British mainstream. *PR* published Miroslav Holub, repeatedly, alongside Jaan Kaplinski, Piotr Sommer and Nobel laureates Miłosz and Szymborska. But the Forbes years are perhaps best characterised by 1994's New Generation promotion, based on the very successful *Granta Best of Young British Novelists* (1983, 1993, and indeed 2003). Of course, there are many more publishing resources, and readers, for fiction than for poetry. While the New Gen promotion, which was intended to resist 'the last gasp of a system of patronage',[22] made the careers of the twenty baby-boomers it nominated, it also sucked necessary oxygen from the rest of British poetry. A generation of arts administrators and teachers of poetry growing up on the *Review* lost a wider sense of what else was going on, especially among older and younger poets.

Culturally, though, this was an interesting moment. Not only did it mark the ascendancy of league-tables and the arrival of sales-trump-all in poetry; it was also the first time that a generation or group emerged which was not driven by shared artistic agenda but constructed by external forces, in particular a narrative about 'success'. Not surprisingly, when Peter Forbes moved on, the *Review* experienced a rebound. From 2002 to 2005, *PR* was steered in a rigorously anti-poetry-lite, criticism-led direction by an academic, David Herd, and a member of the *TLS* editorial team,

Robert Potts. Potts and Herd were interested in post-modernity, critical intelligence and intersections with sophisticated visual culture. They were unafraid of seriousness and risk, elements which were at enough of a premium for their editorial policies to be read, sometimes, as more uncompromising than they in fact were.

Since 2005, the magazine has attempted to reconcile dual responsibilities: to represent the whole range of good practice in the country, and to steer and shape the mainstream. To show what's going on and influence it at the same time may sound paradoxical; but responsive leadership – a bit like an elective democracy – makes of canon-formation something incremental, and organic, achieved through quarterly development rather than the hit-and-run intervention of an anthology. As an early Monro editorial 'Notes and Comments' says:

> We continue to hope, however, that the existence in England
> of a periodical organised, unlike any other English periodical,
> for the publication of only good poetry (when such is forth-
> coming), regardless of subject or style, may act as a stimulus and
> an encouragement to English poets, both known and unknown.[23]

What will *Poetry Review* look like over its next century? It's difficult, and perhaps even beside the point, to speculate.[24] As Pound said in an early issue, 'To give sound criticism of a man's work after it is published is so difficult a task that we find it rarely done well, but to criticise a man's work before it is written is a task so very difficult that even I hesitate before the undertaking.'[25] Whatever shifts are taking place in British poetry at the moment – greater poetic diversity, the renaissance of the through-composed collection and verse-novel, neo-Romanticism and its engagement with the authentic, or spiritual – will be way-markers for the next five years at most. Editors are often asked what new talent they've 'discovered'. But, unlike the editor of a book-list, whose work *is* to nurture the individual development of particular poets, the magazine editor's task is not *primarily* to discover and nurture *individual* talent, but to support *all* fine poets in writing well at every stage in their careers. Movements in poetry arise at particular cultural-historical moments, rather than continually. The editor's role is to help keep the whole field healthy and vibrant. The radical, disciplined attention he or she employs includes the ability to concentrate that attention wherever it's needed: incidentally the best insurance that the next thing, whatever it will be, can emerge undistorted.

To read with this active sense of responsibility requires a strong sense of the reading self, that reflexive experience of consciousness and its agency which used to be called subjectivity. Editors are, after all, primarily readers – albeit of a peculiarly committed kind. Whatever professional discipline they bring to bear, each has an individual's perspective on what is influential, what over-rated, and what unmissable. To edit is to participate in the culture of the day. And so, as this shows, is to read.

Fiona Sampson
January 2009

Notes

1 For example, 'On the Reviewing of *The Poetry Review*', PR 17:4 (1926), pp. 277–9; or Yevgeny Vinokurov's 'Poetry Editor', *PR* 92:1 (2002), pp. 5–6.

2 These include Ernest Hartley Coleridge's memoir 'The Genesis of the Ancient Mariner' (*PR* 2:1 (1913), pp. 11–15); Rosalind Wade's memoir 'The Parton Street Poets' (*PR* 54:4 (1963–4), pp. 290–7); Ruthven Todd's 'Memories of Norman Cameron' (*PR* 76:1–2 (1986), pp. 95–7).

3 *PR* 1:11 (1912), pp. 519–20.

4 *PR* 1:10 (1912), p. 484.

5 Marvin Magalaner, 'Harold Monro and "The Poetry Review"', *PR* 40:5 (1949), pp. 340–7.

6 Magalaner, p. 342.

7 Devonshire Street, off Theobald's Road, has since been flattened and renamed Boswell Street.

8 Yet 'Prufrock' was to be published less than four years after the magazine's foundation – and, what's more, by *Poetry*, the *Review*'s American peer. Harold Monro: 'We welcome with enthusiasm the foundation in Chicago of *Poetry*, a "Magazine of Verse, to be published for the encouragement of the art."' ('Notes and Comments', *PR* 1:9 (1912), p. 423). Stephen Phillips: '*Poetry*, the Chicago magazine of verse which is in the happy position of being handsomely guaranteed and assured of a comparatively long life' (*PR* 3:6 (1913), p. 296).

9 So it is ironic that it was Monro who had been accused of just this policy in a stinging review by *The New Age*: 'Each month this *Review* belauds verse-writers whose achievements should have been kept as a private family joy' (*PR* 1:8 (1912), p. 353).

10 *PR* 5:5 (1914), pp. 185–9.

11 Mary Holliday, 'Verse-Writing in Schools', *PR* 36 (1945), pp. 225–9.

12 'The Totalizer', *PR* 84:3 (1994), pp. 58–9.

13 'Strathspeys and Death Metal', *PR* 85:1 (1995), pp. 32–3.

14 'At the Helm', *PR* 91:1 (2001), pp. 61–2.

15 Extracted here on pp. 227–9.

16 *PR* 37:2 (1946), pp. 165–7.

17 *PR* 39:1 (1948), p. 4.

18 Muriel Spark, *Loitering with Intent* (London, Virago, 2007), pp. 4–5.

19 Although Tracy Warr co-edited Mick Imlah's first three issues.

20 Cf. Peter Barry, *Poetry Wars: British Poetry of the 1970s and the Battle of Earls Court* (Cambridge, Salt, 2006).

21 *PR* 73:4 (1984), p. 37. The 'woman' was Carol Ann Duffy.

22 According to Peter Forbes in *PR* 84:1 (1994), pp. 4–6.

23 *PR* 1:9 (1912), p. 423.

24 And questions about digital format are beside the point here: *Poetry Review* will be published in whatever format equivalent texts appear.

25 *PR* 1:10 (1912), p. 481.

A Note on the Text

The styles and conventions used in *Poetry Review* have varied throughout a hundred years of publication. In general, the pieces collected here are reproduced as they were originally published. Typographic conventions such as the use of double or single quotation marks and the style for dashes have been standardised, and minor typographical errors in the originals have been silently corrected. Any other editorial interventions are shown in square brackets, except in 'Adrienne Rich in conversation with Sarah Maguire', pp. 246–9; Anne Stevenson, 'Sylvia Plath's Word Games', pp. 249–54; 'Ian Hamilton in conversation with Gregory LeStage', pp. 271–5; and Marjorie Perloff, 'It Must Change', pp. 352–7, where annotations in square brackets are as the original. Where texts have been excerpted, the omissions are indicated by ellipses in square brackets. Notes to poems, essays and articles are original, although the bibliographic notes to reviews have been made consistent in format.

Sources of texts are cited by volume, issue number and year. Different systems have been used during the lifetime of the magazine, and intervals of publication have varied, so references do not always appear in a consistent format. Many early issues of *Poetry Review* have been bound into volumes without their title pages, so precise dating has not always been possible.

A Century of
Poetry Review

from the Preface to the first issue, *Poetry Review*
Harold Monro

[...]

Time is ripe for the forging of a weapon of criticism, and for an emphatic enunciation of literary standards. Poetry should be, once more, seriously and reverently discussed in its relation to life, and the same tests and criteria be applied to it as to the other arts.

This periodical will aim not so much at producing poetry as at stimulating the desire for it. We shall strive to create an atmosphere. We shall attempt to co-ordinate the bases of thought from which poetry at last emerges. We shall seek to encourage the poets, and dissuade the poetasters from rushing into print. We believe the multiplicity of useless books a most melancholy weakness of the time, and we deplore the loss of an instinct for appreciation, and the consuming appetite for self-expression.

But we do not believe in destructiveness, nor do we propose to waste our energy in deploring what is, and thundering what might be. We shall try to avoid platitudes and windy denunciations: our attitude is that of the smiling philosopher. We shall discuss, not rant and quibble: we are earnest, but not too grave. Above all we hope we shall never be dull.

Poetry is said to be unpopular – generally by those who dislike it themselves. Good poetry is as much read now as at any time since the invention of printing, and bad poetry is certainly read a great deal too much. Discrimination might well be inculcated, but poetry cannot be popularized. The good might be more appreciated, the bad less read, and the merely mediocre should be always ignored.

[...] Therefore we believe in personality before we believe in books, and in life rather than in letters. We admire sincerity more than originality; we are not deceived by names: we believe in the matter rather than the signature. [...]

PR 1:1, 1912

1 The Old Vicarage, Grantchester
Rupert Brooke

Café des Westens, Berlin. May, 1912

Just now the lilac is in bloom,
All before my little room;
And in my flower-beds, I think,
Smile the carnation and the pink;
And down the borders, well I know,
The poppy and the pansy blow...

Oh! There the chestnuts, summer through,
Beside the river make for you
A tunnel of green gloom, and sleep
Deeply above; and green and deep
The stream mysterious glides beneath,
Green as a dream and deep as death.
– Oh, damn! I know it! And I know
How the May fields all golden show,
And, when the day is young and sweet,
Gild gloriously the bare feet
That run to bathe...
                    Du Lieber Gott!
Here am I, sweating, sick, and hot,
And there the shadowed waters fresh
Lean up to embrace the naked flesh.
Temperamentvoll German Jews
Drink beer around; – and *there* the dews
Are soft beneath a morn of gold.
Here tulips bloom as they are told;
Unkempt about those hedges blows
An English unofficial rose;

PR 1:9, 1912

And there the unregulated sun
Slopes down to rest when day is done,
And wakes a vague unpunctual star,
A slippered Hesper; and there are
Meads towards Haslingfield and Coton,
Where *das Betreten*'s not *verboten*!

εἴθε γενοίμην... would I were
In Grantchester, in Grantchester! –
Some, it may be, can get in touch
With Nature there, or Earth, or such.
And clever modern men have seen
A Faun a-peeping through the green,
And felt the Classics were not dead,
To glimpse a Naiad's reedy head,
Or hear the Goat-foot piping low:...
But these are things I do not know.
I only know that you may lie
Day long and watch the Cambridge sky,
And, flower-lulled in sleepy grass,
Hear the cool lapse of hours pass,
Until the centuries blend and blur
In Grantchester, in Grantchester...
Still in the dawnlit waters cool
His ghostly Lordship swims his pool,
And tries the strokes, essays the tricks,
Long learnt on Hellespont, or Styx.
Dan Chaucer hears his river still
Chatter beneath a phantom mill.
Tennyson notes, with studious eye,
How Cambridge waters hurry by...
And in that garden, black and white,
Creep whispers through the grass all night;
And spectral dance, before the dawn,
A hundred Vicars down the lawn;
Curates, long dust, will come and go,
On lissom, clerical, printless toe;

And oft betwixt the boughs is seen
The sly shade of a Rural Dean...
Till, at a shiver in the skies,
Vanishing with Satanic cries,
The prim ecclesiastic rout
Leaves but a startled sleeper-out,
Grey heavens, the first bird's drowsy calls,
The falling house that never falls.

God! I will pack, and take a train,
And get me to England once again!
For England's the one land, I know,
Where Men with Splendid Hearts may go;
And Cambridgeshire, of all England,
The shire for Men who Understand;
And of *that* district I prefer
The lovely hamlet, Grantchester.
For Cambridge people rarely smile,
Being urban, squat, and packed with guile;
And Royston men in the far south
Are black and fierce and strange of mouth;
At Over they fling oaths at one,
And worse than oaths at Trumpington;
And Ditton girls are mean and dirty,
And there's none in Harston under thirty,
And folks in Shelford and those parts
Have twisted lips and twisted hearts,
And Barton men make cockney rhymes,
And Coton's full of nameless crimes,
And things are done you'd not believe,
At Madingley, on Christmas Eve.
Strong men have run for miles and miles,
When one from Cherry Hinton smiles;
Strong men have blanched, and shot their wives,
Rather than send them to St Ives;
Strong men have cried like babes, bydam,
To hear what happened at Babraham.

But Grantchester! ah! Grantchester!
There's peace and holy quiet there,
Great clouds along pacific skies,
And men and women with straight eyes,
Lithe children lovelier than a dream,
A bosky wood, a slumbrous stream,
And little kindly winds that creep
Round twilight corners, half asleep.
In Grantchester their skins are white;
They bathe by day, they bathe by night.
The women there do all they ought;
The men observe the Rules of Thought.
They love the Good; they worship Truth;
They laugh uproariously in youth;
(And when they get to feeling old,
They up and shoot themselves, I'm told.)...

Ah, God! To see the branches stir
Across the moon at Grantchester!
To smell the thrilling-sweet and rotten
Unforgettable, unforgotten,
River-smell, and hear the breeze
Sobbing in the little trees.
Say, do the elm-clumps greatly stand
Still guardians of that holy land?
The chestnuts shade, in reverend dream,
The yet unacademic stream?
Is dawn a secret shy and cold
Anadyomene, silver-gold?
And sunset still a golden sea
From Haslingfield to Madingley?
And after, ere the night is born,
Do hares come out about the corn?
Oh, is the water sweet and cool
Gentle and brown, above the pool?
And laughs the immortal river still
Under the mill, under the mill?

Say, is there Beauty yet to find?
And Certainty? And Quiet kind?
Deep meadows yet, for to forget
The lies, and truths, and pain?... oh! yet
Stands the Church clock at ten to three?
And is there honey still for tea?

2 *from* **Le Futurisme**
F.T. Marinetti

We will sing the love of danger, the habit of energy and of temerity.

The essential elements of our poetry are audacity and revolt.

Literature having hitherto magnified pensive immobility, ecstasy and sleep, we will exalt aggressive movement, feverish insomnia, the step of the gymnast, the somersault, the smack in the face, and the blow of the fist.

We declare that the splendour of the world has been enriched with a new beauty, the beauty of speed...

The poet must expend himself with heat, vividness and prodigality, in order to augment the enthusiastic fervour of the primordial elements.

There is no beauty except in strife. No masterpiece without an aggressive character. Poetry must be a violent assault upon the unknown forces, summoning them to crouch before man.

We are on the extreme promontory of the centuries!... Of what use to look behind us, since now we must needs break in the mysterious folding doors of the impossible! Time and space died yesterday. We are living already in the absolute, since we have already created the eternal, omnipresent speed.

PR 1:8, 1912

We will glorify war – the only hygiene of the world – militarism, patriotism, the destructive gesture of the anarchists, the beautiful ideas that kill, the contempt for women.

We will sing the great crowds agitated by work, pleasure, or revolt; the multi-coloured and polyphonic surf of revolutions in modern capitals; the nocturnal vibration of arsenals, and of dock-yards, beneath their violent electric arcs; the gluttonous stations swallowing smoking serpents; the factories suspended to the clouds by the threads of their smokes; the bridges leaping like gymnasts over the diabolical cutlery of sunny rivers; the adventurous liners that sniff the horizon; the great chested locomotives that paw the rails like enormous steel horses bridled with long tubes; and the gliding flight of aeroplanes, whose screw flaps like flags and the plaudits of enthusiastic crowds...

Translated by F.S. Flint.

3 Credo *from* Prolegomena, *and* Sub Mare
Ezra Pound

Credo

Rhythm. – I believe in an 'absolute rhythm,' a rhythm, that is, in poetry which corresponds exactly to the emotion or shade of emotion to be expressed. A man's rhythm must be interpretative, it will be, therefore, in the end, his own, uncounterfeiting, uncounterfeitable.

Symbols. – I believe that the proper and perfect symbol is the natural object, that if a man use 'symbols' he must so use them that their symbolic function does not obtrude; so that *a* sense, and the poetic quality of the passage, is not lost to those who do not understand the symbol as such, to whom, for instance, a hawk is a hawk.

Technique. – I believe in technique as the test of a man's sincerity; in law when it is ascertainable; in the trampling down of every convention that impedes or obscures the determination of the law, or the precise rendering of the impulse.

Form. – I think there is a 'fluid' as well as a 'solid' content, that some poems may have form as a tree has form, some as water poured into a vase. That most symmetrical forms have certain uses. That a vast number of subjects cannot be precisely, and therefore not properly rendered in symmetrical forms.

'Thinking that alone worthy wherein the whole art is employed,'[1] I think the artist should master all known forms and systems of metric, and I have with some persistence set about doing this, searching particularly into those periods wherein the systems came to birth or attained their maturity. It has been complained, with some justice, that I dump my notebooks on the public. I think that only after a long struggle will poetry attain such a degree of development, of, if you will, modernity, that it will vitally concern people who are accustomed, in prose, to Henry James and Anatole France, in music to De Bussy. I am constantly contending that it took two centuries of Provence and one of Tuscany to develop the media of Dante's masterwork, that it took the Latinists of the Renaissance, and the Pleiade, and his own age of painted speech to prepare Shakespeare his tools. It is tremendously important that great poetry be written, it makes no jot of difference who writes it. The experimental demonstrations of one man may save the time of many – hence my furore over Arnaut Daniel – if a man's experiments try out one new rime, or dispense conclusively with one iota of currently accepted nonsense, he is merely playing fair with his colleagues when he chalks up his result.

1 Dante in, I think, 'Il Convito'.

No man ever writes very much poetry that 'matters.' In bulk, that is, no one produces much that is final, and when a man is not doing this highest thing, this saying the thing once for all and perfectly, when he is not matching Ποικιλόθρο', ἀθάνατ', Ἀφρόδιτα, or 'Hist – said Kate the Queen,' he had much better be making the sort of experiments which may be of use to him in his later work, or to his successors.

'The lyf so short, the craft so long to lerne.' It is a foolish thing for a man to begin his work on a too narrow foundation, it is a disgraceful thing for a man's work not to show steady growth and increasing fineness from first to last.

As for 'adaptations'; one finds that all the old masters of painting recommend to their pupils that they begin by copying master-work, and proceed to their own composition.

As for 'Every man his own poet.' The more every man knows about poetry the better. I believe in every one writing poetry who wants to, most do. I believe in every man knowing enough of music to play 'God bless our home' on the harmonicum, but I do not believe in every man giving concerts and printing his sin.

The mastery of any art is the work of a lifetime. I should not discriminate between the 'amateur' and the 'professional,' or rather I should discriminate quite often in favour of the amateur, but I should discriminate between the amateur and the expert. It is certain that the present chaos will endure until the Art of poetry has been preached down the amateur gullet, until there is such a general understanding of the fact that poetry is an art and not a pastime; such a knowledge of technique; of technique of surface and technique of content; that the amateurs will cease to try to drown out the masters.

If a certain thing was said once for all in Atlantis or Arcadia, in 450 Before Christ or in 1290 after, it is not for us moderns to go saying it over, or to go obscuring the memory of the dead by saying the same thing with less skill and less conviction.

My pawing over the ancients and semi-ancients has been one struggle to find out what has been done, once for all, better than it can ever be done again, and to find out what remains for us to do, and plenty does remain, for if we still feel the same emotions as those which launched the thousand ships, it is quite certain that we come on these feelings differently, through different nuances, by different intellectual gradations. Each age has its own abounding gifts, yet only some ages transmute them into matter of duration. No good poetry is ever written in a manner twenty years old, for to write in such a manner shows conclusively that the writer thinks from books, convention and *cliché*, and not from life, yet a man feeling the divorce of life and his art may naturally try to resurrect a forgotten mode if he find in that mode some leaven, or if he think he see in it some element lacking in contemporary art which might unite that art again to its sustenance, life.

In the art of Daniel and Cavalcant, I have seen that precision which I miss in the Victorians – that explicit rendering, be it of external nature, or of emotion. Their testimony is of the eye-witness, their symptoms are first hand.

As for the nineteenth century, with all respect to its achievements, I think we shall look back upon it as a rather blurry, messy sort of a period, a rather sentimentalistic, mannerish sort of a period. I say this without any self-righteousness, with no self-satisfaction.

As for there being a 'movement' or my being of it, the conception of poetry as a 'pure art' in the sense in which I use the term, revived with Swinburne. From the puritanical revolt to Swinburne, poetry had been merely the vehicle – yes, definitely, Arthur Symons' scruples and feelings about the word not withholding – the ox-cart and post-chaise for transmitting thoughts poetic or otherwise. And perhaps the 'great Victorians,' though it is doubtful, and assuredly the 'nineties' continued the development of the art, confining their improvements, however, chiefly to sound and to refinements of manner.

Mr Yeats has once and for all stripped English poetry of its perdamnable rhetoric. He has boiled away all that is not poetic – and a good deal that is. He has become a classic in his own lifetime and *nel mezzo del cammin*. He has made our poetic idiom a thing pliable, a speech without inversions.

Robert Bridges, Maurice Hewlett and Frederic Manning are in their different ways seriously concerned with overhauling the metric, in testing the language and its adaptability to certain modes. Ford Hueffer is making some sort of experiments in modernity. The Provost of Oriel continues his translation of the *Divina Commedia*.

As to Twentieth century poetry, and the poetry which I expect to see written during the next decade or so, it will, I think, move against poppy-cock, it will be harder and saner, it will be what Mr Hewlett calls 'nearer the bone'. It will be as much like granite as it can be, its force will lie in its truth, its interpretative power (of course, poetic force does always rest there); I mean it will not try to seem forcible by rhetorical din, and luxurious riot. We will have fewer painted adjectives impeding the shock and stroke of it. At least for myself, I want it so, austere, direct, free from emotional slither.

Sub Mare

It is, and is not, I am sane enough,
Since you have come this place has hovered round me,
This fabrication built of autumn roses,
Then there's a goldish colour, different.

And one gropes in these things as delicate,
Algae reach up and out beneath
Pale slow green surgings of the under-wave,
'Mid these things older than the names they have,
These things that are familiars of the god.

& *from* The Function of Poetry in the Drama
Lascelles Abercrombie

[...] What I am concerned with is to ask, What, in the name of *aesthetics*, does this desire to get close to life really mean? At bottom, it means, surely, nothing but this: that drama, like all art, *must be credible*: otherwise you might just as well not write it. Furthermore, the stuff of drama must be made out of actual experience, that is to say, of appearances: there is nothing else out of which it can be made. Must it not be, therefore, that in order to be credible, drama must imitate those appearances which we call reality? Plainly, it must do some imitation; and at first it would seem that the difference between poetry plays and prose plays in the matter is something like this: for a poetry play, only so much imitation is employed as to keep the poetizing of experience credible, recognizable as a supposed representation of life. Whereas in a prose play, imitation is the chief of the business, only such formalization being used as will make the imitation bearable. There is truth in this, but not the whole truth. It only applies to direct or external imitation. But more than that is possible, and I think we ought to agree that, if thorough imitation is a crucial point, the poetry play does better than the prose play. [...] For every word spoken in a play must do at least two things: characterize and help on the action. But that is not what words do in life. [...]

But what is it exactly that drama has to imitate? The answer is not simple, because reality is not simple. Those appearances which we call reality are like a set of Chinese boxes, an inner one still fitting inside the last one opened. There is the sensible reality of deeds and words – the outward gestures of character; then there is the reality of reasoned motive and conscience – so to speak, the inward gestures of character; then character itself; then passion, then the social reality: I don't profess to have taken the puzzle to pieces in the right order. Anyhow, the innermost reality, the one with which art is most dearly concerned, is what is commonly called the spiritual reality. For the purpose of this discussion, however, let me use a name which allows it to be more easily handled. Let me call it the emotional reality; by which I do not entirely mean the plane of such named and recognizable emotions as love, anger, hate, but rather the general substratum to all existence, emotion nameless and unappointed. This is the layer of flame which is the closest we can get to the central fire, to the Will to live, or whatever you like to call it. And an impression of this profound emotional reality is what art must convey, together, of course, with its concentric apparatus or expression of all the other realities – the named emotions, reason, the habit of conscience, action, and the rest. Now the great difference between prose drama and poetry drama is that the first concentrates its imitation on the outermost reality, the second on the innermost. Prose drama gives you an imitation of the ready-made boot of existence, gives it you as exactly as it can; and trusts to your famil- iarity with it, to your knowledge that the boot does contain something, to enable you to *infer* there from the inner reality on which it is constructed. And if you cannot perform that inference, the boot, as far as art is concerned, might certainly just as well be thrown at you empty.

Poetry drama, however, except only for preserving the necessary cred- ibility, neglects the outer shells of reality, and directly seeks to imitate the core. Or rather, it seeks to imitate in you the *effect* which would be pro- duced if you perceived with certainty and clarity the grand emotional impulse driving all existence. For this kind of drama uses for its texture a verbal process which, with its numerous provocative and evocative devices, such as imagery, and deliberate metaphor, and consistent metre, is inescapably recognizable as *symbolic* of the emotional reality of life. [...] It is here that the wonderfully important function of metre comes in; for metre gives to the poet's words a *form* which is itself a direct expression of the emotion which the words enclose. Not only does the underlying consistent beat keep our answering emotions in the necessary state of excitation, but the sudden varieties and modulations of metre, the momentary deviations from consistency, are most powerful suggesters of shifting changes and unexpected upward rushes of emotion. [...]

[...] So the true explanation of the appeal of drama is, that to witness a spectacle which instinct knows for a genuine symbol of life *does* cause a person to be triumphantly aware of the personality in him. For a genuine symbol of life is, metaphysically, a symbol of our desires for life; it is, therefore, life made orderly and significant; and to see life thus artis- tically refashioned, makes us keenly aware of our hidden desires by means of this very satisfaction, and so, keenly aware of ourselves. Life cannot satisfy our desires for life; but drama can; and by so doing seems more real than life, and we by witnessing it seem more real ourselves. Hence the fundamental importance of drama is its power of forcing us into a state of astonishment – astonishment that glows to perceive with unex- pected force that terrific splendid fact, the fact *that we do exist.*

[...]

A Paper read before the English Association of Manchester.

& *from* Robert Bridges: The Classical Poet
Henry Newbolt

'The one classical poet we have is Mr Bridges.' So I read, but before I consent I must ask what is meant exactly by the adjective. It has half a dozen meanings, and we use them, as a rule, not singly, but in more or less subtle combinations. 'Classical, of the first class' – we almost always add to this the idea of recognition, of established reputation. That would seem to imply a certain amount of popularity: yet again we say of good work that it is 'classical rather than popular,' meaning that it appeals mainly to a cultivated mind or a highly developed taste. In all these senses the poetry of Mr Bridges is classical: he has not pleased all, but he has pleased many, and the many include the best judges. 'The taste of the public,' said Southey, 'may better be estimated from indifferent poets than from good ones: because the former write for their contemporaries, the latter for posterity.' Mr Bridges has written, as indeed, with Southey's leave, every good poet writes, for his own contemporaries: but he has succeeded as few do in gaining, during his lifetime, a recognition which seems likely to be supported on appeal.

There is another common usage which need not trouble us. 'Learned in, or devoted to the Classics' – that is obviously true of the author of *Eros and Psyche*, *The Return of Ulysses*, *Achilles in Scyros*, *The Feast of Bacchus*, *Demeter*, and the two parts of the tragedy of *Nero*. But in the rest of his work, and above all in his shorter poems, he is so English and so essentially modern that the word classical in this sense would be a misdescription. Shakespeare himself, it may be remembered, wrote *Antony and Cleopatra*, *Julius Caesar*, and *Coriolanus*, besides *Lucrece* and *Venus and Adonis*. But there is yet a meaning for 'classical' which may bring us into controversy. To inherit from the Greeks and Latins is one thing, to be a partisan in the war between Classical and Romantic is another. In England at any rate we regard that struggle as over, and he who should attempt to continue it would run the risk of being exiled as a belated and unjustifiable guerrilla. 'A general agreement as to first principles, when it is not a vital instinct, is apt to harden into formulas, and to hinder the free action of the mind,' – 'of the spirit' Mr Symons might have said. Who now would attempt to bind art by any such agreement, any such formulas? We no longer revolt against those bonds: we broke

PR 1:4, 1912

them in the age of Wordsworth and Coleridge. There are still critics who now and again threaten us with 'the iambic pentameter' or adjure us to be 'more objective' and 'study form': but they gesticulate unheeded by our poets, who are happily intent on finding their own form, every one of them.

Is Mr Bridges an exception – the solitary exception, 'the one classical poet' in this sense?

Take down the books – the volumes of the *Shorter Poems*, of the *Elegies*, of the sonnet sequence called *The Growth of Love*. It is true that there is here that quality of 'order in beauty' which Pater declared to be 'the essentially classical element': but the beauty and the order of it spring directly from a personality, and from no other source – they are the work of a creative mind which has remade the world in its own image. Not remote regions and little-known fragments of the world, but the old and great and long inhabited centres of it. Joy, Sorrow, Nature, Love – his songs are of these, and in these the poet has gone, as the new Age must go, not further, but deeper. His sorrow is a wrestling, not an abandonment: *sunt gemitus rerum* might stand at the head of the lines *On a Dead Child*, or of those called *Pater Filio* and *Winter Nightfall*. That Joy should live with such insight is wonderful, but the joy that abounds in these poems is from a bluer heaven than any other that has shone over England.

[...]

Of the poems on Nature I have no space to quote even a line: like the rest they are songs of things that all men know, but none have ever seen before, and they say what all would wish to say but none would ever have said like this. [...]

4 A Song of the Soldiers

Thomas Hardy

What of the faith and fire within us
    Men who march away
    Ere the barn-cocks say
    Night is growing gray,
To hazards whence no tears can win us;
What of the faith and fire within us
    Men who march away?

Is it a purblind prank, O think you,
    Friend with the musing eye
    Who watch us stepping by,
    With doubt and dolorous sigh?
Can much pondering so hoodwink you!
Is it a purblind prank, O think you,
    Friend with the musing eye?

Nay. We see well what we are doing,
    Though some may not see –
    Dalliers as they be! –
    England's need are we;
Her distress would set us rueing:
Nay. We see well what we are doing,
    Though some may not see!

In our heart of hearts believing
    Victory crowns the just,
    And that braggarts must
    Surely bite the dust,
March we to the field ungrieving,
In our heart of hearts believing
    Victory crowns the just.

PR 5:4, 1914

Hence the faith and fire within us
    Men who march away
    Ere the barn-cocks say
    Night is growing gray,
To hazards whence no tears can win us;
Hence the faith and fire within us
    Men who march away.

&   *from* **Argument in Verse**
    The Right Hon. A.J Balfour MP

[...] I have tried to show that there are three great advantages which everybody would admit that poetry has over prose in dealing with any subject, I mean the melody, the pleasure which the comments on the material give, and the enrichment which that particular form of literature permits and even encourages.

But there is another attribute of poetry which is relevant, I think, to the subject argued in verse, and that is the power of compression, the power of producing intensity which poetry possesses in a degree far exceeding prose in its ordinary and most appropriate use. I am not sure that this quality of intensity or compression always receives sufficient attention from critics and students of literature. It seems to me to lie at the root of much more than we are apt to think. Men of science are quite familiar with the idea that the amount of time taken, acceleration, intensity, that these things are of the utmost importance for accounting for natural phenomena, but I do not think we always quite grasp how widely spread through all literature is this quality of intensity, and how much it stands for and by how many means men of letters try and attain to it. We are apt to talk as if the same meaning that had been put in a compressed form, could be expanded and explained and drawn out at unlimited length, and that then you would have the same meaning in two shapes. But that is inaccurate. Mere dilution alters quality. The mere extension, the mere explanation, the mere enriching of the thing destroys its most essential attributes and even destroys its higher qualities. You come upon a line or a couplet in a poet which for some reason seems obscure. You read a long note about it. The note explains what the poet meant. It does not tell you what the poet said – it does not give you the meaning of the poet. You might as well suppose that some medicine or some tonic would produce its effect if diluted with an infinite quantity of water. The tonic is there and is unchanged, but for all practical purposes it is an utterly and entirely different thing. Poetry does permit of this increase of tension, this augmentation of intensity and concentration, in a way which prose does not admit.

It is one of the reasons why we may hope that arguments might be presented with efficiency and force in poetry which prose is incapable of affording. Indeed, there is some truth in that; but before I touch upon that perhaps I had better indicate the methods by which this sort of intensity is reached. These methods are many. The simplest of all are what I may call telegraphic concentration. Sometimes some one sends a telegram which consists of the substance of the message, but there is no preposition, and you are expected to fill up all the gaps and to translate the message into some form more easily comprehended. That kind of concentration is possible in poetry in a manner which you could never tolerate in prose. Poets have used it and abused it. There are passages in the 'Essay on Man' most obscure, not perhaps greatly worth unravelling; but the obscurity comes from the fact that the poet has used almost a telegraphic system. He had left out too much and expects his readers to put it in. And a much greater man, and in some respects a much greater poet, than Dryden, was a still greater sinner in that respect, and that is Robert Browning. Browning has left difficulties – difficulties which every reader who tells the truth finds in following his line of thought, because of the fact that he so recklessly and unscrupulously used this telegraphic weapon of concentration, and a most laborious task it very often is. When not carried to excess I do think this power of compressing is an asset for those poets who are bold enough to try argument in prose. No prose writer would dare to use it – he is expected, and rightly expected, to expand his article to a point which is immediately intelligible to any ordinarily instructed reader. And in that respect the poet has the advantage over him.

[...]

5 The Incense Bearers
Ivor Gurney

Toward the sun the drenched May-hedges lift
White rounded masses like still ocean-drift,
And day fills with heavy scent of that gift.

There is no escaping that full current of thick
Incense; one walks, suddenly one comes quick
Into a flood of odour there, aromatic,

Not English; for cleaner, sweeter, is the hot scent that
Is given from hedges, solitary flowers, not
In mass, but lonely odours that scarcely float.

But the incense bearers, soakers of sun's full
Powerfulness, give out floods unchecked, wonderful
Utterance almost, which makes no poet grateful,

Since his love is for single things rarely found,
Or hardly: violets blooming in remote ground,
One colour, one fragrance, like one uncompanied sound

Struck upon silence, nothing looked-for. Hung
As from gold wires this May incense is swung,
Heavy of odour, the drenched meadows among.

First published in P.J. Kavanagh's *Collected Poems of Ivor Gurney* (OUP, 1982).

6

from **After Death**
Rabindranath Tagore

[...]
He is gone! Let him go!
Let him be forgotten, then.

I know not why we come here,
    And why we work:
And why, at the end of our work,
Our worn out lives leave the
    Shore of this world.

We care not whether we are appreciated
    By those we leave behind,
    We do not barter,
    We cannot order,
        Our lives.

Why do we come and go? –
    Why do we meet?
Why do we make friends and foes?
Why do we feel hope and love and hatred
In our heart, when life is
        So short?
Why so much sorrow and happiness
        In life?
Why are we tied down
    To numerous duties?

What was unfinished here,
What was checked and discouraged,
    Could that be finished,
        Somewhere hereafter?

PR 8:2, 1917

What seemed meaningless and unreal in life,
And scattered about in pieces,
Has Death gathered them together in his basket
　　And filled them with
　　Meaning and reality now?

Translated by Ranee Mrinalini.

7 On the Function of the Poet
Aleksandr Blok

Even from our childhood years, we cherish in memory a cheering
name: Pushkin. It is a name which occupies our thoughts for many
of our living days. The names of emperors, of generals, of inven-
tors of lethal weapons, of life's tormentors and of life's tormented,
are sinister sounds in our ears. And along with these, the gentle
name of Pushkin.

Pushkin succeeded in bearing the burden of his creative genius
quite easily and cheerfully, although the role of poet is neither easy
nor cheerful. It is tragic. Like a great master, Pushkin moved
grandly, confidently, and fully at ease in his part. And yet we are
often moved to tears when we think of Pushkin, and of the festive
and triumphant progress of this poet who could not interfere with
the world outside because his was an inner, a cultural task. It was
a progress to be interrupted only too often by the surly interven-
tion of people to whom a cooking-pot meant more than God.

We know of Pushkin the man, Pushkin the friend of the
monarchy, Pushkin the associate of the Decembrists. All these pale
into insignificance before Pushkin the poet.

The poet's importance never diminishes. His diction and idiom may become obsolete, but the spirit of his work can never go out of date.

The public is liable to turn its back on the poet and his vocation. To-day it erects monuments in his name; to-morrow it wants to 'cast him from the ship of contemporaneity'. Both these actions betray the limitations of the public, but not those of the poet. The spirit of poetry, as of all the arts, is eternal. This or that treatment of poetry by outsiders is ultimately of no consequence.

To-day we are honouring the memory of Russia's greatest poet. It seems to me appropriate to discuss the function of the poet, and to substantiate what I am going to say with Pushkin's own ideas on the subject.

What is a poet? A man who writes verse? No, of course he is not. He is not called a poet because he writes verse; he writes verse – that is to say, produces an harmonious arrangement of words and sounds – because he is a poet, a son of harmony.

What is harmony? Harmony is the concord of world forces; it is the order of world life. Order is cosmos, as opposed to disorder, or chaos. The Ancients taught that cosmos, or world, is born out of chaos. Cosmos is akin to chaos, as the resilient waves of an inland sea are akin to the massy billows of the ocean. A son may not resemble his father in any way, save in one single hidden characteristic; but this alone is enough to guarantee a resemblance between father and son.

Chaos is primeval, elemental anarchy; cosmos is organised harmony, or culture. Cosmos is born out of chaos. The element nurses within itself the seeds of culture. Harmony is created out of anarchy.

World life consists in the continual creation of new varieties, new species. They are rocked in the cradle of anarchical chaos; culture rears them and thins them out; harmony gives them shapes and forms, which dissolve once more into the mists of anarchy. The meaning of this is incomprehensible to us and its true significance obscure. We console ourselves with the thought that the new species is better than the old. But the wind extinguishes this tiny little candle with which we attempt to illuminate the world night. The order of the world is disquieting; it is the legitimate offspring of disorder, and might not conform to our ideas of what is good and what is bad.

One thing we do know: the species which arrives to replace another is new; the one it replaces is old. We observe eternal changes in the world, and ourselves take part in the substitution of species. Our participation is, on the whole, passive; we are born, we grow old, we die; but we are rarely active in the process. We occupy some sort of place in world culture, and assist personally in the formation of new species.

The poet is the son of harmony, and he is given a kind of role to play in world culture. Three tasks are assigned to him: first, the liberation of sounds from their natural, anarchical element; second, the production of an harmonious arrangement of these sounds and their embodiment in form; third, the presentation of this harmony to the outside world.

Sounds which have been ravished from their element, arranged into harmony, and presented to the outside world begin to do their own work independently. 'A poet's words are the *raison d'être* of his vocation.' They reveal unexpected power. They put human hearts to the test and make a selection, as it were, from the slag-heaps of humanity. Perhaps they are re-assembling parts of an old species bearing the name of 'man,' – parts which are suitable for the creation of new species; for the old one, evidently, rapidly declines, degenerates, and dies.

It is impossible to withstand the power of the harmony which the poet presents to the world. To struggle with it is beyond all human strength, individual and united. 'Oh for the time when all might feel the power of harmony thus!' Salieri pines away on his own. But it *is* felt by all, only by mortals otherwise than by god; – or Mozart. When poetry points with its finger and confers a name, that name, like death itself, is unescapable; and it is never bestowed without just cause.

For instance, the poet never stigmatizes those who are simply a piece of the element, – who are neither allowed to understand, nor meant to. People are not called rabble for resembling the soil they plough, the scrap of mist from which they emerged, or the beast which they hunt. On the other hand, those who do not want to understand (although they ought to understand a great deal, being servants of culture) are stigmatised with the infamous name of the rabble. Even death cannot deliver them from this name. It is one which survives death itself, even as it survived Count Benckendorff, Timovsky, Bulgarin, and all those who prevented the poet from carrying out his mission.

In the unfathomable depths of the spirit, where man ceases to be man, in depths inaccessible to the state and the society created by civilisation, roll waves of sound permeating the universe like the natural processes which form mountains, winds, marine currents, and the vegetable and animal world.

These depths of the spirit are screened off by the phenomena of the outside world. Pushkin says that they are screened off from the poet more, perhaps, than from other people. 'Perhaps, amid the world's weak children, he is the weakest of them all.'

The first task required of the poet by his office is to quit the 'worries of this busy world' in order to lift the outer covering and reveal the depths. This necessity isolates the poet from the company of the 'world's weak children':

Half-wild, half-grim, his spirit harassed
By sounds and dark dismay, he flees
To lonely shores of boundless seas
And to the leafy-murmuring forest.

Wild, grim, harassed by dark dismay, because the revelation of the depths of the spirit is as difficult as the act of giving birth. To the sea and to the forest, because only there in solitude can he summon up all his strength and participate in the 'natural chaos', the anarchical element which sets the waves of sound in motion.

The mysterious act has been performed; the covering has been lifted; the depths revealed; the sound received into the soul. The second law of Apollo stipulates that this sound, raised from the depths and still strange to the outside world, should be confined in the abiding and tangible form of words. Sounds and words should form a unified harmony. This belongs to the domain of technical skill. Technical skill needs inspiration just as much as participation in the 'native chaos'. 'Inspiration,' said Pushkin, 'is that state of the soul in which it is most ready to receive impressions, to consider ideas, and subsequently to organise these impressions and ideas into comprehensible language.' It is impossible, therefore, to draw any exact demarcation line between the first and second tasks of the poet. The one is intimately bound up with the other. The more coverings raised, the more intense the participation in chaos, and the more difficult the act of giving birth to sound – the more he strives to achieve clarity of form, and the more persistent, musical, and unremitting he becomes in his persecution of the human ear.

It is now time for the third task of the poet. The sounds which have been received into the soul and arranged into harmony have to be presented to the outside world. Here occurs the famous conflict of the poet with the rabble.

It is doubtful whether the common folk have ever been called rabble by a poet. Surely only those deserving of the title have applied it to ordinary people. Pushkin collected folk-songs, wrote in the folk style, and had a very intimate friend in his old country nurse. One must therefore be either stupid or malicious to think that Pushkin could have meant the common people when he spoke of the rabble. A Pushkin concordance will clarify this point, should there ever be a re-birth of Russian culture.

By rabble, Pushkin understood approximately what we do. He often qualified this noun with the epithet 'high-born', thus conferring a collective noun on that ancestral court aristocracy which had nothing to justify its existence except noble rank. But Pushkin could already see with his own eyes the ancestral nobility being replaced by the bureaucrats. It is these officials with whom we are concerned; these are our rabble; the rabble of yesterday and to-day: not beasts, not clods of clay, not scraps of mist, not bits of the planets, not demons and not angels. Without the addition of the particle 'not', there is only one thing to be said of them: they are at least human beings. This is not particularly flattering. Human beings: – vulgar little men of affairs whose spiritual depths are hopelessly and completely screened off by the 'cares of the busy world'.

The rabble expects the poet to serve that which it serves itself: the outside world. It expects him to be 'useful', as Pushkin so simply expresses it. It expects the poet to 'sweep the muck off the streets,' 'enlighten the hearts of his fellow brethren,' and the like.

From its own point of view, the rabble is right in its expectations. In the first place, it will never be able to enjoy the fruits of that toil, somewhat more important than sweeping the muck off the streets, which is expected of the poet. Secondly, it instinctively senses that this labour is, in some way or other, going to lead sooner or later to its own downfall. The testing of human hearts with harmony is not a restful occupation; nor is it one which assures a level, and therefore (for the rabble) desirable flow of events in the outside world.

The rabble class, which is no different from any other class of human beings, progresses very slowly. For instance, in spite of the fact that the human brain during the last few centuries has become puffed up to the detriment of all the other bodily organs, the public has only thought of obtaining one single instrument from the state – the censorship – to protect the order of its world as expressed in state routine procedure. By this means it has placed an obstacle on the third path of the poet only – the path leading to the presentation of harmony to the world. It might occur to it, apparently, to place obstructions on the first and second paths as well. It might investigate means of muddling up the very sources of harmony. What it is that prevents it – slow wittedness, timidity or conscience – we do not know. Could it be that such means are already being investigated?

The vocation of the poet, however, is, as we have seen, quite incommensurable with the outside world. The tasks of the poet are universally cultural, to use a phrase now in common use. His work belongs to history. Consequently, the poet has the right to say with Pushkin:

I little worry whether the press is free
To rail at fools, or whether the censorship
Restrains the would-be satirist in its grip.

In saying this, Pushkin was maintaining the rabble's right to establish a censorship, for he presumed that the number of fools was not likely to diminish.

It is by no means the poet's business to knock at the door of every fool without exception until it is opened unto him. On the contrary, the harmony created by him selects from amongst the fools in order to obtain something more interesting than the human average from the human slag-heap. This aim is, of course, sooner or later achieved by true harmony. No censorship in the world can hinder this essential function of poetry.

We are not, on a day devoted to the memory of Pushkin, going to dispute whether Pushkin was right or wrong in distinguishing between the liberty which we call personal and the liberty which we call political. We know that he demanded a 'different', a 'secret' liberty. To us, this means personal liberty; but to the poet it is something more than just personal liberty.

> ... To know your life's your own
> By right; to serve and please yourself alone;
> Never, for worldly power and rank, to trade
> Your conscience, your intentions, or your pride;
> To wander at your whimsy, and rejoice
> At smiling nature's heaven-sent loveliness,
> And to be lost in rapturous contemplation
> Before the best of art and inspiration –
> That's happiness ! That's freedom !

He said this shortly before his death. In his youth, Pushkin spoke of the very same thing:

> Deep love and *secret liberty*
> Breathed to the heart a simple hymn.

This *secret liberty,* this *whimsy* – a word which was to be reiterated afterwards by Fet more loudly than by anybody else ('The crazy whimsies of the bard!') – is not just personal liberty. It is something more than that. It is closely connected with the first two tasks which Apollo requires of the poet. All the things mentioned in Pushkin's lines are conditions essential for the liberation of harmony, and although he allowed interference in his third task, the testing of human hearts with harmony – Pushkin could not allow interference in the first two; and those are not personal ones.

Meanwhile, Pushkin's life, now on its decline, was being more and more impeded by obstacles standing in his way. Pushkin was weakening, and so was the culture of his time – the only cultural epoch in the Russia of the last century. The fatal forties were drawing near. The childlike lisp of Belinsky could be heard over Pushkin's death-bed. To us, this lisp seemed to be saying something utterly contradictory and utterly hostile to the polite voice of Count Benckendorff. It seems so to us even now. It would be only too painful for us if it were otherwise. And even if it is not entirely so, we shall continue to think, all the same, that it is not by any means the case. For the time being, of course:

> To us, one thrilling lie is dearer
>> Than countless unexciting truths.

In the second half of the century, what has been heard in the childlike lisp of Belinsky was being roared forth by Pisarev at the top of his voice.

I shall refrain from further comparisons, for it is impossible to clarify the picture just now. Perhaps behind the web of time will be revealed something quite different from what glimmers in my fleeting thoughts, and yet at the same time quite different from what is being maintained by those with viewpoints contrary to my own. We shall have to live through events of some kind or other before then. The final word in this matter is in the hands of the future historian of Russia.

Pushkin died. But 'for children, the Posas never die,' said Schiller. And Pushkin was killed, not merely by the bullet of D'Anthès, but by want of air as well. And with him, his culture died also.

> 'Tis time, my friend, 'tis time! The weary heart seeks peace!

This is Pushkin's death-bed sigh; and it is also the death-bed sigh of the culture of Pushkin's age.

There is no joy on earth, but there is peace and freedom.

Peace and *freedom*. They are essential to the poet in his work of liberating harmony. But peace and freedom can also be taken away. Not eternal peace, but creative peace. Not the child's freedom, not the freedom to play the liberal, but creative freedom, secret liberty. And the poet dies, because there is no air for him to breathe. Life has lost its meaning.

As for those dear officials who hindered the poet from testing human hearts with harmony – they have earned for themselves the name of rabble for all time. But they only interfered with the poet in the execution of his third task. When Pushkin put human hearts to the test with the whole range of his poetry, he missed them out entirely.

Let them have a care, those officials who intend to direct poetry down a sort of special channel, thus encroaching on its secret liberty and obstructing it in the performance of its mysterious function. They will earn that most despicable of all names – rabble.

We die, but art remains. Its final cause is unknown to us, and cannot be known. It is consubstantial and indivisible.

I would like, for amusement, to utter three simple truths. There are no such things as specialised arts. What has not been acknowledged as art should not be designated as such. In order to create works of art, it is necessary to be able to do so.

In these cheering, commonsense truths, before which we stand so guilty, we can swear by the cheering name of Pushkin.

11 Feb., 1921

Translated by A.L. Miller.
Delivered at a ceremonial meeting on the 84th anniversary of Pushkin's death.

& *from* Modern American Poetry
Harriet Monroe

In the United States to-day the poet is rarely able to devote his best energies to his art because, unlike his fellow artists in painting, sculpture and architecture, he cannot make it yield him even a bread-and-water living. In addition to this disadvantage, which he shares with most of his European confrères, he suffers from the decentralization of literary taste and authority. His world is not a coterie in a capital, with an entrenched group of critics whose judgment, right or wrong, arouses comment; but a few inaccessible readers scattered over a wide area, and served by journalists who usually misconceive or ignore poetry altogether. Moreover his public is still sufficiently colonial in taste to distrust its own opinion and listen too eagerly for the verdict of London or Paris.

Thus the poet of serious purpose detects a response so slight, or of such foggy vagueness, that his voice may be gradually muffled. Even a hero cannot lead to victory without an army behind him, and the most heroic artistic vocation is powerless against public apathy. Yet the apathy is more apparent than real. The people are intensely imaginative, with deep dreams calling for a truly interpretive modern poet. Public sympathy is not dead, but remote and scattered and unaware. An organized effort to unite and inform it may be the one thing most needful; perhaps this will be one of the century's important achievements.

[...]

PR 1:10, 1912

8

from Subtlety of the Serpent?
Osbert Sitwell

Now the serpent was more subtle than any beast of the field which the Lord God had made.

                                                    Gen. iii.I

Through the green masses of the undergrowth,
Pools of silent water
Where float huge flowers and patches of white light,
Crawls the Serpent, subtle, sad,
And tired of well-doing;
Never more will he help humanity.
Venomously he hisses at the Cherubim,
Whose flaming sword scars the heavens,
A sword whose flame turns every way
To keep the path of the tree of life.
A tropic spring, this first one,
With leaves like spears and banners,
But the ground is sweet with falling petals
Of great blossoms,
That heave their hot breath at the droning insects.
The air is full of the twittering of birds,
Whose innocence already appeals to Adam,
– Outside the Garden.
High up in their swaying green cradles
The monkeys carry on their high-pitched chatter.

The Serpent reasoned thus,
'For a long time have I been at war
With the ape-tribe;
Small apes with clutching hands,
Great apes (how hideous they are!)

Whom the God of Man has made in the image of Man.
They tried to kill me;
I tried to kill them;
But Adam and Eve deceived me.
Looking scornfully at the great apes,
They pretended to be different.
For a time I loved them,
Fascinated by their words,
By their story of the Creation –
But now give me a good, old fashioned ape, every time.
– An ape who tries to kill me,
Without a chatter of clean hands, law-and-order,
Crime passionel, the right-to-kill,
Self-defence, or helping-me-to-help-myself;
I may be a snake in the grass,
But I am not a hypocrite.
I may change my skin,
But I am not ashamed of it.
I have never pretended to be a super-snake.
I have never pretended to walk, except on my belly.

It is not the ignorance of good or evil
That raises the monkey above the man,
But the fact that the monkey
Cannot yet disguise the good with bad words,
Or the bad with good ones.

Never before have I been cursed
But the God of Man has cursed me with evil words.
Now will I curse mankind.
[...]

9

The Fires
Rudyard Kipling

Men make them fires on the hearth
   Each under his roof-tree,
And the Four Winds that rule the earth
   They blow the smoke to me.

Across the high hills and the sea
   And all the changeful skies,
The Four Winds blow the smoke to me
   Till the tears are in my eyes.

Until the tears are in my eyes
   And my heart is wellnigh broke
For thinking on old memories
   That gather in the smoke.

With every shift of every wind
   The homesick memories come,
From every quarter of mankind
   Where I have made me a home.

Four times a fire against the cold
   And a roof against the rain –
Sorrow fourfold and joy fourfold
   The Four Winds bring again!

How can I answer which is best
   Of all the fires that burn?
I have been too often host or guest
   At every fire in turn.

PR 21:1, 1930

How can I turn from any fire,
　　On any man's hearthstone?
I know the wonder and desire
　　That went to build my own!

How can I doubt man's joy or woe
　　Where'er his house-fires shine,
Since all that man must undergo
　　Will visit me at mine?

Oh, you Four Winds that blow so strong
　　And know that this is true,
Stoop for a little and carry my song
　　To all the men I knew!

Where there are fires against the cold,
　　Or roofs against the rain –
With love fourfold and joy fourfold,
　　Take them my songs again!

This Prelude to *Collected Verse* (Hodder and Stoughton) [was] published by the special permission of Mr Rudyard Kipling as a contribution to [the] issue of *Poetry Review* which marks the twenty-first anniversary of the Poetry Society's foundation.

& *from* The New Criticism
Michael Roberts

The new volume of *Scrutinies* by the *Calendar* group attempts to reveal
the merits of certain of the middle-aged writers of to-day just as the first
volume attempted to assess the permanent value of work of the older
generation. Although the present book contains nothing so acute as
Robert Graves' discussion of Rudyard Kipling's 'philosophy of life', the
essays on Wyndham Lewis (by Edgell Rickword) and Virginia Woolf (by
William Empson) are nevertheless notable.

[…] At a time when theories of criticism have shown the possibility of
estimating a work solely by its elegance, the efficiency with which it fulfils
a chosen purpose, we find ourselves confronted with a literature, the
moral and religious attitudes of which are of the greatest importance.
D.H. Lawrence, for example, whose attitude to life and literature can only
be compared to that of Blake, was essentially a 'prophetic' writer, he was
obsessed by notions of liberty and the 'natural life'. But liberty, the
absence of restraint, is a negative thing and a 'movement towards self-
completion', an act in defiance of accepted codes and obedient to
primitive impulses, may in fact result in self-diminution, a feeling of
degradation. The human being is more complex than Mr Brian Penton,
who writes a 'Note on Form in the Novel', understands. Mr Penton
understands 'booze and kisses' and judges novels by the amount of booze
and kisses which they recommend. […] The poetry of Mr Eliot is not read
by people corresponding to those who read Scott or Tennyson or
Swinburne. It resembles the poetry of Gerard Manley Hopkins and the
later poetry of Shakespeare in so far as it is born of intense spiritual
anguish, not lyric rapture. It is religious poetry, but not religious in the
sense in which the work of Crashaw, Vaughan or Herbert was religious.
It is not the expression of joy in a faith, but the history of a journey toward
a faith. The lyric impulse is continually hampered and thwarted until it
finally triumphs.

Criticism of such poetry naturally tends to become a sort of spiritual
history, and the critic tends to identify his own problems with those of
the author. Mr McGreevy, on the few pages when he is not digressing or
simply quoting Mr Eliot, succumbs to that temptation. The fact that he
frequently has to rate the end of Mr Eliot's poems lower than the begin-

ning might have warned him that he was misinterpreting the attitude of
that careful artist. He imagines that Mr Eliot, in writing 'The Waste
Land', was acting as a Christian. Consequently he does not understand
the bitterness of an artist who sees what he knows by his own standards
to be ugliness and wickedness and yet has no faith which would reveal
some purpose in the whole process of the universe. Failing to understand
this, Mr McGreevy naturally finds nothing but sterility in 'Ash Wednes-
day'. If Mr Eliot always had been a Christian that poem could never have
been written, for its significance and intense emotive power arise from
its joyful acceptance of the fact that 'things are as they are', its suddenly
realized conviction that life is worth while despite the pain and shabbi-
ness. That is to say, it records the sudden vanishing of the question, 'What
is the purpose of all this misery?' That question is one which no Christian
would ever ask with the bitterness and intensity with which Mr Eliot, like
others of this generation, has asked it.

Mr Edmund Wilson, in an illuminating series of essays on Messrs
Yeats, Joyce, Eliot, Stein, Proust and Valery, says, 'I believe therefore that
the time is at hand when these writers, who have largely dominated the
literary world of the decade 1920–30, though we shall continue to admire
them as masters, will no longer serve us as guides. Axel's world of the
private imagination in isolation from the life of society seems to have
been exploited and explored as far as for the present is possible.' He recog-
nizes that 'The question begins to press us again as to whether it is
possible to make a practical success of human society, and whether, if we
continue to fail, a few masterpieces, however profound or noble, will be
able to make life worth living even for the few people in a position to
enjoy them,' but he does not see that he is here pressing his hypothesis
too far. He has assumed that the writers with whom he deals would, like
the heroes of the Symbolists, 'rather drop out of the common life than
struggle to make themselves a place in it.' It is a fruitful hypothesis, it
gives form to the best volume of criticism which has appeared for twelve
months, but it is not entirely true. That isolation from common life has
in some cases resulted from a lack of faith, not from hypochondria, and
if some faith can be reintegrated (as Mr Eliot appears to have reintegrated
his) then we need not fear that poetry will become more and more
'precious' and remote from ordinary life.

Scrutinies II, by various writers (Wishart); *Axel's Castle*, by Edmund Wilson
(Scribners); *T.S. Eliot: A Study*, by Thomas McGreevy (Chatto and Windus).

&   *from* On Verse-Speaking
Edith Evans

[...] What I cannot understand, after coming several times here, is why most of you get the over-colouring of your poems. When you first take up a poem how do you work on it? Very few of you seem to make any pattern. Do you read your poem through several times to get the shape, as it were, the pattern of it? If it is going to be recited very slowly without any pattern we are hypnotized by words and are half asleep after about ten lines. That is the kind of thing that kills interest in poetry speaking. What our Society is after is not only the speaking of poems but to revive interest in and love of poetry. Now you have a great love of your poems but you love them so much that you gloat over them. You seem to hug them to you. There is no discipline. *You* are having a marvellous time but *we* are not! You must work to 'beat'. Most of you get hypnotized by the words, they must affect you but not hypnotize you. You can read some poems as you would read the alphabet and get far more out of them than by overdoing them. You don't let the poet come out, you do it all for him. You must, must, must keep to the beat otherwise you would be speaking prose. Most of you could say your poems beautifully if you said them at twice the pace you did before. You should want to tell it out. I find that mistake with everybody. You should look through the poem and see when the poet has stopped one thought and begun another, otherwise it is a slow beating out of words of one colour. I find in listening to most of you if you have to say a word like 'ocean' the picture seems to be too much for you. You try to give the impression of the ocean. Say the word, don't dramatize it too much; let *us* picture the ocean. You must remember, too, that the sonnet has a very definite form. You must not put in so much of what you think, you must find out the form and keep to it; if you don't keep to the metre we are not getting poetry but prose. You should never stop in the middle because you break the poet's metre. Don't you all of you hear the metre beating in the words when you read them? It is poetry, it is song. You must keep to it. It is so tremendous that you feel you must put all this into it. If you would only speak with more rhythm it would be very difficult to judge you, but most of you have the same faults. You are nearly all given to too much emphasis. Do 'get on with it'. Let the poem swing you along; don't try to swing the poem. Also you are nearly all inclined to go up and down with your voices in your speech. It makes for slack speaking and it worries us by beating on us too much. You ask us to follow you up and down, up and down the whole time. Think of the words the poet has used. He has used those words for a definite purpose. You must not take their words and give them the wrong colour. You should let the words speak for themselves, don't try to act the words. You must not stop in the middle. If you were singers you would know what I mean. The conductor would not let you slow up like this, you would have to follow his beat. The poet is your conductor; he has made the beat and you must find it and keep to it. You should speak poetry naturally as though you were dying to tell somebody about it, quietly, naturally, evenly.

& *from* The English Lyric
Laurence Binyon

Every successful poem has its own predestined form, the form in which its matter is displayed to the most advantage. Every syllable in it, every vowel and consonant, has its value in the whole effect. We cannot separate the form from the matter and treat of it in the abstract. Nor can we separate the matter from the form, since the sound, the rhythm, are an essential element in the meaning.

[...]

The English genius, with its instinctive passion for freedom, is impatient of rules and set patterns; and no sooner was the sonnet introduced into England than our poets began making variations on the Italian pattern. One only of these variations has survived as an alternative and independent form, the quiet [*sic*] distinct form adopted by Shakespeare, with its three quatrains clinched by a concluding couplet. Both forms have triumphantly justified themselves. But in between them we find variations which sometimes may have been conscious attempts to improve on the Italian pattern, but, I think, more often are due to laziness, and impatience at the necessity of finding so many rhymes as are required. The fact remains that the strict form is the most successful...

The song is the simplest form of lyric. It is the purest and most immediate expression of the impulse which is fundamental in all forms of art and is allied to the dance. I think we should all agree that a song suggests something that seems to sing itself, something that we feel was made for music or has such music in itself that it does not need the enhancement of actual notes. A certain brevity then seems essential, or rather singleness and simplicity of motive... We recognize at once the singing voice.

[...]

It is of course in the ballads, of which we have so magnificent a store, that the refrain is oftenest employed. The peculiar value of repetition and refrain are eminently seen in one of the greatest of all these ballads, 'Edward, Edward'. It is like strokes of a hammer driving the tragedy of the situation into the mind with repeated blows. It makes for intensity as nothing else could do...

[...] Just as song merges into lyric, so lyric merges into ode. In neither case is there a defined boundary; and yet there are certain poems which we could not call by any other name than that of ode. [...] We do not always remember that ceremony is one of the arts; a great art and one in which we English, I think, have often excelled. The ode, then, we may say, is the lyric at its most complex and exalted, a public rather than a private utterance, and having in its most developed form a sort of orchestral character. [...]

In recent years there has been a growing movement in favour of the public speaking of poetry. Having had a good deal of experience of this art, I can testify that it supplies a sort of automatic criticism of the poems spoken; it is a test which shows up defects and weaknesses and at the same time discloses unsuspected beauties. There has been also a very interesting development of choric speaking. Now if poets were to compose with a view to such performances, I think it might infuse into the ode a new vitality. Occasions of ceremony might be enhanced by poetry.

[...]

& Three Drawings
Keith Douglas

Reproduced by permission of the owner, Stanley Christopherson

10 A Day in December
Edmund Blunden

The haze upon the meadow
  Denies the death of a year,
For the sun's within it, something bridal
  Is more than dreaming here.
There is no end, no severance,
No moment of deliverance,
  No quietus made,
Though quiet abounds and deliverance moves
  In that sunny shade.

What is winter? a word,
  A figure, a clever guess.
That time-word does not utter at all
  This drowsy wakefulness.
The secret stream scorns interval,
Though the calendar shouts one from the wall –
  The spirit works always;
And death is no more dead than this
  Flower-haunted haze.

PR 34:1, 1943

11

The Chink
Robert Graves

A sunbeam on the well-waxed oak,
   In shape resembling not at all
The ragged chink by which it broke
   Into this darkened hall,
   Swims round and golden over me,
   The sun's plenipotentiary.

So may my round love a chink find:
   With such address to break
Into your grief-occluded mind
   As you shall not mistake
But, rising, open to me for truth's sake.[1]

---

1 LETTERS TO THE EDITOR
   Sir,
      Will you please assure my readers that the mysterious 'writhing' in the last
   line of my poem 'The Chink' is the work of a printer's devil with a lisp. I wrote
   'rising', and should be obliged if you filled his mouth with soap.
   Yours,
   ROBERT GRAVES

   We apologise to Mr Graves, and repeat his poem in its correct text. – Ed.

PR 40:4, 1949

& *from* The Journey of Sidney Keyes
Richard Hoggart

Until you have crossed the desert and faced that fire
Love is an evil, a shaking of the hand,
A sick pain draining courage from the heart.
                              'The Wilderness'

[...] Auden's generation had had time to argue; to consider detailed polit-
ical processes for the staving-off of defeat; to debate the technique of
social improvement. They had time to be clever. Keyes and his friends
had to jump; they *knew* that very soon they would be in the infantry. That
is perhaps the essential difference, and it is that which ensured that the
spokesman of the period, whoever he was, would be intense and broody,
a little humourless. I do not believe that Keyes, at any time, would have
written 'social' poetry; he just was not built that way. The interest lies in
the fact that the times were ripe for a personal, a cosmic poet, and that
they found it in Keyes. His 'historic' interest for us is probably therefore
almost as great as our interest in him personally. But it was definitely not
good that Keyes should see himself as a significant figure in history.
Now and again in fact, he did try to be a conscious spokesman of the
period, and wrote bad poetry (see 'Timoshenko', a downright failure).
Obviously, he was to work by implication. [...]

Thus we come to the beginning of 1943 when Keyes was twenty, and
a subaltern in the West Kents. At this point he wrote 'The Wilderness'
which is, although one or two minor pieces were written later, essentially
his last poem. In it Keyes faced, for the first time clearly, fully, and
economically, this problem on which he had worked for so long. The
thought is controlled as it was not in 'The Foreign Gate'; and, almost
throughout, the speech matches the thought. It possesses a significance,
a historical aptness beyond itself; because of that it is as much the poem
of a decade as 'The Waste Land' was.

It appears, from a draft which has remained, that he began by writing
the poem, as he had written its predecessors, in the second person plural.
Then, after three stanzas, he crossed out all the 'you's' and substituted
'I's'. In fact, as the poem develops it becomes obvious that this time it
could only have been written personally. But why the change after three

stanzas? Did Keyes realize only at this point and in the very progress of his last poem that he would, after all, have to go through alone? The first stanza, as originally written, echoes very plainly the 'Foreign Gate' and 'Advice for a Journey'. It was amended, leaving

> The red rock wilderness
> Shall be my dwelling place.

The decision had been made. Keyes had crossed the bar. The lovers were left in the garden; the journey through the desert and to the phoenix bird must be a solitary one,

> I turn my face to the sun, remembering gardens
> Planted by others – Longinus, Guillaume de Lorris
> And all love's gardeners, in an early May.
> O sing, small ancient bird, for I am going
> Into the sun's garden, the red rock desert.

There is, it will be seen even from that fragment, a haunting sense of loss. During the first two of the five sections of the poem this nostalgia alternates almost equally with the statement of the argument. But so much has Keyes' technique improved that the nostalgia is made use of by being introduced in a lighter key from that in which the main statements are made; in lyric quatrains as against blank verse. By this means the sense of loss is accentuated, and the lines given the childlike quality of a song heard a long way off,

> And all the poets of summer
> Must lament another spirit's passing over,

(and then the key changes)

> O never weep for me, my love,
> Or seek me in this land:
> But light a candle for my luck
> And bear it in your hand.

[…] Here, especially in the final section, Keyes felt himself in sight, in expressible sight, of a synthesis. The poetry has the lankness, the tensed bareness of the decision which it states: –

> We go now, but others must follow:
> The rivers are drying, the trees are falling,
> The red rock wilderness is calling.

And they will find who linger in the garden
The way of time is not a river but
A pilferer who will not ask their pardon.

[...]

And so, a few weeks after writing 'The Wilderness', Keyes sailed for Africa; and but a very few more weeks and he was dead. There is no doubt that for that journey he had prepared himself; he had worked it out and reached a momentary assurance. He had been able, at the end, to make a clear statement: –

Flesh is fire, frost and fire:
Flesh is fire in this wilderness of fire
Which is our dwelling.

12 Herm
Kathleen Raine

Blind I know with senses rising from fern and tree,
Blind lips and fingers trace a god no eyes can see,
Blind I touch love's monster form that bounds
My world of field and forest, crowns my hills.
Blind I worship a blind god in his hour
Whose serpent-wand over my soul has power
To lead the crowding souls back from the borders of death,
Heaven's swift-winged fiat, earth's primeval monolith.

PR 39:3, 1948

13
Swift
Walter de la Mare

That mighty mind!
Those bleak, undaunted eyes,
Never to life or love resigned! –
How strange that he who abhorred cant, humbug, lies,
Could be deceived by such simplicities
As age, as ordure, and as size!

14
The Death of Antonio Torres Heredia, known as 'El Camborio'
Roy Campbell

after Federico García Lorca

Voices of death along the river
Are heard. Old voices, croaking death,
Surround and trap the manly voice
With the carnations in its breath.
He bit the boots that kicked his ribs
With slashes of a tusky boar;
He bucked the soapy somersaults
Of dolphins, slithering in his gore;
He dyed in his opponents' blood
The crimson necktie that he wore,
But then there were four knives to one
So, in the end, he could no more.

PR 40:1, 1949
PR 39:2, 1948

*

When in the grey bull of the waters
Stars strike their javelins: in the hours
When yearling calves are softly dreaming
Veronicas of gillyflowers,
Voices of death reechoed screaming
Along that riverbank of ours.

*

'Antonio, of Camborio's clan,
Who have blue manes both thick and strong
With olive skins, like moonlight green,
And red carnations in their song,
Beside the Guadalquivir's shore,
Who took your life? Who could it be?'
'The Four Heredias, my Cousins,
The children of Benamejí.
Things that they did not grudge to others
Were things for which they envied me –
My boots of bright Corinthian hue,
My medals made of ivory,
And this fine skin wherein the olive
And jasmine both so well agree.'

'Alas, Antonio el Camborio,
So worthy of an Empress high,
Remember now to pray the Virgin
Because you are about to die.'
'Oh Federico García Lorca,
Go quickly while there's time, and raise
The Civil Guard: for I am wilting
And broken, like a stalk of maize.

*

He had three leakages of blood
And then, in profile, there he died –
Live currency of gold, whose like
Can never be again supplied.
A withered angel came and placed
A pillow underneath his head,
While others, with a weary flush,
Lit up a candle for the dead.
And when the four Heredia cousins
Back to Benamejí had come,
Voices of death along the river
Ceased to be heard, and all was dumb.

15 Desert
Hilaire Belloc

I stood in the desert and I watched the snows
Of Aurès, in their splendour from the west.
Sahara darkened: and I thought of those
That hold in isolation and are blest.

They that in dereliction grow perfected:
They that are silent: they that stand apart:
They that shall judge the world as God's elected:
They that have had the sword athwart the heart.

PR 40:1, 1949

16 The Raven
Sylvia Townsend Warner

As rivers through the plain
Widen and turn not back again
Descending man forgot
The ark on Ararat.

Grounded before the gale,
Its swarthy timbers split and failed.
Its voyaging profile was
Blunted with vines and moss;

And emptied of all the prayers
Hymns and Te Deums of its passengers
No voice remained in it
But Noah's old she-cat

Praising her spotted young;
Till long years later came a long
Slow wing-beat through the dark
And closed upon the ark.

Presently, there spoke
The raven, dying: Out, alack!
News of Elysium
I bring – but they are gone.

PR 40:2, 1949

17

A Meeting
Frances Cornford

Who has not seen their lover
Walking at ease,
With usual feet that cover
A pavement under trees;
Not singular, apart,
But featured, footed, dressed,
Approaching like the rest,
In the same dapple of the summer caught;
And thought:
There comes my heart.

&

from Some Post-War Poets – An Appreciation
F. Pratt Green

The wit who said: 'Nowadays only poets read poetry and even they read only their own,' was near enough the truth to score a hit, the truth probably being that more people are writing poetry than buying it. It is no secret that at a time when few papers and periodicals give space to poetry, when publishers complain they cannot sell it, and poetry magazines wink out like bubbles, no less than ten thousand poems were submitted to the editors of *New Poems, 1954*, representing, one supposes, at least a thousand poets! The struggle for recognition, under such conditions, must be severe.

This question of recognition is worth pondering. A poet, unless he is as odd a creature as Emily Dickinson, hopes for recognition because poetry is a communication of experience; he needs a public to share the experience, to stimulate him, to criticize him. If he fails to gain recogni-

PR 40:2, 1949
PR 45:2, 1954

tion, he may be tempted to lower his aesthetic standards, or retire to an ivory tower, or express himself in some other, and less frustrating, medium. Recognition, on the other hand, confirms him in his vocation and thereby fortifies him in the task of fulfilling it. Not that success alone is evidence of genuine talent; luck and influence play too large a part in what a friend of mine calls 'this poetry racket' for success to be the criterion.

Now the war, and its continuing effect on publishing, delayed recognition for some poets who are at last finding their public. A new poet, for this reason, may be a man of thirty-five. He arrives, so to speak, with the poet of twenty-five, who has not been kept waiting in the cold. Among the older poets who have won recognition since the war we may mention Charles Causley, Robert Conquest, Ursula Wood, Rob Lyle, Michael Hamburger, Kingsley Amis, James Kirkup, John Wain, Dannie Abse, David Wright, and even then we should leave out a dozen others worthy of a place; among the younger poets we would specially commend Charles Higham and Thom Gunn. It is noteworthy that all these poets have in common a capacity to write freshly within the tradition and a distaste for mystification and obscurity. The period of intense experimentation would seem to have ended and its lessons to have been assimilated. But it will be some time before those who ceased to read poetry in the experimental period discover that the rough places are once more being made plain.

[…] Four post-war poets, as yet unnamed by me, whose work strikes me as having exceptional significance and interest [are] D.J. Enright and Thomas Blackburn from the older group, Elizabeth Jennings and W.S. Merwin from the younger.

[…]

18

Deus Loci (Forio D'Ischia)
Lawrence Durrell

'era nel tempo quendo Filomena...'

1

All our religions founder, you
remain, small sunburnt deus loci
safe in your natal shrine,
landscape of the precocious southern heart,
continuously revived in passion's common
tragic and yet incorrigible spring:
in every special laughter overheard,
your specimen is everything –
accents of the little cackling god,
part animal, part insect, and part bird.

2

This dust, this royal dust, our mother
modelled by spring-belonging rain
whose soft blank drops console
a single vineyard's fever or a region
falls now in soft percussion on the earth's
old stretched and wrinkled vellum skin:
a footprint in of the god, but out of season,
yet in your sudden coming know
life lives itself without recourse to reason.

PR 41:6, 1950

3

On how many of your clement springs
the fishermen set forth, the foresters
resign their empty glasses, rise,
confront the morning star, accept
the motiveless patronage of all you are –
desire recaptured on the sea or land
in the fables of fish, or grapes held up,
a fistful of some champion wine
glowing like a stained-glass window
in a drunkard's trembling hand.

4

All the religions of the dust can tell –
this body of damp clay that cumbered so
Adam, and those before, was given him,
material for his lamp and spoon and body:
to renovate your terra cotta shrines
whose cupids unashamed
to make a fable of the common lot
curled up like watchsprings in a kiss,
or turned to *putti* for a lover's bed,
or *amorini* for a shepherd's little cot.

5

Known before the expurgation of gods
wherever nature's carelessness exposed
her children to the fear of the unknown –
in families gathered by hopeless sickness
about a dying candle, or in sailors
on tilting decks and under shrouded planets:
wherever the unknown has displaced the known
you encouraged in the fellowship of wine
of love and husbandry: and in despair
only to think of you and you were there.

6

The saddle-nose, the hairy thighs
composed these vines, these humble vines,
so dedicated to themselves yet offering
in the black froth of grapes their increment
to pleasure or to sadness where a poor
peasant at a husky church-bell's chime
crosses himself: on some cracked pedestal
by the sighing sea sets eternally up,
item by item, his small mid-day meal,
garlic and bread, the wine-can and the cup.

7

Image of our own dust in wine!
drinkers of that royal dust pressed out
drop by cool drop in science and in love
into a model of the absconding god's
image – human like our own. Or else in other
mixtures, of breath in kisses dropped
under the fig's dark noonday lantern, yes,
lovers like tenants of a wishing-well
whose heartbeats labour though all time has stopped.

8

Your panic fellowship is everywhere,
not only in love's first great illness known,
but in the exile of objects lost
to context, broken hearts, spilt milk,
oaths disregarded, laws forgotten:
or on the seashore some old pilot's
capital in rags of sail, snapped oars,
water-jars choked with sand,
and further on, half hidden, the fatal letter
in the cold fingers of some marble hand.

9

Deus loci, your provinces extend
throughout the domains of logic,
beyond the eyes watching from dusty murals,
or the philosopher's critical impatience
to understand, to be done with life:
beyond even the mind's dark spools
in a vine-wreath or an old wax cross
you can become the nurse and wife of fools,
their actions and their nakedness –
all the heart's profit or the loss.

10

So today, after many years, we meet
at this high window overlooking
the best of Italy, smiling under rain,
that rattles down the leaves like sparrow-shot,
scatters the reapers, the sunburnt girls,
rises in the sour dust of this table,
these books, unfinished letters – all
refreshed again in you O spirit of place,
Presence long since divined, delayed, and waited for,
and here met face to face.

19

The Gift Outright
Robert Frost

The land was ours before we were the land's.
She was our land more than a hundred years
Before we were her people. She was ours
In Massachusetts, in Virginia,
But we were England's, still colonials,
Possessing what we still were unpossessed by,
Possessed by what we now no more possessed.
Something we were withholding left us weak
Until we found out that it was ourselves
We were withholding from our land of living
And forthwith found salvation in surrender.
Such as we were we gave ourselves outright
(The deed of gift was many deeds of war)
To the land vaguely realizing westward,
But still unstoried, artless, unenhanced,
Such as she was, such as she will become.

First published in *The Witness Tree*, 1942 (US). Poem read by the author at the ceremonial induction of Joseph Kennedy [*sic*] as President of the United States, January 20, 1961.

20 T.S. Eliot Speaks
An interview with Donald Hall

INTERVIEWER   *Perhaps I can begin at the beginning. Do you remember the circumstances under which you began to write poetry in St Louis when you were a boy?*

ELIOT   I began I think about the age of fourteen, under the inspiration of Fitzgerald's *Omar Khayyam,* to write a number of very gloomy and atheistical and despairing quatrains in the same style, which fortunately I suppressed completely – so completely that they don't exist. I never showed them to anybody. The first poem that shows is one which appeared first in the *Smith Academy Record,* and later in *The Harvard Advocate,* which was written as an exercise for my English teacher and was an imitation of Ben Jonson. He thought it very good for a boy of fifteen or sixteen. Then I wrote a few at Harvard, just enough to qualify for election to an editorship on *The Harvard Advocate,* which I enjoyed. Then I had an outburst during my junior and senior years. I became much more prolific, under the influence first of Baudelaire and then of Jules Laforgue, whom I discovered I think in my junior year at Harvard.

INTERVIEWER   *Did anyone in particular introduce you to the French poets? Not Irving Babbitt, I suppose.*

ELIOT   No, Babbitt would be the last person! The one poem that Babbitt always held up for admiration was Gray's *Elegy.* And that's a fine poem, but I think this shows certain limitations on Babbitt's part, God bless him. I have advertised my source, I think; it's Arthur Symons's book on French poetry [*The Symbolist in Modern Literature*], which I came across in the Harvard Union. In those days the Harvard Union was a meeting place for any undergraduate who chose to belong to it. They had a very nice little library, like the libraries in many Harvard houses now. I liked his quotations and I went to a foreign book-shop somewhere in Boston (I've forgotten the name and I don't know whether it still exists) which specialized in French and German and other foreign books and found Laforgue, and other poets. I can't imagine why that bookshop should have had a few poets like Laforgue in stock. Goodness knows how long they'd had them or whether there were any other demands for them.

INTERVIEWER *When you were an undergraduate, were you aware of the dominating presence of any older poets? Today the poet in his youth is writing in the age of Eliot and Pound and Stevens. Can you remember your own sense of the literary times? I wonder if your situation may not have been extremely different.*

ELIOT I think it was rather an advantage not having any living poets in England or America in whom one took any particular interest. I don't know what it would be like, but I think it would be a rather troublesome distraction to have such a lot of dominating presences, as you call them, about. Fortunately we weren't bothered by each other.

INTERVIEWER *Were you aware of people like Hardy or Robinson at all?*

ELIOT I was slightly aware of Robinson because I read an article about him in *The Atlantic Monthly* which quoted some of his poems, and that wasn't my cup of tea at all. Hardy was hardly known to be a poet at that time. One read his novels, but his poetry only really became conspicuous to a later generation. Then there was Yeats, but it was the early Yeats. It was too much Celtic twilight for me. There was really nothing except the people of the nineties who had all died of drink or suicide or one thing or another.

*

INTERVIEWER *I understand that it was Conrad Aiken who introduced you and your work to Pound.*

ELIOT Yes, it was. Aiken was a very generous friend. He tried to place some of my poems in London, one summer when he was over, with Harold Monro and others. Nobody would think of publishing them. He brought them back to me. Then in 1914, I think, we were both in London in the summer. He said, 'You go to Pound. Show him your poems.' He thought Pound might like them. Aiken liked them, though they were very different from his.

INTERVIEWER   *Do you remember the circumstances of your first meeting with Pound?*

ELIOT   I think I went to call on him first. I think I made a good impression, in his little triangular sitting-room in Kensington. He said, 'Send me your poems.' And he wrote back, 'This is as good as anything I've seen. Come around and have a talk about them.' Then he pushed them on Harriet Monroe, which took a little time.

INTERVIEWER   *You have mentioned in print that Pound cut* The Waste Land *from a much larger poem into its present form. Were you benefited by his criticism of your poems in general? Did he cut other poems?*

ELIOT   Yes. At that period, yes. He was a marvellous critic because he didn't try to turn you into an imitation of himself. He tried to see what you were trying to do.

*

INTERVIEWER   *What sort of thing did Pound cut from* The Waste Land? *Did he cut whole sections?*

ELIOT   Whole sections, yes. There was a long section about a shipwreck. I don't know what that had to do with anything else, but it was rather inspired by the Ulysses Canto in *The Inferno*, I think. Then there was another section which was an imitation *Rape of the Lock*. Pound said, 'It's no use trying to do something that somebody else has done as well as it can be done. Do something different.'

INTERVIEWER   *Did the excisions change the intellectual structure of the poem?*

ELIOT   No. I think it was just as structureless, only in a more futile way, in the longer version.

INTERVIEWER   *I have a question about the poem which is related to its composition. In* Thoughts After Lambeth *you denied the allegation of critics who said that you expressed 'the disillusionment of a generation', in* The Waste Land, *or you denied that it was your intention. Now F.R. Leavis, I believe, has said that the poem exhibits no progression; yet on the other hand, more recent critics, writing after your later poetry, found* The Waste Land *Christian. I wonder if this was part of your intention.*

ELIOT   No, it wasn't part of my conscious intention. I think that in *Thoughts After Lambeth* I was speaking of intentions more in a negative than in a positive sense, to say what was not my intention. I wonder what an 'intention' means! One wants to get something off one's chest. One doesn't know quite what it is that one wants to get off the chest until one's got it off. But I couldn't apply the word 'intention' positively to any of my poems. Or to any poem.

INTERVIEWER   *I have another question about you and Pound and your earlier career. I have read somewhere that you and Pound decided to write quatrains, in the late teens, because* vers libre *had gone far enough.*

ELIOT   I think that's something Pound said. And the suggestion of writing quatrains was his. He put me on to [Gautier's] *Émaux et Camées.*

INTERVIEWER   *I wonder about your ideas on the relation of form to subject. Would you then have chosen the form before you knew quite what you were going to write in it?*

ELIOT   Yes, in a way. One studied originals. We studied Gautier's poems and then we thought, 'Have I anything to say in which this form will be useful?' And we experimented. The form gave the impetus to the content.

INTERVIEWER   *Why was* vers libre *the form you chose to use in your early poems?*

ELIOT   My early *vers libre*, of course, was started under the endeavour to practise the same form as Laforgue. This meant merely rhyming lines of irregular length, with the rhymes coming in irregular places. It wasn't quite so *libre* as much *vers*, especially the sort which Ezra called 'Amygism' [a reference to Amy Lowell, who captured and informed Imagism]. Then, of course, there were things in the next phase which were freer, like 'Rhapsody on a Windy Night'. I don't know whether I had any sort of model or practice in mind when I did that. It just came that way.

INTERVIEWER   *Did you feel, possibly, that you were writing against something, more than from any model? Against the Poet Laureate perhaps?*

ELIOT   No, no, no. I don't think one was constantly trying to reject things, but just trying to find out what was right for oneself. One really ignored Poet Laureates as such, the Robert Bridges. I don't think good poetry can be produced in a kind of political attempt to overthrow some existing form. I think it just supersedes. People find a way in which they can say something. 'I can't say it that way, what way can I find that will do?' One didn't really *bother* about the existing modes.

INTERVIEWER   *Can I ask you if you have any plans for poems now?*

ELIOT   No, I haven't any plans for anything at the moment, except that I think I would like, having just got rid of *The Elder Statesman* (I only passed the final proofs just before we left London), to do a little prose writing of a critical sort. I never think more than one step ahead. Do I want to do another play or do I want to do more poems? I don't know until I find I want to do it.

★

INTERVIEWER   *Do you have any unfinished poems that you look at occasionally?*

ELIOT   I haven't much in that way, no. As a rule, with me an unfinished thing is a thing that might as well be rubbed out. It's better, if there's something good in it that I might make use of elsewhere, to leave it at the back of my mind than on paper in a drawer. If I leave it in a drawer it remains the same thing, but if it's in the memory it becomes transformed into something else. As I have said before, *Burnt Norton* began with bits that had to be cut out of *Murder in the Cathedral*. I learned in *Murder in the Cathedral* that it's no use putting in nice lines that you think are good poetry if they don't get the action on at all. That was when Martin Browne was useful. He would say, 'There are very nice lines here, but they've nothing to do with what's going on on stage'.

INTERVIEWER   *Are any of your minor poems actually sections cut out of longer works? There are two that sound like* The Hollow Men.

ELIOT   Oh, those were the preliminary sketches. Those things were earlier. Others I published in periodicals, but not in my collected poems. You don't want to say the same thing twice in one book.

INTERVIEWER   *You seem often to have written poems in sections. Did they begin as separate poems? I am thinking of* Ash Wednesday, *in particular.*

ELIOT   Yes, like *The Hollow Men* it originated out of separate poems. As I recall, one or two early drafts of parts of *Ash Wednesday* appeared in *Commerce* and elsewhere. Then gradually I came to see it as a sequence. That's one way in which my mind does seem to have worked throughout the years poetically – doing things separately and then seeing the possibility of fusing them together, altering them, and making a kind of whole of them.

INTERVIEWER   *Do you write anything now in the vein of* Old Possum's Book of Practical Cats *or* King Bolo?

ELIOT   Those things do come from time to time! I keep a few notes of such verse, and there are one or two incomplete cats that will probably never be written. There's one about a glamour cat. It turned out too sad. This would never do. I can't make my children weep over a cat who's gone wrong. She had a very questionable career, did this cat. It wouldn't do for the audience of my previous volume of cats. I've never done any dogs. Of course, dogs don't seem to lend themselves to verse quite so well, collectively, as cats. I may eventually do an enlarged edition of my cats. That's more likely than another volume. I did add one poem, which was originally done as an advertisement for Faber and Faber. It seemed to be fairly successful. Oh yes, one wants to keep one's hand in, you know, in every type of poem, serious and frivolous and proper and improper. One doesn't want to lose one's skill.

INTERVIEWER *There's a good deal of interest now in the process of writing. I wonder if you could talk more about your actual habits in writing verse. I've heard you composed on the typewriter.*

ELIOT Partly on the typewriter. A great deal of my new play, *The Elder Statesman*, was produced in pencil and paper, very roughly. Then I typed it myself first before my wife got to work on it. In typing myself I make alterations, very considerable ones. But whether I write or type, composition of any length, a play for example, means for me regular hours, say ten to one. I found that three hours a day is about all I can do of actual composing. I could do polishing perhaps later. I sometimes found at first that I wanted to go on longer, but when I looked at the stuff the next day, what I'd done after the three hours were up was never satisfactory. It's much better to stop and think about something else quite different.

INTERVIEWER *Did you ever write any of your non-dramatic poems on schedule? Perhaps the* Four Quartets?

ELIOT Only 'occasional' verse. The *Quartets* were not on schedule. Of course the first one was written in the 1930s but the three which were written during the war were more in fits and starts. In 1939 if there hadn't been a war I would probably have tried to write another play. And I think it's a very good thing I didn't have the opportunity. From my personal point of view, the one good thing the war did was to prevent me from writing another play too soon. I saw some of the things that were wrong with *Family Reunion*, but I think it was much better that any possible play was blocked for five years or so to get up a head of steam. The form of the *Quartets* fitted in very nicely to the conditions under which I was writing, or could write at all. I could write them in sections and I didn't have to have quite the same continuity; it didn't matter if a day or two elapsed when I did not write, as they frequently did, while I did war jobs.

*

INTERVIEWER   *Do you feel that the* Four Quartets *are your best work?*

ELIOT   Yes, and I'd like to feel that they get better as they go on. The second is better than the first, the third is better than the second, and the fourth is the best of all. At any rate, that's the way I flatter myself.

INTERVIEWER   *This is a very general question, but I wonder if you could give advice to a young poet about what disciplines or attitudes he might cultivate to improve his art.*

ELIOT   I think it's awfully dangerous to give general advice. I think the best one can do for a young poet is to criticize in detail a particular poem of his. Argue it with him, if necessary; give him your opinion, and if there are any generalizations to be made, let him do them himself. I've found that different people have different ways of working and things come to them in different ways. You're never sure when you're uttering a statement that's generally valid for all poets or when it's something that only applies to yourself. I think nothing is worse than to try to form people in your own image.

INTERVIEWER   *Do you think there's any possible generalization to be made about the fact that all the better poets now, younger than you, seem to be teachers?*

ELIOT   I don't know. I think the only generalization that can be made of any value will be one which will be made a generation later. All you can say at this point is that at different times there are different possibilities of making a living, or different limitations on making a living. Obviously, a poet has got to find a way of making a living apart from his poetry. After all, artists do a great deal of teaching, and musicians too.

INTERVIEWER   *Do you think that the optimum career for a poet would involve no work at all but reading and writing?*

ELIOT   No, I think that would be – but there again one can only talk about oneself. It is very dangerous to give an optimal career for everybody, but I feel quite sure that if I'd started by having independent means, if I hadn't had to bother about earning a living and could have given all my time to poetry, it would have had a deadening influence on me.

INTERVIEWER *Why?*

ELIOT I think that for me it's been very useful to exercise other activities, such as working in a bank, or publishing even. And I think also that the difficulty of not having as much time as I would like has given me a greater pressure of concentration. I mean it has prevented me from writing too much. The danger, as a rule, of having nothing else to do is that one might write too much rather than concentrating and perfecting smaller amounts. That would be *my* danger.

INTERVIEWER *Do you consciously attempt, now, to keep up with the poetry that is being written by young men in England and America?*

ELIOT I don't now, not with any conscientiousness. I did at one time when I was reading little reviews and looking out for new talent as a publisher. But as one gets older, one is not quite confident in [one's] own ability to distinguish new genius among younger men. You're always afraid that you are going as you have seen your elders go. At Faber and Faber now I have a younger colleague who reads poetry manuscripts. But even before that, when I came across new stuff that I thought had real merit, I would show it to younger friends whose critical judgment I trusted and get their opinion. But of course there is always the danger that there is merit where you don't see it. So I'd rather have the younger people to look at things first. If they like it, they will show it to me, and see whether I like it too. When you get something that knocks over younger people of taste and judgment and older people as well, then that's likely to be something important. Sometimes there's a lot of resistance. I shouldn't like to feel that I was resisting, as my work was resisted when it was new by people who thought that it was imposture of some kind or other.

INTERVIEWER   *Do you feel that younger poets in general have repudi-*
ated the experimentalism of the early poetry of this century? Few poets
now seem to be resisted the way you were resisted, but some older critics
like Herbert Read believe that poetry after you has been a regression to
outdated modes. When you talked about Milton the second time, you
spoke of the function of poetry as a retarder of change, as well as a maker
of change, in language.

ELIOT   Yes, I don't think you want a revolution every ten years.

INTERVIEWER   *But is it possible to think that there has been a counter-*
revolution rather than an exploration of new possibilities?

ELIOT   No, I don't see anything that looks to me like a counter-
revolution. After a period of getting away from the traditional
forms, comes a period of curiosity in making new experiments
with traditional forms. This can produce very good work if what
has happened in between has made a difference; when it's not
merely going back, but taking up an old form, which has been out
of use for a time, and making something new with it. That is not
counter-revolution. Nor does mere regression deserve the name.
There is a tendency in some quarters to revert to Georgian scenery
and sentiments: and among the public there are always people who
prefer mediocrity, and when they get it, say 'What a relief! Here's
some real poetry again'. And there are also people who like poetry
to be modern, but for whom the really creative stuff is too strong
– they need something diluted.

    What seems to be the best of what I've seen in young poets is
not reaction at all. I'm not going to mention any names, for I don't
like to make public judgments about younger poets. The best stuff
is a further development of a less revolutionary character than
what appeared in earlier years of the century.

INTERVIEWER   *I have some unrelated questions that I'd like to end with.*
In 1945 you wrote 'a poet must take as his material his own language as
it is actually spoken around him'. And later you wrote, 'the music of
poetry, then, will be a music latent in the common speech of his time'.
After the second remark, you disparaged 'standardized BBC English'.
Now isn't one of the changes of the last fifty years, and perhaps even more

of the last five years, the growing dominance of commercial speech through the means of communication? What you referred to as 'BBC English' has become immensely more powerful through the ITA and BBC television, not to speak of CBS, NBC, and ABC. Does this development make the problem of the poet and his relationship to common speech more difficult?

ELIOT   You've raised a very good point there. I think you're right; it does make it more difficult.

INTERVIEWER   *I wanted you to make the point.*

ELIOT   Yes, but you wanted the point to be *made*. So I'll take the responsibility of making it: I do think that where you have these modern means of communication and means of imposing the speech and idioms of a small number on the mass of people at large, it does complicate the problem very much. I don't know to what extent that goes for film speech, but obviously radio speech has done much more.

INTERVIEWER   *I wonder if there's a possibility that what you mean by common speech will disappear.*

ELIOT   That is a very gloomy prospect. But very likely indeed.

INTERVIEWER   *Are there other problems for a writer in our time which are unique? Does the prospect of human annihilation have any particular effect on the poet?*

ELIOT   I don't see why the prospect of human annihilation should affect the poet differently from men of other vocations. It will affect him as a human being, no doubt in proportion to his sensitiveness.

INTERVIEWER   *Another unrelated question: I can see why a man's criticism is better for his being a practising poet, better although subject to his own prejudices. But do you feel that writing criticism has helped you as a poet?*

ELIOT   In an indirect way it has helped me somehow as a poet – to put down in writing my critical valuation of the poets who have influenced me and whom I admire. It is merely making an influence more conscious and more articulate. It's been a rather natural impulse. I think probably my best critical essays are essays on the poets who had influenced me, so to speak, long before I thought of writing essays about them. They're of more value, probably, than any of my more generalized remarks.

INTERVIEWER   *G.S. Fraser wonders, in an essay about the two of you, whether you ever met Yeats. From remarks in your talk about him, it would seem that you did. Could you tell us the circumstances?*

ELIOT   Of course I had met Yeats many times. Yeats was always very gracious when one met him and had the art of treating younger writers as if they were his equals and contemporaries. I can't remember any one particular occasion.

INTERVIEWER   *I have heard that you consider that your poetry belongs in the tradition of American literature. Could you tell us why?*

ELIOT   I'd say that my poetry has obviously more in common with my distinguished contemporaries in America, than with anything written in my generation in England. That I'm sure of.

INTERVIEWER   *Do you think there's a connection with the American past?*

ELIOT   Yes, but I couldn't put it any more definitely than that, you see. It wouldn't be what it is, and I imagine it wouldn't be so good; putting it as modestly as I can, it wouldn't be what it is if I'd been born in England, and it wouldn't be what it is if I'd stayed in America. It's a combination of things. But in its sources, in its emotional springs, it comes from America.

INTERVIEWER   *One last thing. Seventeen years ago you said, 'No honest poet can ever feel quite sure of the permanent value of what he has written. He may have wasted his time and messed up his life for nothing.' Do you feel the same now, at seventy?*

ELIOT   There may be honest poets who do feel sure. I don't.

First published in *The Paris Review* 21, Spring/Summer 1959 (France and US).

21

MCMXIV
Philip Larkin

Those long uneven lines
Standing as patiently
As if they were stretched outside
The Oval or Villa Park,
The crowns of hats, the sun
On moustached archaic faces
Grinning as if it were all
An August Bank Holiday lark;

And the shut shops, the bleached
Established names on the sunblinds,
The farthings and sovereigns,
And dark-clothed children at play
Called after kings and queens,
The tin advertisements
For cocoa and twist, and the pubs
Wide open all day;

And the countryside not caring:
The place-names all hazed over
With flowering grasses, and fields
Shadowing Domesday lines
Under wheat's restless silence;
The differently-dressed servants
With tiny rooms in huge houses,
The dust behind limousines;

PR 52:4, 1961

Never such innocence,
Never before or since,
As changed itself to past
Without a word – the men
Leaving the gardens tidy,
The thousands of marriages
Lasting a little while longer:
Never such innocence again.

22 *from* Scottish Literature Today
Hugh MacDiarmid

It is natural to write in one's own language. Only in Scotland is it
regarded as unnatural. This is because Scotland has become so
Anglicized. But that applies only to the middle and upper classes.
The working class still speaks Scots. True, it is a Scots that has
become sadly impoverished, disintegrated into dialects. Yet it
retains a tremendous hold. That is why our music-hall comedians
use it. That is why the use of a Scots phrase in a political speech
can galvanize a Scottish audience as all the surrounding eloquence
in English has failed to do. But so far as literature is concerned it
may be argued that to write in Scots is to confine oneself to a very
small public compared with the immense reading-public of the
English-speaking world. That is true. It is true even of the relatively
small Scots-speaking public itself, for though they speak a form of
Scots they cannot read it. They are used to seeing only English in
print.

But the same argument against Scots as a literary medium was
levelled against Burns by the Edinburgh *literati*. Yet Burns persisted
in writing for the most part in Scots and despite his Anglicized

admonishers achieved a greater international currency than any other poet in the history of literature perhaps. The recent world-wide celebrations of his bicentenary show that Burns would not have done his great work if he had thought it was to end the Scots literary tradition and that his vociferous admirers would never-theless let the language in which he wrote die out and much of his work become unintelligible as a consequence. On the contrary, he wanted Scotland to have a succession of bards to carry on that tradition to endless generations, with, as he said, 'more poetic fire'. His only successors, however, have been wretched imitators who have brought the tradition down to unparalleled depths of doggerel. Burns's devotees have regarded him as the be-all and end-all of Scots poetry. They have bitterly opposed any Scots writing not slavishly based on Burns's models. In exalting Burns they have excluded all his predecessors in the Scots literary tradi-tion to whom he owed so much, and thus they have cut off the object of their idolatry from the past, on the one hand, and off from the future on the other, and thus made Burns a sort of Melchisedek without ancestry or offspring.

Scots pride themselves on their perfervid love of country, yet they are the only people in the world who have acquiesced in the virtual elimination of their own history, literature, and native languages (Scots and Gaelic) from the curricula of their schools and colleges, and given a monopoly to the history, language, and liter-ature of another and very different country. Even yet there is no Chair of Scottish Literature in any of Scotland's four Universities, and a lectureship in the subject (established no more than a few years ago) only in one of them. How is this paradox to be explained? How is the paradox of the tremendous idolizing of Burns to be explained when it is set against the failure of his devo-tees to follow his lead in language, politics, and everything else?

It is not a matter of the loss of Scots as a medium for the whole range of contemporary literary purpose, although many leading writers of various nationalities have recognized that many things can be said in Scots which cannot be expressed in English at all. It is not only that Burns is ceasing to be read, since more and more of the Scottish population do not understand his Scots words, and

that previous Scots literature, by Dunbar, Henryson, and the other
great Scots poets of the fifteenth and sixteenth centuries, is a closed
book to them. But most of our balladry and great treasury of folk-
song is in Scots and that, too, must pass out of ken and with all that
the whole great repertoire of songs in Scots. Much of Sir Walter
Scott, too, will be lost, for his best work, like 'Wandering Willie's
Tale', is in Scots.

Gaelic is already gone so far as all but a tiny fraction of our
people is concerned. Yet as I have said in one of my poems:

> ...We must return
> To the ancient classical Gaelic poets. For in them
> The inestimable treasure is wholly in contact
> With the immense surface of the unconscious. That is how
> They can be of service to us now – that is how
> They were never more important than they are today.

> Our Gaelic forbears possessed their great literature.
> As nothing is possessed by peoples today,
> And in Scotland and Ireland and Wales
> There was a popular understanding and delight
> In literary allusions, technical niceties, and dexterities of
> > expression
> Of which the English even in Elizabethan times,
> Had only the poorest counterpart,
> And have since had none whatever
> And have destroyed it in the Gaelic countries too.

There is a consensus of opinion among critics that, wherever
modern Scottish writers have written in Scots or Gaelic and in
English, by far their best work has invariably been done in the
former. It was this fact that was one of the bases of the Scottish
Literary Movement initiated about 1920 and which has led since
then to the production of one of the finest bodies of Scots verse
any period in our literary history has to its credit. To achieve this
the poets had to enrich their linguistic medium by reviving much
lapsed vocabulary. They had also to make a synthesis of many
dialects (as Burns himself did), and they had to go back behind

Burns to Dunbar and the other great medievals. These were all learned men.

So are our contemporary poets. One of their main objectives was to oust the horde of analphabetic village rhymesters who, following Burns, had reduced our tradition to such a pitiful pass. Above all, they repudiated the common notion that poetry is all a matter of inspiration – not an art in which miracles are only vouchsafed to a prepared mind. Burns himself is thought to have been a perfect example of the simple spontaneous poet. What nonsense! As Burns himself said:

> I have no great faith in the boastful pretentions to intuitive propriety and unlaboured elegance. The rough material of Fine Writing is certainly the gift of Genius; but I as firmly believe that the workmanship is the united effort of Pains, Attention, and repeated Trial.

Above all, the quotation from Burns's own writings that can stand best as the slogan of the whole Scottish Literary Movement today is the following: 'Let our National Muse preserve its native features. They are, I own, frequently wild and unreduceable to the modern rules; but on that very eccentricity, perhaps, depends a great part of their effect.'

Certainly it cannot be denied that so far as poetry is concerned, Scottish poets who have written in English have seldom done better, relative to the best poetry in Scots, than Burns himself did in his English poems, which were virtually worthless. Dr Kurt Wittig, in *The Scottish Tradition in Literature* – by far the best book on the subject – shows conclusively that the concept that Scottish literature is a tributary to the larger English stream cannot be defended for a moment, but that there is a Scottish tradition in poetry if not in prose and that it is largely independent of developments in English verse. Far from being provincial, the Scottish tradition is, if anything, more closely linked with the culture of France, Holland, and Europe in general than the English ever was.

[...]

23

FEATURE
from Poetry in Scotland

Introduction and a Selection
Norman MacCaig

It's impossible to talk about contemporary Scottish poetry without talking almost all the time about Hugh MacDiarmid. After nearly two centuries, during which hundreds of tiny poets wrote thousands of tiny non-poems, imitating the worst of Burns and never taking a peep over the Kailyard wall, he took the Scots language by the scruff of the dictionary, reviving words that were obsolescent or obsolete, and sent them out, fat and lively again, to discuss matters that had lain outside the scope of Scottish poetry for centuries and to introduce others that the old Makars had never heard of. The point is, in his best poems, and there are a lot of them, there is no whiff of *pedantry*. The language is alive and lively. And what it deals with is of a range and scope unparalleled in Scottish writing.

When he had done what he wanted to do in Scots, he took on English. Here again, linguistically and thematically, his range is extraordinary. An all-inclusive 'poetry of ideas' is what he is after and he, who first made his name with tiny lyrics in Scots, has pursued that aim in a number of enormously long poems in English.

He is a good man at making enemies as well as friends, so it isn't surprising that, while many literary sleepwalkers in Scotland got very rude awakenings indeed, others were stimulated by his atrocious energy to find out what they could do themselves. The result has been called by a big name, the 'Scottish Renaissance', and if it's big, it's not altogether absurd. One would have to go far back to find a time when the level of Scottish poetry was as high as it has been in the last thirty years, in two important respects, and this is due to MacDiarmid. He demonstrated the importance of technical

PR 56:3, 1965

expertise, and showed that to be Scottish was not enough – one had to be international as well. He says 'Back to Dunbar!' But he also preaches the necessity to look abroad, to know what is being done elsewhere, to extend the range of one's informations and responses, to be the opposite of parochial.

[...]

Beachcomber
George Mackay Brown

Monday I found a boot –
Rust and salt leather.
I gave it back to the sea, to dance in.

Tuesday a spar of timber worth thirty bob.
This winter
It will be a chair, a coffin, a bed.

Wednesday I fought with Ikey the tinker
Over a can of Swedish spirit.
We got drunk then behind the rock.

Thursday I got nothing, seaweed,
A whale bone,
Wet feet and a loud cough.

Friday I held a seaman's skull,
Sand spilling from it
The way time is told on kirkyard stones.

Saturday a barrel of sodden oranges.
A Spanish ship
Was wrecked last month at the Kame.

Sunday, for fear of the elders,
I sit on my bum.
What's heaven? A sea chest with a thousand gold coins.

Sounds of the Day
Norman MacCaig

When a clatter came,
It was horses crossing the ford.
When the air creaked, it was
A lapwing seeing us off the premises
Of its private marsh. A snuffling puff
Ten yards from the boat was the tide blocking,
Unblocking a hole in a rock.
When the black drums rolled, it was water
Falling sixty feet into itself.

When the door
Scraped shut, it was the end
Of all the sounds there are.

You left me
Beside the quietest fire in the world.

I thought I was hurt in my pride only,
Forgetting that,
When you plunge your hand in freezing water,
You feel
A bangle of ice round your wrist
Before the whole hand goes numb.

By Wauchopeside
Hugh MacDiarmid

Thrawn water? Aye, owre thrawn to be aye thrawn!
I ha'e my wagtails like the Wauchope tae,
Birds fu' o' fechtin' spirit, and o' fun,
That whiles jig in the air in lichtsome play
Like glass-ba's on a fountain, syne stand still
Save for a quiver, shoot up an inch or twa, fa' back

Like a swarm o' winter-gnats, or are tost aside,
   By their inclination's kittle loup,
   To balance efter hauf a coup.

There's mair in birds than men ha'e faddomed yet.
Tho' maist churn oot the stock sangs o' their kind
There's aiblins genius here and there; and aince
'Mang whitebeams, hollies, siller birks –
     The tree o' licht –
         I mind
I used to hear a blackie mony a nicht
Singin' awa' t'an unconscionable 'oor
Wi' nocht but the water keepin 't company
(Or nocht that ony human ear could hear)
– And wondered if the blackie heard it either
Or cared whether it was singin' tae or no'!
O there's nae sayin' what my verses awn
To memories like these. Ha'e I come back
To find oot? Or to borrow mair? Or see
Their helpless puirness to what gar'd them be?
     Late sang the blackie but it stopt at last.
     The river still ga'ed singin' past.

O there's nae sayin' what my verses awn
To memories, or my memories to me.
But a'e thing's certain; ev'n as things stand
I could vary them in coontless ways and gi'e
Wauchope a new course in the minds o' men,
The blackie gowden feathers, and the like,
And yet no' cease to be dependent on
The things o' Nature, and create insteed
     Oot o' my ain heid
     Or get ootside the range
        O' trivial change
Into that cataclysmic country which
Natheless a' men inhabit – and enrich.

For civilization in its struggle up
Has mair than seasonal changes o' ideas,
Glidin' through periods o' floo'ers and fruit,
Winter and Spring again; to cope wi' these
Is difficult eneuch to tax the patience
O' Methuselah himsel' – but transformations,
Yont physical and mental habits, symbols, rites,
That mak' sic changes nane, are aye gaen on,
Revolutions in the dynasty o' live ideals
– The stuff wi' which alane true poetry deals.
Wagtail or water winna help me here,
(That's clearer than Wauchope at its clearest's clear!)
Where the life o' a million years is seen
Like a louch look in a lass's een.

Thrawn: contrary, stubborn; *kittle*: ticklish; *coup*: tumble; *aince*: perhaps; *louch*:
suspicious, equivocal.

**For the 'International Poetry Incarnation', Royal Albert Hall,
11 June 1965
Edwin Morgan**

Worldscene! Worldtime! Spacebreaker! Wildship! Starman!
Gemini man dangles white and golden – the world floats
on a gold cord and curves blue white beautiful below him –
Vostok shrieks and prophesies, Mariner's prongs flash –
to the wailing of Voskhod Earth sighs, she shakes men loose at last –
out, in our time, to be living seeds sent far beyond
even imagination, though imagination is awake – take
poets on your voyages! Prometheus
embraces Icarus and in a gold shell with wings

he launches him up through the ghostly detritus
of gods and dirty empires and dying laws,
he mounts, he cries, he shouts, he shines, he streams
like light new done, his home is in a sun

and he shall be the burning unburned one.
In darkness, Daedalus
embraces Orpheus, the dark lips caked with earth and roots
he kisses open, the cold body he rubs
to a new life – the dream
flutters in a cage of crumbling bars, reviving
and then beginning slowly singing of the stars.

Beginning singing, born to go.
To cut the cord of gold. To get
the man new born to go.

24 A Loss
C. Day Lewis

'You *are* nice' – and she touched his arm with a fleeting
Impulsive gesture: the arm that had held her close
And naked a year ago. She was not cheating,
But it falsified their balance of profit and loss.

Her gesture saluted a magnanimity shown
When he asked if she was happy with her new
Lover. That cool touch scalded him to the bone:
The ingenuous words made all words ring untrue.

Their love had never been one of creditor-debtor;
But he felt her hand, reaching to him across
The year he had spent in failing to forget her
And all they'd shared, simply wrote off a loss.

PR 52:4, 1961

Why Publish Poetry?
Rupert Hart-Davis, Charles Monteith, Diana Athill, Colin Franklin and Erica Marx

EDITOR   *Whenever one reads anything about publishing poetry one is told that it is published at a loss. Why is it then, that publishers, who aren't philanthropists, publish it at all? Is it because they are really devoted to the art or are there any other reasons?*

CHARLES MONTEITH   Well, I straight away challenge the first part of this. In our experience it's not true that as a general rule poetry is published at a loss.

DIANA ATHILL   Isn't it? If you are starting a poetry list, as we have been doing, then you *do* publish it at a loss except on very rare occasions. I think we have three poets we do pretty well with, and the rest – well, if we just *get home* with them, financially, we think ourselves very lucky. So that the money isn't the essential thing. You still want to have a poetry list because you think poetry ought to be published.

CHARLES MONTEITH   Yes. When you start looking for the real reasons why you publish poetry, you get involved in some rather embarrassing psychological self-examination. But I suppose you can sum it up by saying that you publish poetry because you enjoy doing it; then if you build up a decent poetry list in the end your poetry makes a profit. But the profit's not the main reason why you do it.

RUPERT HART-DAVIS   I agree with that. I think some publishers even *enjoy* poetry! Indeed, I think you must enjoy it if you are going to publish it. I think there may be a baser emotion occasionally – that you think writers who are now poets might later on write other things. Faber must have gone very steady for many years on Lawrence Durrell, and I think we are all delighted to see that he suddenly comes through and makes them some money and that is a side to remember; that wasn't their motive in publishing him, I'm sure, but it is a very gratifying thing to have happened.

CHARLES MONTEITH   Yes. It's a very nice unexpected lollipop we've been given. When we took on Lawrence Durrell, which I suppose was twenty-five or thirty years ago, we published first of all two or three slim volumes of poetry which Eliot took on because he thought they were good, and we went on publishing poetry by Durrell – at a loss, I imagine. We did one or two novels which didn't do frightfully well and probably the first books of his we made anything out of at all were those travel books, *Prospero's Cell* and *Reflections on a Marine Venus*, which made real but modest profits. The financial turning point came with *Bitter Lemons*, his book about Cyprus. And then suddenly he produced *The Alexandria Quartet*. But I'm certain that it never crossed anyone's mind at Faber's when we took on that first slim volume that twenty-five years later we would have a world bestseller.

EDITOR   *No. But the fact that this does happen, might it mean that publishers who see that in fact poets often do become big sellers – Richard Church wins a* Sunday Times *Award, Laurie Lee writes* Cider with Rosie, *etc…*

ERICA MARX   What I want to say, Charles, is that I think you've slid out of a rather important point, because I think the very reasons why you publish poetry are the reasons that it *does* entail a sort of exploratory revelation of one's self; this is essential to the real reasons why one does it at all. That is what we should go into if we want to discuss the question deeply.

CHARLES MONTEITH   I think we are all terribly liable to think out hard-headed *ex-post facto* explanations for publishing it at all, but really we don't think about those possibilities at the time we are publishing it.

DIANA ATHILL   To go back to Rupert's 'baser emotion', I know what ours was when we started ten years ago – I remember quite clearly – we were sitting in a café in Thayer Street and André Deutsch said, 'You know it would be rather nice, if we could publish two or three volumes of poetry every year'. At the time we had nothing. Chiefly we wanted to do this for fun, but partly, and this was a beginner's point of view, we wanted to be the kind of publisher who publishes poetry; a sort of prestige bid as well as for pure pleasure.

COLIN FRANKLIN   But why does poetry give the idea of prestige?

DIANA ATHILL   I suppose because we all know that poets are the really serious writers and that poetry is what we *should* be publishing.

ERICA MARX   After music it is surely the greatest art.

EDITOR   *Is the fact that you want prestige because you hope to attract to your list other writers of serious importance? Colin, you have a lot of poets who write excellent books of criticism which you publish.*

COLIN FRANKLIN   Yes. Taking up the prestige point – it's always a word one loathes in a way; it is like the kind of schoolmaster who says 'you learn Latin because it is good mental exercise' and I used to think, aren't there other mental exercises that are rather more useful and enjoyable! And I wonder if there aren't more useful forms of publishing which give the sort of prestige or reputation you want. If only a hundred or two people buy the average book of poems it's among very few people you gain this prestige.

DIANA ATHILL   But it's the kind of prestige you want; it's also fun. I mean if you say to yourself 'I want to be a *prestigious* publisher, therefore I will start publishing works of some higher form of criticism or other', if this isn't your line, what is the point?

CHARLES MONTEITH   Well, here we all are doing something that most people regard as foolish and so we try to produce reasons for doing it to justify ourselves: (a) to gain prestige, (b) we may get a good prose work afterwards. In fact, I'm certain that it is simply that we *want* to publish poetry.

ERICA MARX   It certainly never has anything to do with prestige as far as I am concerned.

COLIN FRANKLIN   In any case I think there is something outdated about this prestige idea. When I was at school – a sixteen-year-old – I spent half my term's pound, which I thought a very mean allowance to go back with – on a Faber book of poems, and Faber were my favourite poetry publishers for this reason. Now that was a sensible sort of prestige: they had it not because they asked for it but there it was, by virtue of their list. Well, now I think the idea of poetry being linked with this sort of reputation has gone on but the thing itself hasn't. I doubt if there are schoolboys now who buy poets in the way one bought them then because I don't think the poets are there to buy. They know nobody in the way we knew, say, Spender, Auden, MacNeice and so on. I very much doubt – but maybe this dates me – whether a sixteen-year-old at school now reads your poets in the way we did or could quote them in the way we can still quote those.

DIANA ATHILL   It's very difficult to know. But I think they do buy – not poets that I publish perhaps – but say Christopher Logue, or at least they buy his records reading to Jazz – and they probably buy his books. I think they probably do have poets they buy with equal passion, as we did our favourites then.

CHARLES MONTEITH   Perhaps you're right, Diana, over this. When we were at school in the thirties a new poem by Auden in *The Listener* was an enormously exciting occasion. One had read it and one had almost learnt it by heart without knowing; and I remember waiting with terrific impatience for the Faber 3s. 6d. library to bring out a Selected Auden. But after that – in the forties – the excitement seemed to go flop. But I sense as you do that in the last three or four years poetry is again becoming a rather exciting thing.

EDITOR   *What we don't have is the Faber 3s. 6d. library. Isn't price perhaps one of the problems?*

DIANA ATHILL   These teenagers who are buying, they buy 35s. gramophone records without turning a hair.

CHARLES MONTEITH   After all, 3s. 6d. in those days was the equivalent of 10s. 6d. now.

ERICA MARX   I think sometimes this business of establishing a price is all wrong anyway. It can sometimes work the other way. I have always complained about it to the Poetry Book Society – which I feel entitled to do since I was once a member of the board. They like the price of a book to be 10s. 6d. and if you want to produce a book at 3s. 6d. they don't really like it – at least it does really prevent you from submitting it – it causes so much paper work and disorganization.

RUPERT HART-DAVIS   Charles, do you think, as the publisher who has probably published more poetry than anyone else, that people are reading or buying more poetry now than a few years ago?

CHARLES MONTEITH   I certainly think so. We publish for instance two very good young poets, Ted Hughes and Thom Gunn. Ted Hughes has published two books of adult verse, the first one, *The Hawk in the Rain*, has been reprinted and the second one, *Lupercal*, has been reprinted twice. Thom Gunn's first book that we published, *The Sense of Movement*, has been reprinted once and the second one is selling, for poetry, very well and I'm sure it will be reprinted soon. And we are going to try as an experiment this spring doing a paperback, *Selected Poems of Ted Hughes and Thom Gunn*, at 5s.

RUPERT HART-DAVIS   Ah, that's better. How many pages will that have?

CHARLES MONTEITH   Sixty-four, which I think is good value.

RUPERT HART-DAVIS   Going back to the question of why publishers do it.

This spills over from poetry to other things. I think that if publishers have any sort of literary conscience they publish things because they think they ought to be published. I remember old Algernon Blackwood telling me that he couldn't get anyone to take on his first book and eventually he went to see old Sir Frederick Macmillan who was very gruff with him and said: 'This book cannot possibly make us a penny, Mr Blackwood, but we think it deserves a hearing; we therefore intend to publish it!' Now this is a thing I believe in very much; and I think a lot of people do in fact publish books, even if they sometimes don't personally like them very much, if they think they are good enough, they think they ought to be published. This certainly goes for poetry.

COLIN FRANKLIN   I quite agree with that. What you are saying in a way is that the publisher is likely to be interested in good writing, and I suppose that of all the kinds of good writing poetry is historically one of the high forms – so one must be interested in that.

RUPERT HART-DAVIS   Mind you, it's not always easy to explain this attitude to the big-business boys, or your own accounting side. They say, 'Well, look at these returns! Look at this loss, look at that…'

EDITOR   *Erica, did you find the fact that your Poems in Pamphlet series was so cheap affected the sales?*

ERICA MARX   When I first started that particular enterprise I would have been able to make it pay if I had sold every copy that I published at 1s., but I must say I started at a very unfortunate period because within two months of the first issue coming out the costs of printing and the cost of paper went up, and I didn't dare raise the price – I was doing so well with it. My object, of course, was to propagate poetry at the time. I couldn't put the price up, so in the second year I had to change the quality of the paper.

RUPERT HART-DAVIS   By our standards of course you had practically no overheads.

ERICA MARX   No, certainly not. I had a half-part-time secretary…

RUPERT HART-DAVIS   But you proved something by it, undoubtedly.

ERICA MARX   You see, I can never understand why (I'm not talking about big publishing enterprises), but whenever people get together to try to start something, their first thought is that they must have an office; you *cannot* persuade a group of people sitting round a table to be simple about starting something that might in the end be quite big – they *must* have an office and they *must* have a secretary; this is surely the wrong way to do it.

EDITOR   *And you really found that by keeping the price down you could sell.*

ERICA MARX   Yes. In fact I even found that in one or two places where I didn't sell it was because certain booksellers said it was too cheap! But on the whole, yes, the price made an enormous difference. In fact I had to go closely into this business of self-examination as far as the poetry was concerned, the *quality* of the poetry, and try to play that off against the price. I wanted to find out whether it was really the poetry that was the selling factor or merely the cheapness of the pamphlets. Now I am indulging in an immense enterprise which is an anthology of American Negro Poetry, contemporary, and I am going to do it in a very big way and I can't publish it under 7s. 6d. even if I do it as a paperback.

RUPERT HART-DAVIS   How many pages roughly?

ERICA MARX   About two hundred.

RUPERT HART-DAVIS   Well, that's damn cheap at 7s. 6d.

ERICA MARX   But I've got to sell ten thousand to make it pay. I think I probably shall sell them.

DIANA ATHILL   Why the usual price is about 12s. 6d. is that when one is doing a volume of verse one automatically steps up the standard of production and printing above that of the novel, say; you have a nicer paper and perhaps get an outside designer in – well, *we* sometimes do – the result of a sort of reverent feeling about poetry! that it should look right. We probably could publish the same number a shilling or two cheaper on rather nasty paper, but I don't think it would make any difference to sales.

RUPERT HART-DAVIS   I don't think it would make any difference at all.

EDITOR   *You wouldn't be interested in the possibility of using 'near-print' methods which are now really remarkable, and really getting the price down to rock bottom?*

CHARLES MONTEITH   No, because then you are up against printing numbers. With a slim volume by a young poet you can't print more than a small number.

RUPERT HART-DAVIS   What do you print, Charles?

CHARLES MONTEITH   Well, we would usually start off with a printing of a thousand.

RUPERT HART-DAVIS   I always start with a thousand copies.

CHARLES MONTEITH   With some we have started with two thousand because of a Poetry Book Society Choice or something like that.

DIANA ATHILL   Yes, but these are people with some sort of reputation. Starting from scratch, surely a thousand copies is the absolute outside…

RUPERT HART-DAVIS   What's the lowest you've ever sold, Charles? I think I've sold two hundred.

CHARLES MONTEITH   I don't know. Certainly less than a thousand. Four hundred, five hundred, six hundred, something like that.

COLIN FRANKLIN   Oh, I think we could come down quite a bit from that!

DIANA ATHILL   I could break all records on this. We really have had the most terrible shock over a poet. He was an American and no one knew anything about him here; no one would pay any attention. We have sold forty-nine copies!! No one will take him to exist. I have several manuscripts in now and one of them very good is by an American, but I simply dare not do anything about it.

ERICA MARX   But that doesn't astonish me at all. When I first published one very good young poet, over a couple of years I'd only sold fifty copies.

COLIN FRANKLIN   I think I know who you mean, Erica, because we publish him now and although he is good he still doesn't sell much.

CHARLES MONTEITH   And of course one *does* have to be careful. We get on an average ten books of poems submitted to us a week!

DIANA ATHILL   I have been trying to think up a scheme for building up an American poet before publishing him over here.

CHARLES MONTEITH   I'll tell you what we do with American poets – we publish half a dozen or so. Eliot's strategy about it has always been to wait until an American poet has already got three or four volumes to his credit in America and has a really solid reputation there. Then he usually asks him to do a small Selected for publication in this country. We did this with Richard Wilbur and Lowell, for example. And then we follow this up with individual volumes as they come out, but I don't think we've ever to my knowledge taken on for a start a single volume of poems.

DIANA ATHILL That's our problem; this other American poet I mentioned has never yet had a volume published in America.

ERICA MARX I imagine Hutchinson did quite well with Lawrence Ferlinghetti. I think his book is so good – *A Coney Island of the Mind*.

DIANA ATHILL He comes in the Beat wave, too, which is not quite fair.

CHARLES MONTEITH Yes, possibly his sales could be accounted for by being part of the Beat wave.

ERICA MARX I think all that is so irritating.

EDITOR *But it does help to sell. Isn't it true to say that perhaps Faber, rather like, at the other extreme, Mills and Boon, sell because of the overall quality of the kind of thing they do in that field.*

CHARLES MONTEITH We like to think so. We have after all, thanks to Eliot, built up a pretty reputable list.

RUPERT HART-DAVIS Yes, surely the imprint itself helps there. In that respect Faber are *hors concours* in this discussion because I think we would agree that they are the only publishers, except you, Erica, whose books are bought because they are somebody's publication. No other list has this pull. Therefore it is slightly outside the argument.

EDITOR *How much is this affected by production? I know for instance that one of the things which made me buy Faber books was because I could not put them back on the shelf; they all looked so beautiful.*

DIANA ATHILL Me too! in my young days. The Faber slim volume in those early days was very potent.

EDITOR *I know during the war, for instance, that when everyone was producing books that looked as if they were produced during the war because you couldn't get any other material Faber used exactly the same material, and it looked as if they had deliberately chosen it. If a book came out looking as if it was printed on old sacking from Faber you thought – 'Goodness, that's rather interesting, they've printed it on old sacking!'*

COLIN FRANKLIN Is there a time in the history of publishing when people could have had such a discussion as this – 'Well, because there are so many people interested and because it is passionately important and that kind of thing!' Here we are in the doldrums and I am just wondering how long this can go on, to publish poetry as a mildly respectable thing like joining a club, and whether if it continues to be as unimportant as it is now, whether publishers will as a dilettante matter still continue. What do you think?

RUPERT HART-DAVIS   But they have always got, you see, the odd chance of the bonanza like Betjeman or something – this is one in a million admittedly; this has become an enormous best seller: no one was more surprised I'm sure than John Murray. But I think it will go on as long as publishing goes on unless the whole aspect of the thing changes.

CHARLES MONTEITH   I believe that as long as good literature is written it will get published.

DIANA ATHILL   It is not all the fault of the publishers. Poets have for some time now been writing in a sort of inward way, in a very uncommunicative way – this is something which happens and will pass and will change; I mean poetry will go on being poetry surely; will go on being, as you say, Erica, next to music the highest art form, the purest form of expression, but it has gone through a difficult stage.

ERICA MARX   It was particularly so just before I started because I deliberately chose a certain kind of poetry, I mean I wasn't always choosing poetry that I loved best myself, but I was trying to interest the public again in this very important subject. Poetry is a non-material art.

DIANA ATHILL   I'm interested in this thing of how one chooses one's poetry. There I feel terribly at sea; I know where I stand when I'm reading prose; when I'm reading a novel I know exactly what I want and how I feel, but reading poetry I feel it all becomes very subjective, very personal, and I'm terrified that I am making mistakes, that it is some private reason of mine that I happen to like this man. What can one do about it except to say well, all right, I *like* it, and then X and Y whom I ask also agree he's not bad so…

RUPERT HART-DAVIS   But that's the only way, Diana, of taking it; once you take it for any other reason – if you take it because you think it's what people will like but you don't like it yourself, you're lost. If you like it it's possible that someone else may.

DIANA ATHILL   Therefore I tend now to go for the poets I get fairly easily, the not too obscure, or difficult, or knotty, poet.

CHARLES MONTEITH   We are the only people who can do to poetry what an ordinary person can do to pictures, that is go out and buy the original.

Deciding to publish a volume of poetry gives the same sort of rather terrifying thrill that one gets on deciding to spend a lot of money on buying a picture. For an ordinary member of the public all he's got to spend to get his volume is 12s. 6d., but we've got to spend a lot of money... and this is the fun of it in a way.

COLIN FRANKLIN   I think you are very lucky, Charles, in a way, because I wouldn't say that 'we all want to publish poetry' necessarily goes for my colleagues at all...

ERICA MARX   But I think you have put your finger on the heart of the whole operation and that is that you really do... it is a form of self-examination as to what type of poetry you publish and in order to find out in yourself why you are publishing it you've got to see that you are isolated from all sorts of fashionable points of view, that you're not doing X because the Beat is in vogue at the moment or that something else is; you've got to come to terms with yourself and find out whether this is you, really you liking what you are reading, or whether something else has infiltrated into you while you're reading it; you've got to isolate yourself from any kind of extraneous influence.

DIANA ATHILL   And this is the only form of publishing where one does it to that extent. Because, after all, with fiction you're always thinking, 'Well, after all, a good many people are going to be getting their entertainment from this, they may love it and value it and enjoy it even if I don't'; you've got to bring this into account, whereas with poetry one can't do it.

RUPERT HART-DAVIS   I think Charles said something very important just now which is never mentioned in all the manuals of publishing which you can read about how to run a publishing business, what they never say is that it is *fun*, *fun* or romantic or exciting or anything like that; but this is all part of it, without being highfaluting in any way, it is. And poetry is a particular form of romance or fun. Erica is looking shocked.

ERICA MARX   No, I agree only I think it's *agony* and it's fun! But it's what one wants to do. It's the gamut of what is going on; its poetry; that's the difference.

EDITOR   *That means, though, that in any large company you've got to have one person who feels very strongly about it, because I can't believe that nine people on the board of a large publishing company are all passionately interested or devoted or recognize the latest* avant garde *poet.*

COLIN FRANKLIN   Do you have fearful opposition in Faber if you want to publish a poet...

CHARLES MONTEITH   Not at all, no. If Eliot says 'I want to publish this volume of poems', then none of us would dissent. But I do agree that there is absolutely no point in a large publisher taking on poetry unless at least one member of the board genuinely enjoys poetry himself, and wants to publish it not simply because he wants to make a profit or get a bestselling novel.

EDITOR   *Very well, we've decided that all publishers publish poetry because they want to. Are they satisfied with the way in which it sells? It does seem to me that, as Colin said, we are all saying in this period of history that we publish poetry because we want to but the public don't appear to be passionately involved; now this seems to me odd because we are surely not unrepresentative. A great deal is due to the fact that it has a small sale anyway and because it has a small sale the resistance of booksellers out of London to stocking it is immense. Isn't the distribution of poetry something we need to look into?*

CHARLES MONTEITH   And of course we can only publish the poetry that is sent to us to publish. I think poetry – new poetry – was extremely exciting in the twenties and thirties. Then it became much less exciting from about the beginning of the war up to about three or four years ago. Now I think it's getting much more exciting again and the sales depend on the quality of the poetry that is published.

COLIN FRANKLIN   No.

ERICA MARX   Oh! No. No.

RUPERT HART-DAVIS   Well, I agree with a lot of that, but while we all agree that more people are reading poetry now I feel that an awful lot of people who have paid 15s. or 12s. 6d. for a book and can't understand a word are now jolly chary of buying any more books until they know it well enough or there is a background of opinion to make them confident of buying it. They've been had, and I've been had; very often myself I've bought a book of poems that I really can't make head or tail of, it seems to me like private notes or something.

ERICA MARX   But I think that period is past now.

DIANA ATHILL   Yes, but I do think it has made us as publishers pretty defeatist. I think that we publish our poems saying to ourselves, 'well, all right, now this is fun for us', and it doesn't occur to us that we are going to be able to sell more than seven hundred or a thousand copies. I sometimes think that we are making this gesture, we're saying, well, here are the books and then let the public get on with it; we don't really do a great deal afterwards.

RUPERT HART-DAVIS   What can we do?

DIANA ATHILL   Well, we perhaps run to Christine Foyle and say let's have a reading – to which people *always* come and surely this might be something we ought to be able to exploit more. No one could call them comfortable occasions; one sits in a draught on that dusty floor while people read their poetry, but there's always a fairly full house.

RUPERT HART-DAVIS   Yes, but they never buy the books, Diana.

ERICA MARX   They never seem to buy the books. There is only one thing that *sells* poetry and that is a really good review in *The Sunday Times*, *The Observer*, *The Times Literary Supplement*; these are the things that sell, and unfortunately the gentlemen reviewing find very little space for it and have very little time, except for certain kinds of poetry; they won't even look at most of the poets, or they treat them with contempt.

EDITOR   *Yes, surely this is where the whole question of fashion arises. You just said, Charles, that you thought poetry was very exciting in the thirties and then became interesting again a few years ago; and this is a very current feeling. The forties are out. But surely it is unquestionable that Edwin Muir and Robert Graves and Dylan Thomas and George Barker all published their greatest books slap in the middle of the forties, but we write that period off.*

CHARLES MONTEITH   But they started earlier. We don't think of them as forties poets.

EDITOR   *Yes, but those books were produced in the written-off period. Surely poetry was exciting then. It was to me.*

CHARLES MONTEITH   Well, of course. After all the *Four Quartets*, a very great poem, was published during the war.

DIANA ATHILL   You've raised a point, Erica, that I have always wondered about. Who ought to review poets? It ought not to be other poets because that's where the cliquishness comes in.

RUPERT HART-DAVIS   I agree with that entirely.

DIANA ATHILL   Poetry relies on reviews more than any other form.

RUPERT HART-DAVIS   Of course it is a very difficult thing to do, reviewing poetry.

DIANA ATHILL   Yes, it is a very terrifying thing to do; and people feel like I do, they don't know enough to review it except on the basis of I like this – unless they are a poet, and then they become pompous and school-masterish, and they go through other people's poetry with a red pencil because he does not write in the way they write, they rap him over the knuckles...

COLIN FRANKLIN   Yes, a startling example of this occurred a little while ago when some poems I thought were rather good, by a young man called Michael Baldwin, were published and Betjeman reviewed them in the *Telegraph,* and without it seemed to me making any effort to get inside the poet. He wrote rather a carping little review and then said, but two or three lines in one of the poems showed what he could do, and the two or three he quoted were about the sea front at Herne Bay! That's exactly what you're describing.

DIANA ATHILL   Yes, they all tend to do it. Roy Fuller who is the nicest, most generous man, when he is reviewing a poet who doesn't happen to be on his wave-length, he can be almost brutal. Alvarez sometimes strikes me as doing this, too.

COLIN FRANKLIN   I have an impression that if you talk to old people you get the feeling that they took the poets in their undergraduate youth as the main source of philosophy and vision and ethics and mental excite-ment; I think it is merely nothing to do with poets or publishers that there are now so many alternatives to these things at the appropriate time of the day, and especially I think it may be we shall discover that instead of going on turning out our few poets, that music has considerably taken over this particular function; that at the time of evening when a man puts aside his job and whatever he is doing and turns to something in the hour before bed it isn't a book of poems; he turns on his tape recorder for some Beethoven or he may look at television; this sort of thing has so much taken over that the undergraduate or post-graduate function of poetry in 1900 has quite passed away.

DIANA ATHILL   I was going to say that when we were talking about records – that people are going to records for the same thing we used to go to poets for.

ERICA MARX   But this is something, as publishers, we should contend with.

EDITOR   *Colin, Routledge possibly publish more criticism of poets than the other publishers here. Do you find that the work which is non-poetic is what gives the poet his large audience; are there many poets – who achieve a wide audience simply by their poetry and not by something else? Betjeman after all is a public figure and other poets, perhaps Kingsley Amis, for instance, I mean his wide public is for his novels which must spill over into his poetry public. Laurie Lee's books of poems are now presumably bought by many more people after the success of* Cider with Rosie. *And it was very noticeable with Dylan Thomas after* Milk Wood.

CHARLES MONTEITH   We had to reprint Durrell's *Collected Poems* after *The Alexandria Quartet.*

COLIN FRANKLIN   John Wain's poems, I would say, after the success of his novels.

DIANA ATHILL   It is certainly usually something extraneous. Dylan Thomas, it was certainly his reputation as a person; after all many of his poems are very difficult and obscure for the general reader.

EDITOR   *Yes, the number of people who said after* Milk Wood *'this is absolutely marvellous, I must go and get this man's poems', and then they sit there with popping eyes because they can't understand a word of so many of them.*

COLIN FRANKLIN   Well, certainly it is the criticism by our poets that does enormously better than the poetry. I can't think of a poet / critic whose poetry is particularly successful from the sales point of view. I think of John Holloway, he may be lucky and get a Poetry Book Society choice or something, but otherwise I think his poetry is not successful – successful in the way you mean; I think his poetry is good and successful as poetry. Then Donald Davie, a good poet, but his criticism does a great deal better.

RUPERT HART-DAVIS   Yes, if you can make a person a national figure – Radio, TV, perhaps a gimmick, then people will go and buy the poetry. And this is infuriating because these people should be able to be got at in some way without all that.

ERICA MARX   Yes, quite cultured people in outskirts had never heard of Dylan Thomas at all until the notoriety – I know a lot of people who certainly should have known it before and didn't.

RUPERT HART-DAVIS   And we don't seem to be able to get to those people; who do so often like it when we do.

EDITOR   *Do you think a new Poetry Bookshop would help?*

CHARLES MONTEITH   Harold Monro and all that sort of thing? No.

ERICA MARX   David Archer tried, didn't he?

DIANA ATHILL   I don't like this 'special' sort of thing; it smacks of the special poetry voice which is the tone of voice that brings death.

RUPERT HART-DAVIS   What Desmond MacCarthy called the Voice Beautiful.

DIANA ATHILL   Yes, terrible.

EDITOR   *Yes, but if you go into the average bookshop they have obviously never heard the word poetry – you must face it that as a whole bookselling is pretty dreary; it is an advantage to have a shop or shops where you know they are going to be; Zwemmers, especially in the old days, was a case in point, because when you went in, there they all were, all the poetry books you could want to look at; this happens less now in general.*

COLIN FRANKLIN   In fact, although we all say we publish poetry because we want to, do we want to enough to put tremendous energy into selling it as well. Are we indulging in a private luxury?

DIANA ATHILL   An expensive one!

CHARLES MONTEITH   I think we could all do more perhaps in that line, but the public and the poets themselves must come some way to help us. Too many people complain that poetry does not sell, but they are just the people who don't buy.

ERICA MARX   If every member of the Poetry Society bought four or five new books of poems a year, think of that!

EDITOR   *But despite all the problems you all care enough to go on?*

CHARLES MONTEITH   Yes, most emphatically. It is a significant part of our list and we certainly are proud of it, and economically not at all unhappy with it.

RUPERT HART-DAVIS   Well, the world would be a poor place without its poetry and while we think that, then I think we shall do our damnedest to keep it alive.

EDITOR   *We've wandered a long way from the first question. I'm not sure what conclusions, if any, we have reached, but I think your views as publishers are most valuable. I shall expect to see a great many slim volumes coming from your firms in the next few years. Thank you.*

Those taking part in this discussion [were] directors of the following publishing companies: Rupert Hart-Davis (Rupert Hart-Davis Ltd); Charles Monteith (Faber & Faber Ltd); Colin Franklin (Routledge & Kegan Paul Ltd); Diana Athill (André Deutsch Ltd); Erica Marx (The Hand and Flower Press). [The editor was John Smith.]

25 The Wedding Photograph
Stevie Smith

Goodbye Harry, I must have you by me for a time
But once in the jungle you must go off to a higher clime,
The old lion on his slow toe
Will eat you up. That is the way you will go.
Oh how I shall like to be alone on the jungle path
But you are all right now for the photograph,
So smile, Harry, smile, and I will smile too
Thinking what is going to happen to you.
It is the death wish lights my beautiful eyes
But people think you are lucky to go off with such a pretty prize.

Ah, feeble me that only wished alone to roam
Yet dared not without marrying leave home,
Ah woe, burn fear, burn in eyes' sheathing
Fan bright fear, fan fire in Harry's breathing.

PR 53:3, 1962

26

Day Trip to Donegal
Derek Mahon

for Paul Smyth

We reached the sea in early afternoon,
Climbed stiffly out. There were urgent things to be done –
Clothes to be picked up, people to be seen.
As ever, the nearby hills were a deeper green
Than anywhere in the world, and the grave
Grey of the sea the grimmer in that enclave.

Down at the pier the boats gave up their catch,
Torn mouths and spewed-up lungs. It seems they fetch
Ten times as much in the city as there,
And still the fish come in year after year –
Herring and whiting, flopping about the deck
In attitudes of agony and heartbreak.

We cannot hope to make them understand –
Theirs is a sea-mind, mindless upon land
And dead. Their systematic genocide
(Nothing remarkable that millions died)
To us is a necessity,
For ours are land-minds, mindless in the sea.

We left at eight, drove back the way we came,
The sea receding down each muddy lane.
Around midnight we changed-down into suburbs
Sunk in a sleep no gale-force wind disturbs –
The time of year had made its mark
On frosty pavements glistening in the dark.

PR 56:3, 1965

Give me a ring, goodnight, and so to bed…
That night the slow sea washed against my head
Performing its immeasurable erosions –
Spilling into the skull, marbling the stones
That spine the very harbour-wall,
Uttering its threat to villages of landfall.

At dawn I was alone far out at sea
Without skill or reassurance (nobody
To show me how, no earnest of rescue),
Cursing my mindless failure to take due
Forethought for this – contriving vain
Overtures to the mindless wind and rain.

& *from* Relief and Admiration
John Lehmann

Mr George Barker is a poet of an extraordinary consistency of style: it is
both his strength and his weakness. From the moment when he appeared
on the general scene, with his volume of *Poems* from Messrs Faber &
Faber, over thirty years ago, he dazzled us in the armour of his romantic,
rhetorical, high-flown manner; and he still wears it. Fashions have
changed since then; but Mr Barker hardly at all. He has in his time written
some poems which, in their reckless, anything-goes unevenness, a bril-
liant and original passage followed by a crash of bathos, are surely among
the worst produced by his generation. He also written others which, for
my money, are among the most memorable of the last three decades. No
one else could have written 'Letter to a Young Poet': I have read it dozens
of times, and am still as grateful for it as I was the first time.

He has an ungovernable addiction to Blakean visions, punning
conceits and paradoxes and personified abstractions. […]

It was with these thoughts in mind that I turned eagerly to his new
collection, *Dreams of a Summer Night,* and to the series of linked elegiac
reflections of the title poem first of all. It is a moving poem, full, it seems

to me, of a desperate sadness and nostalgia; but Mr Barker is still encased
in his armour with its florid baroque devices gaudily embossed upon it,
often to lamentably grotesque effect:

> I have seen
> That stripdance of manic shadows in their St Vitus of life
> Shaking the last vestment of responsible sorrow from their shoulders
> Step out of the sawdust corpse and agonised ego in the dark,
> And then sit smiling in a lotus of joy at ceasing to mean.

At this point I am inclined, rebelliously, to comment that Mr Barker's
poetry ceases to mean also. And yet, when I turned back to the beginning
and read the collection right through, I began to feel that something long
hoped for was indeed happening. He has included five 'Memorials for
Dead Friends', which might have been the occasion for exercises in his
most rhetorical and exalted manner. But nothing could be simpler and
more touching (though still essentially Barkerian) than the short piece on
John Minton; and in the memorial verses for Louis MacNeice he seems
to have been touched by something of his dead friend's easy conversa-
tional style. It is a remarkable example of that very rare thing – an epitaph
of praise and love that is perfectly frank about its reservations. [...]

I also very much liked the undertone of affectionate humour in the
Elegiacs for T.S. Eliot. I wish Mr Barker would indulge in this kind of
writing, relaxed yet seldom losing its poetic tension, more often in the
future. I have a hunch that he may. [...]

Dreams of a Summer Night, by George Barker (Faber).

& *from* Chaucer's Man
Robert Graves

What sort of a man was John Masefield? Gentle, generous, courageous,
unassuming, over-sensitive. [...]

When we first met, half a century ago, he had at last settled down,
after years of knock-about adventure at sea and abroad, as a prosperous
writer. His first book, *Salt Water Ballads* (1902), owed much to Rudyard

Kipling; but though Kipling as a master-journalist could dramatically impersonate tinkers, tailors, soldiers or sailors, he never quite got inside their skins. Masefield *was* a sailor, had served before the mast, and wrote from the heart. To his grief, however, he had been forced to abandon the seas as a profession – like Nelson, he was constantly prostrated by sea-sickness.

[...]

War-time Oxford was where I first met Masefield. He had since written *The Widow in the Bye-Street* and *Dauber*, in much the same personal style as The *Everlasting Mercy*, though with rather less abandon. I was then on sick leave from the Western Front, and training officer cadets at Wadham College. He had been introduced by Dr Robert Bridges, Masefield's predecessor as Poet Laureate, chosen in 1913 – forgive the digression – by Asquith the Liberal Prime Minister, in replacement of Alfred Austin, whose appointment as Tennyson's successor had been generally regarded as a bad Tory joke. The truth was that a Poet Laureate needed to be presentable at Court, and in 1892 few of the better-known poets could have been, say, admitted to the Royal Enclosure at Ascot. Morris was a Socialist, Swinburne a drunkard, Hardy an atheist, Watson had once assaulted the Prince of Wales in a park, Kipling had earned Queen Victoria's anger by disrespectfully calling her 'the widow of Windsor'. So the Queen was asked to settle for Alfred Austin – a respectable Tory journalist, but very small beer as a poet. Bridges, by contrast, was an eminent physician, of unblemished personal life, a sound scholar, an expert of English prosody, and the author of fine rhetorical verse.

> Whither, O splendid ship, your white sails crowding,
> Leaning into the bosom of the urgent west,

survives in anthologies today. The self-educated Masefield – who, though a married man in his middle thirties and the father of two children, had recently served with the RAMC in a hospital ship at the Dardanelles – looked up to Bridges with a huge respect.

[...]

I returned to Oxford in 1920 as a married undergraduate, and Masefield, hearing that I could find no rooms for my family in the crowded City, nobly rented me a cottage at the bottom of his garden at Boars Hill. I grew greatly attached to my new landlord, as also did my neighbour, the poet Edmund Blunden, another young battle-shocked ex-officer. Though members of the rebellious new generation, we refused to ally ourselves with the modernistic Sitwells, Eliot, Pound, H.D., Flint,

Read and the rest. Theirs was a Franco-American movement, and we remained as patriotically rooted in pre-eighteenth-century tradition as Masefield himself. He was Chaucer's man, and is being now laid near him in Poets' Corner.

On Bridges' death, Ramsay Macdonald, the first Labour Premier, proposed Masefield to King George as the new Laureate. King George, an old salt himself, approved. He also, it appears, had looked upon the rum when it was brown, and chuckled over Masefield's 'Old Bold Mate of Henry Morgan':

> Now some are fond of Spanish wine and some are fond of French
> And some will swallow tea and stuff fit only for a wench
> But I'm for right Jamaica till I roll beneath the bench,
>   Said the old, bold mate of Henry Morgan.

These islands have fostered several different poetic traditions. [...] Poet Laureate originally meant someone on whom a University Senate had conferred a degree for proficiency in Latin and Greek verse-composition, his brow being thereafter ritually encircled with Apollo's laurel garland. And until Masefield's time, Laureates, so far as I can find out, had all been University graduates. The worst of their line had been the eighteenth-century court lackeys, who composed sycophantic birthday odes and poems on Royal Occasions. Indeed, so much odium clung to the title even after Wordsworth's and Tennyson's tenures of office, that Bridges had refused to write any verses at all at the Royal request. I will remember the 1913 *New York Times* news heading: KING'S CANARY WON'T SING.

For Masefield, however, job was job. A jongleur, rather than a druid, he felt bound to celebrate Royal occasions with short, loyal, carefully rhymed verses for publication in the centre page of *The Times*, always sending a stamped return envelope in case of rejection. He was, I think, underscoring the continuity of the Royal tradition with which our poetic tradition has been bound for more than two thousand years. I respect him for that, even when his loyal addresses grew more and more laboured down the years, as I also respected Bridges' view that no true poem can be written at request, even at Royal request.

By the outbreak of the Second World War, when modernism had won, when verses were no longer expected to scan, rhyme, or even make grammatical sense, and when long narrative poems had long gone out of fashion, Masefield the poet became, for all but a few of his contemporaries, one of A.E. Housman's

Runners whom their fame outran
And the name died before the man.

[...]

And yet once, at an earlier otherwise dark period, the fierce live flame of poetry had truly burned in him; and though it had seldom since reappeared, he had never lost the supreme poetic quality: of unselfish love for all and sundry... and I recall his shy smile of greeting in 1921 when, spade and refuse-bucket in hand, I used to come up from my cottage and pass his work-shed half hidden among gorse trees in the garden. Though assumed by his energetic Ulster wife to be working hard on *Right Royal* for the family's support, he was, as often as not, idly engrossed in a favourite foc'stle occupation: carving and rigging model sailing-ships. [...]

An extended version of the address given at the Memorial Service for Dr John Masefield, O.M., in Westminster Abbey, on June 20th, 1967.

& *from* Thoughts on the Forties
Derek Stanford

[...]

The indictment of the Forties is something of an old story now. The first attack upon it came in 1949 from the magazine *Nine* edited by Peter Russell. This was more of a whispering campaign than anything of a frontal assault. *Nine* was a journal of neo-classical bent, so that it was natural for it to oppose the, often, neo-romantic theory and practice of the Forties. It did not, however, get much beyond suggesting that Ezra Pound's paper-Fascism was probably a more mature political guide than Dr Alex Comfort's Direct-Action anarchism, and that the Roman poets and Confucius' *Book of Odes* were better models for the tyro writer than Dylan Thomas' uterine frenzies (it was generally the Welsh poet's more murky performances which were imitated by his *aficionados*). Two further reasons for the limited nature of *Nine*'s campaign were: the desire not to soil one's own door-step (two of the Editorial Board were themselves men of the Forties – G.S. Fraser and Ian Fletcher, the former having contributed a critical apologia to *The White Horseman* (1941), a New-

PR 60:3, 1969

Apocalyptic anthology); and an inside knowledge of the period under fire which naturally put them into a position of knowing its strength as well as its weakness.

These first rumours of dissent gave way in the middle Fifties to the rumbling barrage of 'The Movement'. Writing the Introduction to its initial anthology *New Lines* (1956), Mr Robert Conquest declared that 'In the 1940s the mistake was made of giving the Id, a sound player on the percussion side under a strict conductor, too much of a say in the doings of the orchestra as a whole. As it turned out, it could only manage the simpler part of melody and rhythm, and was completely out of its depth with harmony and orchestration. This led to a rapid collapse of public taste, from which we have not yet recovered.' This was, at least, a bright piece of writing though Mr Conquest's analogies had their dangers: what quite were 'harmony and orchestration' when transcribed into poetic terms? (Examining Mr Conquest's own language, one can well see his point in calling the notion 'that poetry *must* be metaphorical' a 'debilitating theory'.) Courtesies aside, however, it may be admitted that Mr Conquest's indictment contained its measure of truth. What was expendable in the poetry of the Forties and what deserved to be conserved was a distinction that did not bother Mr Conquest, however, since it was his task as apologist of 'The Movement' poets to liquidate the Forties and replace them.

Mr A. Alvarez was the next critic of note to take up the cry against the 'dream-rolling forties'. Unlike Dr Leavis with his plea to lock up the Muse in the Senior Common Room, Mr Alvarez had a reasonable measure of respect for Dylan Thomas ('not only a fine rhetorician' but someone who 'in his early poems had something rather original to say'). 'His followers', he tells us, though, 'used his work as an excuse to kiss *all* meaning goodbye.' Who were these followers, one would like to ask, and did they number among themselves any of the good young poets of the time: Alex Comfort, Sidney Keyes, John Heath-Stubbs, John Waller, Norman Nicholson, John Bayliss, Terence Tiller, and Nicholas Moore? Equally, one would look in vain for the reverberation of Thomas in poets of a slightly older age who had, in some cases, made a name for themselves before 1939: Lawrence Durrell, David Gascoyne, Kathleen Raine, and Anne Ridler. Indeed, the only poets of note who seem to have fabricated a style at all Dylanesque were Norman MacCaig and W.S. Graham, the latter strenuously repudiating any over-attribution of Thomas' influence upon his poems. This leaves one, possibly, with Vernon Watkins, a fine craftsman of controlled imagination in whom readers and poets might have believed were Dylanesque notes because of a friendship between the two poets and a nationality shared in common. For Mr John Heath-Stubbs, an all but co-eval of Watkins, the poet worked, not in the manner of Thomas, but 'in the tradition of Yeats'.

When the critical demolition squads are required to instance uninhabitable poems, they invariably stick their 'Condemnation' labels on a snatch of verse by J.F. Hendry – generally drawn from the same poem:

> Crow, wooden lightning, from a sky of thorn
> O cross-ribbed Adam, tumbled hill of blood
> While blinded shell and body's thunder churn
> Ear to worm-ball, tongue to lipless stone.

This is clearly unsuccessful, but Mr Ian Hamilton is surely wrong in calling it 'the sort of typical Forties reflex poem'. It is not a 'reflex' composition, produced by an instinctive or spontaneous reaction. Indeed, it fails through being contrived, and its title gives the clue to its failure: 'Picasso – for Guernica'. What we have, here, is not the break-down of instinctive speech in the face of violent experience, but an attempt to create, by reflection at second-hand, the hot, immediate discontinuous fragmentation of effect in Picasso's painting. Hendry's poem fails, then, through experiment rather than through wayward imagination uncontrolled by intelligence.

[...] The reflective reader may begin to doubt Mr Ian Hamilton's hasty conclusion that 'the forties was indeed a sorry period for English poetry... a period notorious for its abandonment of even the most tentative critical standards'. There are other values, one may briefly remark, than the values of playing safe. [...]

27

A New Year Greeting
W.H. Auden

for Vassily Yanowsky

On this day tradition allots
   to taking stock of our lives,
my greetings to all of you, Yeasts,
   Bacteria, Viruses,
Aerobic or Anaerobic,
   A Very Happy New Year
to all for whom my ectoderm
   is as Middle-Earth to me.

For creatures your size I offer
   a free choice of habitat,
so settle yourselves in the zone
   that suits you best, in the pools
of my pores, in the tropical
   forests of arm-pit or crotch,
in the deserts of my fore-arms
   or the cool woods of my scalp.

Build colonies: I will supply
   adequate warmth and moisture,
the sebum and lipids you need,
   on condition you never
do me annoy with your presence,
   but behave as good guests should,
not rioting into acne,
   or athlete's-foot or a boil.

Does my inner weather affect
    the surfaces where you live?
Do unpredictable changes
    record my rocketing plunge
from fairs when the mind is in tift
    and relevant thoughts occur
to fouls when nothing will happen
    and no one calls and it rains?

I should like to think that I make
    a not impossible world,
but an Eden it cannot be:
    my games, my purposive acts
may turn to catastrophes there.
    If you were religious folk,
how would your dramas justify
    unmerited suffering?

By what myths would your priests account
    for the hurricanes that come
twice every twenty-four hours,
    each time I dress or undress,
when, clinging to keratin rafts,
    whole cities are swept away
to perish in space, or the Flood
    that scalds to death when I bathe?

Then, sooner or later, will dawn
    a Day of Apocalypse,
when my mantle suddenly turns
    too cold, too rancid for you,
appetising to predators
    of a fiercer sort, and I
am stripped of excuse and nimbus,
    a Past subject to Judgement.

28

Mary, Mary Magdalene
Charles Causley

On the south wall of the church of St Mary Magdalene at Launceston in Cornwall is a granite figure of the saint. The children of the town say that a stone lodged on her back will bring good luck.

Mary, Mary Magdalene
Lying on the wall,
I throw a pebble on your back.
Will it lie or fall?

Send me down for Christmas
Some stockings and some hose,
And send before the winter's end
A brand-new suit of clothes.

Mary, Mary Magdalene
Under a stony tree,
I throw a pebble on your back.
What will you send me?

*I'll send you for your Christening
A woollen robe to wear,
A shiny cup from which to sup,
And a name to bear.*

Mary, Mary Magdalene
Lying cool as snow,
What will you be sending me
When to school I go?

PR 61:2, 1970

I'll send a pencil and a pen
That write both clean and neat,
And I'll send to the schoolmaster
A tongue that's kind and sweet.

Mary, Mary Magdalene
Lying in the sun,
What will you be sending me
Now I'm twenty-one?

I'll send you down a locket
As silver as your skin,
And I'll send you a lover
To fit a gold key in.

Mary, Mary Magdalene
Underneath the spray,
What will you be sending me
On my wedding-day?

I'll send you down some blossom
Some ribbons and some lace,
And for the bride a veil to hide
The blushes on her face.

Mary, Mary Magdalene
Whiter than the swan,
Tell me what you'll send me
Now my good man's dead and gone?

I'll send to you a single bed
On which you must lie,
And pillows bright where tears may light
That fall from your eye.

Mary, Mary Magdalene
Now nine months are done,
What will you be sending me
For my little son?

I'll send you for your baby
A lucky stone, and small,
To throw to Mary Magdalene
Lying on the wall.

29

False Image
Roy Fuller

'Driven inshore by weather, huge white birds' –
    Immediately I'm aware
    Of faking in the words:
The Baudelairean trope, portentous air.

And yet the birds were vast and cream, and crossed
    Today on skies of white
    Over still whiter frost:
Unusual visitors, unearthly light.

Eager to find in natural tableaux
    Symbols for feelings that
    As yet I do not know,
I render down the day's superfluous fat,

And leave myself the sawing sabre wings
    That came undoubtedly
    Through cold in search of things
Of which the man-tamed land might make them free.

PR 57:1, 1966

How ignorant the beasts are of our pity!
   The feathers failed to light
   Upon our thick-roofed city
Since what they really craved was blue not white.

Not beyond doubt that into a universe
   Purely of phenomena
   An order might immerse
Itself of more reality by far.

So had the troop descended we could have found
   Angels with emperors' beaks
   On this familiar ground,
Or girl-breasted flutterers scoring our burning cheeks.

& *from* Thoughts after Advent
Edward Lucie-Smith

My first thought, when asked to write about Michael Horovitz's anthology *Children of Albion*, was to do a flip piece and entitle it 'Albert Memorial' […]. My second and wisest thought was to refuse to write about it at all. 'Oh God,' groaned an inner voice, 'the issues which the book raises are really very complicated, and people get so upset about poetry. Better leave the whole thing alone.' On third thoughts, here I am, writing about it.

   […]

   Basically, what [Michael Horovitz] feels is that something important has happened to poetry in Britain in the last few years, and that the trans-formation has been either ignored or denigrated by those who write for the established organs of literary opinion. For him, the key event is the big Albert Hall poetry reading of 1965 – his whole book looks back to this, hence my first thought for a title to this piece. Other key factors were, he feels, the involvement of his own generation with jazz, and the work done by his own magazine *New Departures*, and the readings which he organised around it. Personally, I would contest nearly all of these points.

PR 61:1, 1970

The Albert Hall reading was a spectacular explosion, but I am unrepentant about the words I wrote at the time (and which Horovitz indignantly quotes) in which I implied that it was the explosion of a stock-response which the audience had already prepared within itself. I feel that pop played a more important part than jazz, and that *New Departures* is accorded an unduly important role by its progenitor. But let these things be. Essentially we are in agreement.

[...] One notices a tone of aspiration, an idealism, a straining towards something better, not in poetry, but in the world. [...] There can be no denying the fact that people have suddenly begun to read much more poetry, nor that the *kind* which on the whole they choose to read is the kind which Horovitz presents and advocates. A critic like Alvarez may even be doing the book a very good turn by gunning it down so efficiently in a newspaper like *The Observer*. What better proof could there be that this is the pure milk of the new poetic gospel; a gospel which says, among other things, that the poet must be identifiably an idealist, identifiably the enemy of the *status quo*, political as well as literary?

The real quarrel between the two factions seems to be, not about this poet or that, but about the nature of poetry itself. One side is restrictive. The poet must be prepared to submit his work to the most stringent questions, the most minutely detailed examination of his honesty, both literary and spiritual, as well as of his craftsmanship. If, with the thought of the questions he must answer in his mind, the contemporary poet dare not soar very high or very far, but merely hops from fence-post to fence-post, this defect of modesty may quite possibly be forgiven him. The advocates of this attitude are the professional literary men, proud of the stringency of their judgement, the rigour of their standards. But the audience does not think like that. For them the word poetry has an overtone, an aura, a glamour – call it what you like. Whatever you do call it, the audience (the broad, uncritical, and in the end *essential* audience) expects to find this special quality. Whenever we use the word 'poetry' metaphorically, and we do so fairly often, we are at the same time admitting that there is indeed some justification for the demand I have just described. Horovitz has grasped that at least, and his book is a monument to his realisation that it exists – a monument as weird, as bad in many of its details, and in some ways as characteristic of its age as the monument which the mourning Victoria erected to the memory of the Prince Consort.

Children of Albion, edited by Michael Horovitz (Penguin Books).

& Evening / Sail
Ian Hamilton Finlay, drawn by Michael Harvey

PR 64:2, 1973

30

Buzzard
Frances Horovitz

our connection is silence
   the plunge in the blood

what music he moves to –
   he plays me
from the bed of the lane
he reels out my sight
he turns round the hills
eddies   splits air
lounges like paper
he drops the whole sky

a comet too near the earth
   rabid he crashes
   yellow eye glittering
   savage his absence
   seering the fields

leaves hang in stillness
a breath drawn suspended
our connection is silence
   the plunge in the blood

PR 64:1, 1973

31

**At Briggflatts Meetinghouse: Tercentenary
Basil Bunting**

Boasts time mocks cumber Rome; Wren
set up his own monument.
Others watch fells dwindle, think
the sun's fires sink.

Stones indeed sift to sand, oak
blends with the saints' bones,
Yet for a little longer here
stone and oak shelter

silence while we ask nothing
but silence. Look how clouds dance
under the wind's wing, and leaves
delight in transience.

1975

32

Talking To You Afterwards
Peter Porter

Does my voice sound strange? I am sitting
On a flat-roofed beach house watching lorikeets
Flip among the scribble-gums and banksias.

When I sat here last I was writing my *Exequy*,
Yet your death seems hardly further off. The wards
Of the world have none of the authority of an end.

If I wish to speak to you I shouldn't use verse.
Instead, our quarrel-words, those blisters between
Silences in the kitchen – your plainly brave

Assertion that life is improperly poisoned where
It should be hale: love, choice, the lasting
Of pleasure in days composed of chosen company,

Or, candidly, shitty luck in the people we cling to.
Bad luck lasts. I have it now as I suppose I had it
All along. I can make words baroque but not here.

Last evening I saw from the top of Mt Tinbeerwah
(How you would have hated that name if you'd heard it)
A plain of lakes and clearances and blue-green rinses,

Which spoke to me of Rubens in the National Gallery
Or even Patenir. The eyes that see into Australia
Are, after all, European eyes, even those Nationalist

Firing slits, or the big mooey pools of subsidized
Painters. It's odd that my desire to talk to you
Should be so heart-rending in this gratuitous exile.

PR 67:3, 1977

You believed in my talent – at least, that I had as much
As anyone of a commodity you thought puerile
Beside the pain of prose. We exchanged so few letters

Being together so much. We both knew Chekov on marriage.
The unforgivable words are somewhere in a frozen space
Of limbo. I will swallow all of them in penance.

That's a grovel. Better to entertain your lover with sketches
And gossip in a letter and be ever-ripe for death.
You loved Carrington as you could never love yourself.

I think I am coming within earshot. Each night
I dream comic improvements on death: 'Still live
In Catatonia', but that's no laughing matter!

Perhaps I had Australia in me and you thought
Its dreadful health was your appointed accuser –
The Adversary assumes strange shapes and accents.

And I know, squinting at a meat-eating bird
Attempting an approach to a tit-bit near me,
That our predatoriness is shut down only by death,

And that there are no second chances in a universe
Which must get on with the business of living,
With only children for friends and memories of love.

But you are luckier than me, not having to shine
When you are called to the party of the world. The betrayals
Are garrulous and here comes death as talkative as ever.

lawrence ferlinghetti

THE OLD ITALIANS DYING

For years the old Italians have been dying
all over North Beach San Francisco
For years the old Italians in faded felt hats
have been sunning themselves and dying
You have seen them on the benches
in the park in Washington Square
the old Italians in their black high button shoes
the old men in their old felt fedoras
with stained hatbands
have been dying and dying day by day

You have seen them
every day in Washington Square
the slow bell
tolls in the morning
in the church of Saint Peter + Paul
in the marzipan church on the plaza
toward ten in the morning the slow bell tolls
in the towers of Peter + Paul
and the old men who are still alive
sit sunning themselves in a row
on the wood benches in the park

and watch the processions in and out
funerals in the morning
weddings in the afternoon
slow bell in the morning Fast bell at noon
In one door Out the other
the old men sit there in their hats
and watch the coming + going
You have seen them
the ones who feed the pigeons
                cutting the stale bread
                        with their thumbs + penknives
the ones with old pocketwatches
the old ones with gnarled hands
                        and wild eyebrows
the ones with the baggy pants
                wearing both belt + suspenders
the grappa drinkers with teeth like corn
the Pie'montesi the Genovesi the Sicilianos
                        smelling of garlic + pepperonis
the ones who loved Mussolini
the old fascists
the ones who loved Garibaldi
the old anarchists reading L'Umanita Nova
the ones who loved Sacco + Vanzetti
They are almost all gone now

They are sitting and waiting their turn
and sunning themselves in front t the church
over the doors & which is inscribed
a phrase which would seem to be unfinished
from Dante's Paradiso
about the glory of the One
                    who moves everything...
The old men are waiting
for it to be finished
for their glorious sentence on earth
                    to be finished
the slow bell tolls + tolls
the pigeons strut about
not even thinking of flying
the air too heavy with heavy tolling
The black hired hearses draw up
the black limousines with black windowshades
shielding the widows
the widows with the long black veils
who will outlive them all
You have seen them
madre di terra, madre di mare

The widows climb out of the limousines
The family mourners step out in stiff suits
The widows walk so slowly
up the steps of the cathedral
fishnet veils drawn down
leaning hard on darkcloth arms
Their faces do not fall apart
They are merely drawn apart
They are still the matriarchs
outliving everyone
the old dagos dying out
in little Italys all over America
the old dead dagos
hauled out in the morning sun
that does not mourn for anyone
One by one Year by year
they are carried out
The bell
never stops tolling
The old Italians with lapstrake faces
are hauled out of the hearses
by the paid pallbearers
in mafioso mourning coats + dark glasses

The old dead men are hauled out
in their black coffins like small skiffs
They enter the true church
 for the first time in many years
 in these carved black boats
                    ready to be ferried over
The priests scurry about
                    as if to cast off the lines
The other old men still alive on the benches
watch it all with their hats on
You have seen them sitting there
waiting for the bocci ball to stop rolling
waiting for the bell to stop tolling + tolling
for the slow bell to be finished tolling
telling the unfinished Paradiso story
as seen in an unfinished phrase
                    on the face of a church
as seen in a fisherman's face
in a black boat without sails
making his final haul

33

Why Brownlee Left
Paul Muldoon

Why Brownlee left, and where he went,
Is a mystery even now.
For if a man should have been content
It was him; two acres of barley,
One of potatoes, four bullocks,
A milker, a slated farmhouse.
He was last seen going out to plough
On a March morning, bright and early.

By noon Brownlee was famous;
They had found all abandoned, with
The last rig unbroken, his pair of black
Horses, like man and wife,
Shifting their weight from foot to
Foot, and gazing into the future.

PR 68:1, 1978

34

from Fits and Starts
Paul Auster

after Jacques Dupin

Tongue of black bread and pure water,
When a spade turns you inside out
The sky falls into action.

Our lover's arms darken,
Our worker's arms knot.

Just the force
To topple into the ravine
Our successive cadaver

And my library of stones.

35 Bayonne Entering NYC
Allen Ginsberg

from a long poem of These States

Smog trucks after mile high wire
   Structure leading toward New York along
      black multilane highway's showering lights
      blue city-glare horizoning
         Megalopolis' burning factories,
Bayonne refineries,
      Newark Hell-Light behind,
   truck trains passing trans-continental gas-lines,
blinking safety signs Keep awake –
Giant Giant Giant transformers,
    & electricity Stacks' glowing smoke –
More Chimney fires than all Kansas in a mile,
Sulphur Network smell Humble gigantic by viaduct –
      chemical burning rubber oil –
        'freshens your mouth'
      Railroad rust, deep marsh garbage-fume –
          Nostril horns.
  City announcer jabbering at City Motel,
      Airplanes rumbling overhead
    Flat winking space ships
         by Gorney Gorney Mortuary
Brilliant Signs the
    10 PM clock Churchspire lit in Suburb City,
    New Jersey's colored streets asleep –
High derrick spotlites lamped an inch
         above city
Shoprite lit for Nite people,
Vast Hohokus marshes and Passaic's flat gluey

PR 63:1, 1972

Blackness ringed with lightbulbs.
Blue Newark airport, waiting for Uraguayan Ambassador's
                              body arrive – green bulletshaped brain
        Plane, heart throbbing redlights middriff
           settling down – shark swift –
    toward the 71 million 3 hundred 69
              Lights at field edge,
Robot towers Blazon'd Eastern Air TWA
        above the Lavender-bulbed runway
        'Police say apparently had a heart attack' –
        Crossed barrage of car bridges –

I was born here in Newark,
        Public Service sign of the Twenties
              visible miles away
                      thru grey smoke in grey nite,
My aunts & uncles died in hospitals,
        are buried in graves surrounded by Railroad Tracks,
        Tombed near Winking 3 ring Ballentine Ale
        Where Western Electric has a Cosmic plant,
        & Pitt-Consoles breathes acrid fumes
                      above Flying Service tanks
Where superhighway rises above Montsanto
        Pulaski Skyway hanging in air my childhood
        neighboured with gigantic harbour stacks,
                                   steam everywhere
        Blue Star buses skimming skyroads
        beside th' Antennae mazes
        brilliant by Canalside...

Empire State's orange shoulders lifted over Hill –
New York City visible above the world
                   2 Guys from War put tiger in yr Tank –
        Radio crawling with Rock youngsters,
                              Stop – Pay Toll.
Blue Uniformed attendants rocking on their heels
                      in green booths

Let the hitchhiker off in the acrid Mist-
light Parade everywhere,
      Motel Hotel
      Lincoln Tunnel
      Pittsburgh Shitsburgh
      Seagram's a Sure One
Macdaniels vast parking lot –
cliff rooms, balconies & giant ancient schools,
reptilian trucks on Jersey City approaches
          Manhattan star-spread behind Palisades
evening lights reflected across
             Hudson water –
brilliant diamond-lantern'd Tunnel
      Whizz of bus-trucks shimmer in Ear
      over red brick –
      under Queen Mary & Kammerer's body
under Whitmanic Yawp Harbour Here
   roll into Man city, my city, Mannahatta,
      Lower East Side
grimed with Heroin, shit black from Edison towers
      on East river's rib –
O McGraw Hill Stand'st thou still here
      o'er green Garver's shade,
       & Huncke redeemed?
Green-hattd doormen awaken the eve
      in statuary-niched yellow Lobbies –
Zephyrus' canyons brightlit Empire State
      too small to be God –
Lording over Macy's Seafood City Grant Hotel –
Ho Ho Turn right the Blackman crossing street
     lighting his cigarette, lone on asphalt
     as the Lord in Nebraska –
Down 5th Avenue, brrr – the irregular spine
      of streetlights –
traffic signals all turn'd red at once,
wait silent see your Home
Cemented asphalt, wire roof banked,

canyoned & hived & churched with mortar,
                                morticed with art gas –
          passing Ginsberg Machine Co.
     & th' axehead Antique Flatiron
                building looms old photographs
                     parked in the mind –
     Cannastra's 21st street dark lofts
Tonite 18th street Westside blocked by a bus,
Dusty 16th still stretches
                         Hudson perspectiv'd –
Dali in London, Joe Army jr churches
          loom brownly in time,
               How quiet Washington monument!
& Fairy youth turns head down street
               crossing 5th Avenue trafficlite,
     doorman playing poodledog
     on brilliant-lit sidewalk No. 1 –
               park's dark, one walks,
an old reporter w/ brown leather briefcase
               past shiny pillar'd apartment
Gee it's a Miracle back on this street
     Where strange guy mustache
               stares into windowshield –
lovely the Steak Sign! bleeps on & off
               beneath Woman's prison –
Sixth Avenue bus huge window bright lit
     Lady in kerchief leans backward,
  At Whalen Drugs an old Beret familiar face
                         nods to his girl
Humm, McDougal I lived here,
          Humm perfect, there's empty space,
                    Park by the bright-lit bookstore –
               Where I'll find mail
                    & Harmonium, new from Calcutta
Waiting I come back to New York & begin to Sing.

36 Goings
Elizabeth Jennings

A packet of hurried letters, nervous gestures
To do with fingers, voices high and low
But out of key, eyes afraid to meet eyes –
    All this meaning 'Go'.

A child might hug or rush into its silence.
This is the fear of life not fear of death,
And the promises that distances mean nothing
    Already out of breath.

O our walls are painted with partings we don't notice,
Our minds are galleries of looks averted.
Perhaps the cord was never cut completely
    And those birth pangs were started

In a universe that's vast with a unique
Structure of inter-connections – star and steeple,
Storm and brain cell. We are born to break;
    We are departing people.

PR 72:1, 1982

37 Variations on a Phrase
David Gascoyne

Le lièvre fit sa prière à l'arc-en-ciel à travers la toile de l'araignée...

Rimbaud

The hare sent up his prayer to the rainbow
Through the spider's fine-spun filmy web,
Despite the huntsmen tracking it below.

The hunters set their snares, the norns weave threads,
Hephaestus' net awaits all peccant pairs.
A filament of light through heaven spreads.

A shaft of sunshine transpierces the dust
That rises as the shell's target explodes,
And glorifies it. Deep in mud we must

Unseal our eyes through choking smoke to see
How slaughter and compassion can combine
To trace a liberating filigree.

A hostage prisoned in a stinking cell
For just an instant saw a glinting fly
Above him as a sign from heaven not hell.

In chthonic labyrinth where we now stray
Do Thou in us make peace, O lightbringer.
Submerged in darkness glows the serene day.

While raw-scabbed refugees without end file
Past numbed spectators, an aeon elsewhere
Some insane sanity sustains its smile.

PR 72:3, 1982

Yet jackals howl across the wastes of thyme.
The drunken boat speeds on. The skilled music
Still needed by desire runs out of time.

The Charleville boy ended up peddling guns
In Ethiopia, amnesic of dream.
We can end roasted by our man-made suns.

Regarding the origin of this poem, I should like to acknowledge my indebtedness
to M. André Dhotel's 'Rimbaldiana', a contribution to *La Nouvelle Revue Française*
for May 1982 (No. 352). – D.G.

& Horror Poet
Philip Larkin

In this book Ted Hughes has arranged Sylvia Plath's poems as far as possible
in the order they were written, with about forty pages of juvenilia at the
end. It is therefore possible to read them through, helped by Hughes's
notes, with a fair degree of continuity. For someone hitherto largely un-
familiar with her life and work this is an extraordinary experience.

The first hundred poems (or, to be precise, the first ninety-eight) are
not ultimately very interesting, except insofar as they predicate a remark-
able personality. Plath was prolific and precocious. She seems to have
written compulsively (her annual output between 1956 and her death in
1963 averaged thirty-two poems); when she had nothing to write about
she wrote on set themes, as she had as a student at Smith College. She
threw nothing away. She seems not to have gone through the appren-
ticeship of following different poets for their styles, unless there are
models I do not recognise; her pieces are intellectually conceited, vivid
and resourceful in image and vocabulary. Form was not her strong point:
she rhymed and scanned when it suited her, which was less and less often
as she grew older. Nor was her 'ear' good: 'Each teacher found my touch
/ Oddly wooden' she says of early piano lessons, and one can see what
they meant; at times in 1956 her verse had the denseness of early Dylan
Thomas:

Now in the crux of their vows hang your ear,
Still as a shell: hear what an age of glass
These lovers prophesy to lock embrace
Secure in museum diamond for the stare
Of astounded generations; they wrestle
To conquer cinder's kingdom in the stroke of an hour
And hoard faith safe in a fossil.

They are the poems of a prize pupil, crammed with invention, lacking emotional centre. Hughes recounts illuminatingly her search for a title for her first book: it was called, successively, *The Earthenware Head*, *The Everlasting Monday*, *Full Fathom Five*, *The Bull of Bendylaw*, *The Devil of the Stairs*, and finally *The Colossus*. The effect is almost farcical.

Up till 1959 Plath's poems lack what one looks for in any writer of stature: the individual note or theme by and with which he or she will henceforth be identified. Line by line they are often remarkable: in sum they are unmemorable. But in that year a poem begins

The day she visited the dissecting room
They had four men laid out, black as burnt turkey,
Already half unstrung...

The shock is sudden, and the possibility that she is simply trying on another style is dispelled by the two following pieces, 'Suicide Off Egg Rock' and 'The Ravaged Face'. Plath liked them for their 'forthrightness', a word suggesting the abandonment of literary fancy in favour of plainer realism, and in one sense this was true: she had found her subject-matter. It was, variously, neurosis, insanity, disease, death, horror, terror.

A note by Hughes says that at this time Plath was taken with the work of Theodore Roethke, and 'realised how he could help her'. She certainly picked up his something-nasty-in-the-greenhouse manner; she, too, could find the creepiness in things. In November of that year she wrote 'Mushrooms', a superficially gentle, even Georgian poem, but filled with menace. The following year saw the birth of her first child and a cessation of activity, but by the end of it she was writing

How the balconies echoed! How the sun lit up
The skulls, the unbuckled bones facing the view!
Space! Space! The bed linen was giving out entirely.
Cot legs melted into terrible attitudes, and the nurses –
Each nurse patched her soul to a wound and disappeared.

The pleasurable excitement of watching a young writer gaining command of her predestined material is nullified by the nature of that material and her involvement with it. Hughes's notes have already made it clear that she was mentally unstable; like many Americans, she had a psychiatrist, but, more individually, had also a scar across her cheek from an earlier suicide attempt. For her to exercise her unique talent for the distortions of horror and madness was to risk liberating these forces in herself. She was, to use Henry James's well-worn phrase, immersing herself in the destructive element.

At first the exercise seems deliberate, writing poems with titles such as 'Insomniac', 'Widow', 'The Surgeon At 2a.m.' and 'Fever 103°', or about a hospital for mutilated war veterans, thalidomide children or cutting one's thumb half off. But there are others, in which neutral or even sympathetic subjects are wilfully refracted into something terrible or horrible; 'Zoo Keeper's Wife', according to the notes, came from Plath's frequent visits to Regent's Park Zoo, seemingly a harmless enough recreation, but

> How our courtship lit the tindery cages –
> Your two-horned rhinoceros opened a mouth
> Dirty as a bootsole and big as a hospital sink
> For my cube of sugar: its bog breath
> Gloved my arm to the elbow.

An even more striking example is the series of bee poems. Plath kept bees in Devon, and attended meetings of the local Beekeepers' Association, activities surely not to be undertaken except in a matter-of-fact spirit, but she portrays it as a kind of mythopoeic nightmare:

> Which is the rector now, is it that man in black?
> Which is the midwife, is that her blue coat?
> Everybody is nodding a square head, they are knights in visors,
> Breastplates of cheesecloth knotted under the armpits.
> Their smiles and their voices are changing.
> …
> I am exhausted, I am exhausted –
> Pillar of white in a blackout of knives.
> I am the magician's girl who does not flinch.
> The villagers are untying their disguises, they are shaking hands.
> Whose is that long white box in the grove, what have they
>   accomplished, why am I cold.

Brilliant as this is, as if Hitchcock had filmed the church fête at the beginning of Graham Greene's *The Ministry of Fear*, the reader does not agree that, yes, it must have been terrible; rather, he wonders whether Plath is wilfully hyping up this ordinary event to make a poem, or whether this is really how she saw it, in which case Plath and the reader are about to part company. For a time one inclines to the first view. Hughes quotes an interesting remark by Plath when introducing a broad-cast reading of 'Lady Lazarus' (one of her most celebrated poems, compounded of a suicide attempt, the Lazarus story and German death camps where God is the Commandant) to the effect that the speaker in the poem is Phoenix, the libertarian spirit, a woman who has the gift of being reborn: 'The only trouble is, she has to die first... She is also just a good, plain, very resourceful woman.' One suspects that half the time this is what Plath was. She also sounds ambitious, competitive, compul-sive, the girl most likely to succeed, ready to exploit her own traumas if they would make poems. Mad poets do not write about madness: they write about religion, sofas, the French Revolution, nature, and their cat Geoffry [*sic*]. Plath did: it was her subject, her donnée ('I do it exception-ally well'); together they played an increasingly reckless game of tag.

Of course it might have been all for the best. In 1961 she wrote her novel, *The Bell Jar*, perhaps with the idea of self-therapy and making a fresh start. Early in 1962 she had a second child. In September she and her husband separated. During this year she wrote fifty-six poems, one of them the long and apparently-reconciled piece for voices 'Three Women'. Increasingly divorced from identifiable incident, they seem to enter neurosis, or insanity, and exist there in a prolonged high-pitched ecstasy like nothing else in literature. They are impossible to quote mean-ingfully: they must be read whole. In February 1963 she killed herself.

How far this was due to pressure from within, how far to pressure from without is hard to say. Plath may have taken on more than she could manage and been destroyed by circumstances. Or she may have been committed to such a break-up whatever she did. Or, as I have suggested, she may have indulged her own talent for following a literary fashion (Roethke, Lowell) until she lost control of it and it overwhelmed her. Considering what one takes to be their subject-matter, her poems, partic-ularly the last ones, are curiously, even jauntily impersonal; it is hard to see how she was labelled confessional. As poems, they are to the highest degree original and scarcely less effective. How valuable they are depends on how highly we rank the expression of experience with which we can in no sense identify, and from which we can only turn with shock and sorrow.

38

from Skating: Memories of Childhood
Andrew Motion

[...]

3

What did she look like? Very beautiful. 5 foot 8½ inches ('I could always have joined the police force') with fair hair a bit darker than mine. When I brushed her hair, I had to be careful that the bristles didn't strike the large mole at her crown. This mole used to embarrass her, and the hair would be brushed over it in a long wave. There was a mole on her cheek, too, and you could feel its bump when she kissed you. One nostril was slightly lifted where she had hit her nose falling off a pony. These things used to worry me when I was a child: my brother Kit (who is two years younger than me) and I both thought that they 'spoilt' her. Now they seem to make her more perfect by making her more human. But we were always proud of the way she looked, and enjoyed it. We used to creep into her bed in the morning, as soon as my father had gone off to work. 'You're no good', she'd tell me. 'You're a lamp-post.' (I was hopeless at cuddling.) Then she would dress while we lay and watched her, ostentatiously stripping off her nightdress and lazily padding about hunting for clothes. It was delicious and shocking: I can remember looking away from her to a mad ballet of flies around the lamp-shade. When she was finished, and the hair-brushing began, she would sit at her kidney-shaped dressing table. It had a glass top, and underneath this she had slipped photographs of my father, my brother and myself. You could see the photographs over her shoulder: me in my pram on the mill pond; me in the forest of cowparsley. My vanity and hers were appeased at one and the same time.

PR 73:3, 1983

4

[...]

Because I'd never doubted for a second that my parents adored me, I never really believed that they would send me away. How did they imagine we could live apart? What was the point? If they did try to explain, I have forgotten. (Their friends' children went away to school – that was probably all it was.) Before they left me on my first evening, they pushed me into the company of Greenwell, an older boy I knew vaguely from home. 'You're a Jap,' he said. 'And I'm the Allied Forces,' then chased me round the hall. I was crying so bitterly I could scarcely see where I was going. But when I stopped, and dried my eyes, I looked through the double glass doors which led from the hall to the vestibule, and there was my mother looking in, crying too. I thought she had already gone.

The school was a sandstone Victorian country house with peculiar lead-capped towers at its four corners. It was called (ironically, I thought, when I knew what irony was) Maidwell Hall, and the headmaster was a friend and contemporary of my grandfather's. This meant that the remoteness he had as a teacher was slightly diminished, but I don't think he ever took any special interest in me. His real passion was orchids, and in season the grounds would suddenly become exotic with bizarre blooms. We thought they were rather disgusting, since they reminded us of him. The grounds themselves were large and full of mystery: The Wilderness (a huge – though probably in fact quite small – evergreen wood); Dinkey Farm (a slithery pit where we played with our toys); and The Lake (full of golden orfe and crossed by stepping-stones which only prefects were allowed to use). There were games every afternoon, and I was good at them. From the age of about ten I could run faster than anyone in the school, and this gave me a sense of identity. I traded on it – in a mildly tyrannical way – to the extent that I formed a gang, and on Wednesday and Sunday afternoons (when we had 'Muck-About' and no games) we used to run futilely round the grounds looking for things to do. We also dug a large hole in The Wilderness, roofed it with planks and covered the planks with earth, and called it The Hut. When we weren't running around, we'd retreat to The Hut and smoke pine needles wrapped up in lavatory paper.

So outdoors was more or less all right. It was a haven from indoors, where I had no feeling of purpose or ability, and where whatever successes I'd had at games never helped me. If I'd been unsure of myself at work before I arrived, my nervousness was rapidly intensified by my first teacher, Miss Hangwick. She was tall, grey, and generally considered to be 'a good sort'. But her secret vice, when we disappointed her, was to inflict on us the 'Haggie Hairpull'. Rogers, whose hair came out very easily, was virtually scalped one afternoon. I can still see the large hank in Miss Hangwick's hand.

I can also see now that Miss Hangwick had a tiresome and thwarting life. But in those days (most children have so little sense of adults' cares and responsibilities) I simply disliked her. She made me feel stupid, and feeling stupid made me feel – and be – wet. I looked like a cissy, too, with my fair hair, and I was clearly spoilt by my mother. She sent me, during my first term (twelve weeks long) twenty-six parcels – usually plastic model kits of ships. One Sunday afternoon a group of boys led me outside, took off my shirt, tied me to a cedar tree, and beat me with bamboo canes. I still have the scars on my back – but I don't remember ever telling my mother. I wanted to be a success for her.

Being able to run fast was never really enough. I simply couldn't find any work to do well. By the time I moved on from Miss Hangwick, every subject was terrifying – in my dormitory I kept a Bible on my bedside chair and slept with one hand holding onto it. 'Please God,' I'd pray, 'Let me see the light.' Latin and Maths were especially bad: I used to cheat as hard as I could, and squeeze blood from my bitten finger-nails onto my prep, so that the person marking it could see that I'd been making an effort. English was marginally preferable to other subjects – but only marginally. Spelling and précis were at least only dreary, not actually frightening, and writing essays could be fun, if the title was an exciting one like 'River In Flood', or 'How I Survived The Earthquake'. We rarely got round to writing or talking about poems (I remember producing one which began 'There was an old man in the moon

/ Who wanted to grant the earth a boon...') but we did occasion-
ally have to learn them. I can still recite most of 'The chief defect
of Henry King' and de la Mare's 'Nod'. They never meant much
to me, though: poetry, everyone agreed, was for cissies. But if I
was a cissy, why wasn't it for me? Oh well.

5

Nevertheless, during my last few holidays from Maidwell, I found
myself writing stories. (It was probably to curry favour.) They
were giftless – melodramatic accounts of car accidents and Indian
massacres – but I'd be pleased and surprised by them, and take
them into my mother's bed the morning to read them to her. 'Why
are you so bloodthirsty?' she'd ask – and I'd be unsure whether this
implied praise or the opposite. I can see now that the stories were
ways of imagining the worst: ways of trying to prolong the idyll of
her company by dreaming up some radically appalling alternative.

In fact the pleasures of holidays lasted for years, though their
details are nearly all forgotten. We never did anything which might
be construed as having the remotest connection with school work:
no theatre, no art galleries, no concerts – we simply weren't inter-
ested. We were busily occupied, though: Little Brewers was (in
those days) near unspoilt country, and we led what I suppose is a
typical landed life. It was extremely horsey. Hunting dominated
the winter, and in the summer my mother, Kit and I went for a
long ride each morning. Kit was always much more adventurous
and proficient than I was; I think riding rather scared me. In the
afternoon, my mother rested on her bed for an hour, and we never
gave it a second thought. But the more I think about her now, the
more mysterious her life seems. Was she catastrophically bored?
She was often ill: to what extent was she appealing for more consid-
erate attention from us? What did she do when Kit and I weren't
there? At the time, she seemed to exist entirely for us – after her
rest she would walk the dogs with us, or go shopping with us, or
come for a bike ride with us. She had a vast black upright bike, with
what looked like a dead umbrella over the back mudguard to stop
mud splashing up. Once I threw a stick into the spokes as she was

pedalling along, to see what happened. She fell off, of course. I think I must have thought she was infallible.

In my very earliest memories, my mother is just *there*: entirely trustworthy and always affectionate. But as I grew up, and became aware of her personality, I realised that I liked her very much, as well as loving her instinctively. She was brave, she was sensible, and she made me laugh (she loved filthy jokes). She also made me feel special by sometimes confiding in me as she might have done with an equal. I sensed that her character had exciting reserves which I would discover when I was older. Not that I spent any time articulating such things: when I was with her, I was much too busy enjoying myself. But I do wish that I could now remember more actual incidents – like the time I stopped my pony in a wood, and discovered that I was eye-level with a pigeon on its nest. I can still see the ramshackle platform of twigs, and the bird with its beautiful swollen crop and its wet eye staring me out.

[...]

6

How I passed my common entrance I can't think. I must have been born in the sun. I expected Radley to be an X certificate version of Maidwell, and to start with it seemed so. Everything I did was wrong. I wore a buttoned pull-over (a prefect's privilege); I walked on the grass (also a prefect's privilege); and – worst of all – I smiled at older boys (I was a tart). By the end of my first term, though, good teaching had convinced me that learning wasn't as intimidating as I'd always imagined, and I relaxed. In fact I even started to be quite good at some things – especially English, which consisted largely of writing essays (more rivers in flood and earthquakes), and reading the First World War poets (every English teacher in the school seemed to be addicted to them). Life outside the classroom started to brighten up, too: there was Chapel every day, which I enjoyed – it was bliss to be left alone with one's thoughts – and there was Social Hall. This was the large room that boys shared for their first year, everyone having a wooden enclave called a 'horsebox' where you kept your books and tuck, and did your work. The sort of camaraderie which prevailed in Social Hall was what I imagine the feeling must have been like in a Prisoner of War camp. It was 'us' against 'them', and even our most minor law breakings generated a profound sense of community.

For the first time, I found myself distracted from the thought of home. I still longed for it, and for the two letters a week that my mother wrote me, but my homesickness lost that weak-kneed, stomach-loosening intensity I'd felt almost continuously at Maidwell. It was partly a matter of feeling more confident, and partly that for the first time I made a close friendship – with a boy called Sandy Nairne. He was slightly younger than me, but bigger, cleverer and much more assured. I felt safe with him. (Later we shared a study together, and eventually went to the same college at Oxford. He's still one of my very closest friends.) Sandy also made me think. It never occurred to me until years afterwards, but the fact that he came from a professional background whereas most of my previous acquaintances were from landed families – Maidwell was that kind of school – made an enormous difference to me. When I went to stay with him in the holidays, I joined a society where it was perfectly normal – indeed, it was the done thing – to talk about books and paintings and so on. Although Sandy never wrote poems himself – he drew very well – he encouraged me to feel that there was nothing peculiar about reading them. But to start with it was an illicit sort of pleasure. I used to take books – Keats, usually – to remote parts of the grounds and read them aloud to myself. I remember reading, for the first time, 'Bright Star', and wondering what it would be like to be in love. How would it be different from loving my mother?

When I actually began to write poetry, my parents regarded it with slightly alarmed tolerance as the sign of 'a phase I was going through'. They were quite right: the poems had nothing to do with art, but were simply appeals for attention, attempts to épater les bourgeois, and clumsy efforts at catharsis. Nearly all of them were about outcasts, lepers, and people in woods with no clothes on.

I think my parents may have persuaded themselves that my writing could be justified as an extension of work. At least it was a *serious* sort of activity. But there was no denying the fact that none of their friends' children did it, which made it embarrassing. I remember being driven to a party, once, by one of these children a few years older than myself, and asking her, ridiculously, 'Do you write?' 'Yes,' she answered. 'We have three horses.' What made it all so much worse for my parents was that writing poems seemed to require of me a calculatedly pretentious – I thought it was Romantic – manner. I even, for a short time, owned a cloak. One winter holiday, when I told my parents that I didn't want to go hunting any more, my mother rounded on me and said 'Oh don't be so wet. You'll end up fit to do nothing but run an antique shop.' It's the only irritated, and irritating, thing I can remember her saying to me, and at the time I thought it was a sign that our mutual understanding was coming to an end. Most of my friends (though not Sandy) made a point of complaining about their parents – it was almost a fashion. I didn't suppose I'd remain any different for ever. I was growing up, I told myself. What else could I expect?

7

Then I got rheumatism, and spent most of a year at home: no Kit to compete with, my father away most of every day – just my mother and me together. It was wonderful, and I realise now that if it hadn't existed I would hardly have known her at all. By this time we had moved to the house my father still lives in: a beautiful, high-ceilinged, Georgian ex-rectory in north Essex. It was cut off from the lane by a thick belt of trees (mostly elms – they're dead now) and felt secluded and magical. For the first few months of my illness I had a bed made up downstairs (I couldn't walk), and through the window there was a huge chestnut tree. The lower branches had been rubbed smooth by the horses scratching their backs, and the bark was greasy and covered with hairs.

After her morning ride, my mother would sit with me, or do her chores about the house. I lived her life vicariously: I could hear the radio and the crackle of cooking from the kitchen, and smell the ironing when she did that. I suppose she was denying herself whatever she normally did during term, but she never made me aware that I was a nuisance. I just felt loved and grateful. I also felt, in an accidental sort of way, included for the first time in an adult world which was usually disguised during the holidays proper. There was a large stone fireplace in my bedroom, and when my father came home from work, they'd sit by the fire with me between them. After they had gone to bed I'd watch the fire sinking in the darkness and listen to them undressing upstairs. It had never occurred to me before to ask myself whether they were happy together – now I could see that they were. Immensely.

8

My year at home was so contented that, when I recovered, I asked my parents if I could go to a local day school, and not back to Radley. I never really expected them to say yes, but the request seems significant, now, as a sign that I was discovering – at last, one might well say – a sense of guilt about the privileges of my life. It was never acute enough actually to prevent me from enjoying school, or home, but it made me shifty whenever I stepped outside the confines of the world where I could recognise and play 'the system'. Within the system, I made efforts to seem radical which were well-meant but probably weak-willed, and certainly ineffectual. When Sandy and I adopted attitudes, or voiced opinions, which ran counter to the school's prevailing ideology, the school simply shifted to accommodate us, and contained what we thought was our spirit of rebellion by calling us 'interesting'.

Actually we weren't rebellious at all: our radicalism consisted largely of reading magazines like the *New Statesman* and some Fabian pamphlets that I'd sent off for. There was little chance, anyway, of many people being affected by our Socialist views and much vaunted liberal love for our fellows, since at the first possible opportunity we retreated to a study at the top of a tower and cultivated a mood of faintly embattled, haughty elitism. The only sustained and direct challenge to authority that I went in for was to refuse to give up smoking. But this was entirely self-interested. And anyway, can something be a challenge if no one knows it exists? Most afternoons (I couldn't play games because of my rheumatism) I put a book of poems in one pocket (actually just sticking out in case anyone noticed and was impressed), my fags in the other, and set off for Bagley Wood. In the evenings, in the tower (for Christ's sake) I took snuff, which usually gave me a sore throat.

I think Sandy and I must have worked fairly hard – we both enjoyed it, and I was being taught English by a master I admired and wanted to please. Sandy and I also talked an immense amount – about trivial things mainly, I expect, but also about politics a good deal, and – at the slightest possible excuse – about sex. I'd left Maidwell in a state of prodigious innocence. It was the same (amazingly, it now seems) for every one of my contemporaries there. All we had been given to lighten the darkness of our ignorance was a talk by the headmaster when we were ten – 'The Special' – and another just before we left – 'The Extra Special'. 'The Special' was so unexpected and embarrassing that I can't remember anything about it. The 'Extra Special' meant more detail and a drawing of some wiggly sperms flying into space. 'When you get to public school', the talk ended 'some older boys will probably try to get too friendly with you. On no account let them.' I wasn't so sure that it didn't sound rather interesting.

Soon after arriving at Radley I decided to ignore the advice given me in my 'Extra Special' (it wasn't so much a decision, actually, as merely obedience to my instincts) and the results did wonders for my confidence. It was so marvellous to be admired. But I did want to find out about girls too, and read as many enlighteningly erotic books as I could get my hands on. Once, desperately needing to replenish my stocks, I biked into Abingdon during a three-quarters-of-an-hour break, bought the first filthy-looking book I saw in the bookshop, and tore back to school so as not to miss the next lesson. The book turned out to be a sober account of the life of Mary Magdalene.

When holidays began, though, there was the bewildering prospect of real girls, and not just books about them. How far did they want to go? More to the point, how far did I want to go? I was so engrossed, pottering around at home with my mother and Kit, that I could usually avoid the problem altogether. But there was always the threat of dances. These tended to be large, rather formal affairs which began with a dinner party and ended with half an hour of darkness in which couples staggered about clutching each other. I loathed dances. My shyness (if that's what it was) made my head empty of easy conversation, and fill with unacceptable literary thoughts: 'I wonder what she thinks of Greville's sonnets?' Usually I just hung around trying to be polite, waiting for enough time to elapse before I could decently complain that my rheumatism was hurting, and could I please ring my father and ask him to come and collect me? He and I occasionally had man-to-boy, complicit chats about girls, but if I ever ventured to say that I was keen on anyone, I knew that I was on thin ice. My ineptitude would always mean that soon after confiding in him I would have to tell him that nothing had come of anything. 'Never mind, darling,' my mother would say. 'There are plenty more fish in the sea.'

9

My mother and I never talked much about sex – I think she must have just wanted me to find out about it for myself. I can remember standing beside her at the kidney-shaped dressing table once, when I was going off to stay with a girl in London, and her checking that I knew about contraception. As things turned out, I didn't need to know.

But school – so I was led to believe – was full of people who had 'been the whole way' with girls in the holidays, and it was difficult not to feel that one wanted to do it too. The best chance seemed to be with a girl called Caroline Coleridge. She looked as if she would help if things got tricky, and I liked her – for herself as well as her name. After some unusually (for me) confident manoeu-vrings at a party, I got what I wanted: an invitation to stay. She knew some people who were giving a dance…

I was still about eighteen months away from learning to drive, so on these sort of occasions my mother would either take me herself, or put me on a bus. This time it was to be the bus. After breakfast I packed my case, feeling ill with trepidation. Should I take Caroline a present? There was a whole day together before the dance began: would we have anything to say to one another?

Then my mother and I drove down the lane, through the village, down the long hill with its tunnel of trees, and up to the bus stop on the main road. It was December with occasional blasts of snow, and an east wind was blowing. My mother was hunting with Kit later that day, and she was wearing a stock under her brown jersey. We waited with the engine on, to keep the heater working, 'Have you got everything?' 'Yaaaas' (said in that flat way we'd evolved, meaning 'Don't flap'.) 'I'll meet you here tomorrow.' 'Yaaaas.' When the bus came it was a double-decker. Without knowing why (why didn't I want to assert my independence?) I climbed to the top as quickly as I could and stared through the back window. I saw her car, the green Hillman Estate, pull away from the bus stop and head for the lane home again. As she went, she bibbed her horn, and crouched right down to look up at me. She waved, and I waved, and the car turned out of sight.

Not much survives of my day with Caroline but we got through it all right. In the afternoon we went for a walk, not holding hands, I wearing her father's overcoat because of the cold. By 6.30 I was in the spare-room, changing for the dance. It was a cosy, dark-panelled room, but the bed didn't look very big, and when I sat on it the springs gave a loud lunatic jangle. I tentatively bounced up and down, then stopped, guilty, when there was a knock on the door. 'It's Caroline with a plan,' I thought. But it wasn't. It was her mother.

When I think back over the next few minutes, they seem to be as clear as if I were living them now, and yet profoundly unreal – invented, almost. I suppose a bringer of bad news will almost always talk in clichés: clichés are protective, and they're meant to be easily understood. 'Something terrible has happened,' Mrs Coleridge said, leaning against the wall and looking as if someone had pushed her. 'Your mother has had an accident.'

[...]

39

Working for T.S. Eliot:
A Personal Reminiscence
Anne Ridler

'Il n'y a point de héros pour son valet de chambre', and in general this must be true for a man's secretary also. I can truthfully say, however, that no disillusion overtook my view of T.S. Eliot, hero to the poetasters of my generation, after my years of working as secretary and junior editor in Faber & Faber.

I started there in the production department in 1935, under Richard de la Mare, and later moved to be Eliot's secretary, responsible for seeing the *Criterion* through the press, and monitoring the unsolicited contributions which came in to that quarterly. Also, as there was no rigid delimiting of jobs, I did copy-editing, and reported on manuscripts to the weekly Book Committee.

I lived in Taviton Street, only five minutes' walk from the Faber offices at 24 Russell Square, and before I went into the firm had hung around the door at a likely time to see the great man come out. So, once taken on as an employee, I soon made a pretext to go up in the creaky lift to the second floor on some message to Mr Eliot. The pretext was a query raised by the proof reader on his *Collected Poems 1909–35,* and concerned the gender of a noun in 'Lune de Miel', which he had given wrongly, writing 'le Cène'. 'Well, that depends of course on Italian,' he said, and I was puzzled, informing him of what I was sure he must know, that the Italian was *cena,* feminine. But it occurred to me afterwards that he was probably thinking of the masculine *cenacolo,* as the allusion is to Leonardo's fresco of the Last Supper. Editions of Eliot's poems became known for slight inaccuracies: the proofs were probably too reverentially treated by the correctors (I was responsible for one set, the little *Sesame* selection which I made), while the master himself was always reluctant to linger over past productions of his own.

That eyrie of Eliot's has often been described, with the brass plate on the door saying 'Thomas Stearns' (relic of his maternal grandfather), the clutter of books piled up on floor and table, old snapshots on the mantelpiece which were added to from time to time, and the view down over the trees of Woburn Square. The window looked straight down the square, as No. 24 Russell Square, the corner house, jutted out from the rest, with a black poplar in its garden, especially beautiful in spring with its red catkins. Though 'Lines to a Persian Cat' speaks of the green trees of *Russell* Square, I think when I read it of Eliot looking over Woburn Square, wearily at work in the afternoon:

> Why will the summer day delay,
> *When* will time flow away?

I think it was on the first visit of mine to his room that I noticed with surprise a necktie made of marzipan lying on the desk. When I came to write a piece about Eliot for broadcast to India just after the war, I mentioned this necktie, but cut out the allusion after his comment: 'The necktie of marzipan, I fear, would simply puzzle the earnest Bengalis, and indeed would be a mystery to anyone who had not known Mr F.V. Morley. My own rule with foreigners, except maybe the French and Chinese, is that anything at all humorous must be labelled JOKE and be very simple indeed.'

When I came to take letters from dictation in this room, sitting in the one armchair while Elliot often stood, I was oppressed by the tedium for him of the matters I had to set before him, and must sometimes have made things worse by my tentative approach. 'What must I bear?' I remember his saying, not with a smile, after some preface of mine. There is a distinction to be made between proper awe of a great man and the servile fear which dreads to make a fool of itself. My attitude to Eliot, at any rate in early days, partook of both: the fear he would challenge, sometimes with a deliberate purpose, sometimes because it provoked his instinct for teasing. He certainly took pleasure in what we might now call one-upmanship; on the other hand he liked people to defend themselves vigorously, and once said as much to me. When, after weeks of vetting the mostly-rubbishy poetry sent in to the *Criterion* without finding anything worth his notice, I felt I must pick out something for him to look at, and put a couple of MSS on his desk with his letters, these were held out to me later with a blank look and the monosyllable *Why?* To which I think I found no better answer than that I didn't understand them, so thought they might be good.

Eliot was the most considerate of employers, where his secretary's welfare was concerned, and he had, with all his sophistication, a delightful simplicity in some practical matters. I remember his warm approbation – 'That was very smart of you' – when I had merely thought to enclose a stamped addressed envelope for him to use with something I sent on to him.

He worked at home in the mornings and came to Russell Square after lunch, except on Wednesdays, when the Directors had lunch together in their board room overlooking Russell Square, which was also the office of Frank Morley and Morley Kennerley. Their roast lamb and apple pie was prepared by the caretakers, Mr and Mrs Lister, who lived on the top floor of the building. After lunch came the Book Committee, at which the MSS offered to the firm were considered, though there was a preliminary sorting to discard obvious duds. In the latter part of my time I did this with Alan Pringle, later a Director, and also attended the Book Committee. Written reports were read out at the Committee, or comments made extempore, and a manuscript might be passed for further reports within the firm, or occasionally to an expert outside; if the verdict was favourable, rapid calculations would be made on the spot as to possible returns, at such and such a price and size of edition. Poetry and theology went first to Eliot, of course, and often books in German or French. He affected a certain detachment from the proceedings, and did the *Times* crossword during the meeting, but his business judgements were as shrewd as anyone's – a fact emphasised to me by the Sales Manager, Mr Crawley. However on one occasion, when Eliot had interviewed Geoffrey Grigson about a proposed anthology from Grigson's magazine *New Verse*, he had clearly forgotten to discuss terms, and half-pretended that 'two shy men' had not felt able to approach the delicate subject of money. When tea was brought in by Lister, Eliot, who did not take sugar, would carefully remove the teaspoon from his saucer before it became slopped with tea.

Though he might appear not to listen, he was well aware of the foibles of his colleagues both senior and junior, and when he proffered his *Practical Cats* to the Committee, produced with it a series of mock reports on the script, parodying the style of each member. Mine, I recall, was scathing in tone and peppered with parentheses.

Eliot typed his own reports, and many of his letters, standing up at his typewriter. Some of the MSS he read in the office, sitting in his armchair, others he took home, often a relaxation from more strenuous mental work. 'It is easier to go on reading this book than to stop,' he commented on one; 'especially if one has something better to do.'

When Eliot came to write *The Cocktail Party*, he gave Reilly's secretary the name of Miss Barraway. Barring away was certainly one of the chief functions of his secretary, for not only was there a continuous stream of hangers-on and impecunious poets (never completely barred away), but also the pathetic figure of his estranged wife Vivienne, a 'restless shivering shadow' (the phrase from *The Family Reunion* seemed only too apt), who would sometimes hover in the waiting-room till he came past the window on his way to the entrance. Telephone callers were rarely put through to him, and if he had to speak, his voice had a curiously strangled sound.

In dictation he was measured but fluent: as with his normal speech, the sentences were perfectly formed – there might be a pause, but no humming and ha'ing. Sometimes his extempore criticism in a letter was so interesting that I found it hard to remember that my business was to take it down, not to listen or comment. As when, criticising a friend's story for carrying too obvious a 'message', he said that this essential meaning was thrust at the reader, when it should be absorbed by him unconsciously through attention to the narrative; for objects are seen more vividly at the margins of the eye 'where the rods and cones are less worn, just as one can count more of the Pleiades on a clear night if one is not looking directly at them.'

I remembered this vivid image when, many years later, he wrote to me à propos of fantasy in drama: 'there is... one's deeper fantasy which is one's view of life, or one's own particular way of giving meaning to the apparently meaninglessness of human events and situations; and it seems to me that what one has to do is to get deeper into one's own fantasy so that nothing sticks out: to make the audience partake of one's fantasy, instead of poking it at them here and there.'

Conscientious attention and generous expenditure of time, on any work he thought worth the trouble, were freely given, but equally admirable was the integrity he preserved in giving his opinions. He never resorted to the facile praise or cowardly half-truths which most of us utter, persuading ourselves that we wish to avoid hurting the feelings of others, when our real motive is to leave them with a favourable view of ourselves. Eliot did employ a skilful ambiguity sometimes – I came to know the phrases very well. He could, also, indulge in some mockery of the foolish, or some teasing, behind his *persona* of the grave, judicious public man. As E.W.F. Tomlin put it in a broadcast talk: 'He exploited the drawl – perhaps the last vestige of his Southern accent – in such a manner as to convey infinite nuances of banter and irony.'

'Interviewing waifs and strays, and a few genuine authors' was how he described his week to me, writing after I had left the firm. Of one of the latter sort, who had submitted a script: 'I don't think that X quite understands the nature of the fundamental differences between François Villon and himself.'

Out of recent offerings the best bit is the following:

> This morning the village of Denethorpe, Northants
> Was suddenly roused by ten men in strange pants.

That came with a flattering letter to the author from Richard Church, regretting that Dent's have so little paper, and recommending us. The following is, I think, more poetical, and comes of course from India:

> Whai ho! Who wonneth here?
> 'Tis merrymad magpies Roop and Mary
> Six wet monsoons wedded be we.

'From this' he commented elsewhere, 'you will see that 24 Russell Square is just as much a vortex of lunacy as it was in your time.'

'Sometimes I feel I loathe poetry,' he said wearily to me one day. And seeing him so much pestered, one did not readily inflict one's own work on him. I did not offer my poems to the firm while I was working there – the suggestion that Faber should publish them came from Eliot himself later on – but I have a few manuscripts with his terse and trenchant comments in the margin. In later years when he was my publisher, I knew that if he commented on a script 'I have looked through your manuscript which seems to me all right', I was doing very well. His advice on drama was illuminating, especially in relation to his own work. When I was writing a play for Martin Browne, and confused between my own instinct and what the producer required, he wrote: 'I think that at the present stage, at which there is no *tradition* for verse plays (I mean, not only that every author has to make a fresh start once, but has to make a fresh start with every play – not only other people's work, but one's one previous work, can be a distraction) there is bound to be a certain tug of war between author and producer. It's probably best to give way most of the time to the producer at first, because one does not know where it is one's instinct that is in opposition, and where it is merely one's ignorance of the theatre. But it isn't the producer, or the actor one learns from... but the production.

'I... don't consider *Murder in the Cathedral* as more than a successful tour de force – though a few minor inspirations did come to me in the course of writing it. I don't think I learned much from it that was helpful in writing another play, except a certain self-confidence due to success, which made me more prepared to write what would probably be (and was) a failure.'

Working with Eliot, one was aware of standards of truthfulness higher than the common, and perhaps tried harder for the rest of one's life to be careful of the truth. He was generous with money, to all sorts of people; his tender-heartedness can be guessed from his poetry, though not everyone has seen it. For example, he could not bear to re-read old letters; the emotion they evoked was too strong. 'Occasionally I come across a letter, slipped in among the leaves of a book... from somebody long dead. I usually shut the book up quickly and put it back.'

If it seemed that only disillusion with life could produce such rectitude as his ('Magnanimous despair alone / Could teach me so divine a thing'), the happiness of his last, married, years was splendidly to prove that judgement wrong.

Grateful thanks are due to Mrs T.S. Eliot for permission to quote from her husband's letters.

& The Peter Porter Poem of '83
Gavin Ewart

This is going to be an ordinary friendly poem, nothing very spectacular,
as it lollops along in the domain of what has been called the republic of
the vernacular.

Thirty years ago I first met you at a small party given by Charles Rycroft –
but it wasn't until later that our paths became brothers, like Sherlock
and Mycroft.

At that time I had been more or less 'silent' for almost a quarter of a
century
(as they say of poets) and the likely lads, in Faber fable, tough and
adventury,

were Gunn and Hughes with their loonies in leather, rampageous pigs,
cats, hawks,
all ready to murder you quickly; from lad- and Nature-lovers there
were few protesting squawks.

You on the other hand were into the serious satirical Colonial-in-
London bit,
lighting Latimer candles to Culture – and a good many candles were lit

by the best poems in that first book (*Once Bitten, Twice Bitten*),
which one could certainly call a very fine first book (if not the best
                                            book ever written).

So we were into satire. Our London was brash, immoral, surprising –
'What a city to sack!' – It was sacked by advertising.

We met in pubs halfway between your civilised agency and (much less
                                                        so) mine.
Oh, there was literary laughter, and bottles and bottles of wine!

Later we both worked at Notley's – where no highbrow had to grovel –
and I remember Trevor (with feminine help) xeroxing a whole novel.

'I see you're both working late,' the Managing Director said
as he went off to his routine gin and tonics and dinner and bed.

'A nest of singing birds', Ewart, Porter and Lucie-Smith;
Oliver Bernard had gone before, creating a substantial Bohemian myth.

That satire rings truer now, in the money-mad world of a Thatcher,
and in the rye, alas, we're left without any catcher;

but writers, wrote Wystan (to Christopher?), are ironic points of light.
And I think you've certainly been one, before you go, and I go, and we
                                    all go into that not-so-good night.

40

Bluefoot Traveller
James Berry

Man
who the hell is you?
What hole you drag from
          an follah railway line
          past plenty settlement
          sleep under trees
          eat dry bread an water
          sweat like a carthorse
to come an put body
an bundle down in we village?
How we to feel you not obeahman
          tief
          Judas with lice
          an a dirty mout?
Why you stop here? Get news
Mericans open up dollar place
          in we districk?
Hear we got woman givin way
          to follah-line man
          an water an donkey an lan?
Bluefoot
          I considerin you hard hard
          I point out to you –
move!
It in me bones deep deep –
          better comfort for you man
          pick up possessions.
Walk again –
          an I might even say

PR 63:3, 1972

              God be with you –
an you dont call out
              no battalion of fists
dont pull down
              no hills of rockstone
you dont bring out
              no woods of lickle bumpy sticks
to come an mount you top
              an crack it up.

41

The Manifesto Against Manifestoes*
James Fenton

They appear to have sprung up overnight, these fresh-faced,
pleasant young people with their earnest enquiries as to the State
of the Craft. They have been reading the Morrison-Motion
anthology, and they want to know if they have been correctly
informed. Perhaps a certain scepticism, lightly worn, gives colour
to their opinions, perhaps a modest outrage. At all events there is
a general interest in the hot tip. Should they sell Martians? Should
they buy into The Narrative? What *should* they do? What should
we all do? What is happening?

*

One major change for good or bad: we look to ourselves these days
for the answer. A decade ago we would have defined ourselves in
terms of our American allegiances, but more recently it appeared
that the American Muse had picked up the newspaper and retired
to the *Klo*. Little has been heard since, beyond the occasional groan.

*   [*sic*]

PR 73:3, 1983

*

We look to ourselves. We feed on our differences. We imagine battle-lines drawn and strategies adopted. A friend tells me how he regrets that a projected meeting between myself and the poet Ypsilon failed to materialise. Ypsilon had remarked: 'Still, you know, Fenton and I are of opposing camps.' When I hear this I am most intrigued. I do not know Ypsilon's work. I do not know to which camp I belong. I cannot imagine what the remark means, and alas my friend did not demand clarification. He was afraid of 'getting out of his depth'.

*

To the extent that we are poets, we are all, of course, of opposing camps. But was this what Ypsilon meant?

*

Fleeing from the Cambridge Poetry Festival into the nearest pub, I find the premises crowded with poets who had *once* been associated with the Cambridge Poetry Festival but are now deliberately ignoring it. Indeed one of them has travelled to Cambridge this weekend with the *express purpose* of ignoring it. He proceeds to tell me what he thinks of me. At some time in the past I have shown promise as an exponent of the Middle Way. There was evidence that I had some inkling of what the avant-garde was up to, and that I was striving, after my fashion, to develop in important directions. On the other hand, my recent work has been extremely disappointing. I will not mind his telling me this, he tells me, because he is merely exercising his right as a purchaser of my book. The more he talks, the less I understand. Finally the beer itself becomes incomprehensible.

*

The reality of schools, camps, influences, programmes and manifestoes is grossly exaggerated. When, in an irresponsible fit, I coined the term 'the Martian School', the school in question contained two poets, Raine and Reid. Reid is not Raine. Raine is not Reid. Could a class be composed of two members? I feared not.

But soon the pupils were lining up at the door, while the teachers, quite rightly, had slipped out the back way. The students broke into the classroom and pilfered everything they found. England had not witnessed such wholesale literary robbery for half a century.

★

Considered theft is a considerable tribute. One could wish, though, that the thieves were less prone to smear the walls with their excrement.

★

Two remarkable poet-editors. The first is known for his advocacy of the short, intense, personal lyric. He published many of my longer, rambling and more frivolous poems. The second, celebrated for his way with a metaphor or simile, was happy to take a hundred lines with not a single metaphor or simile. I have always been lucky enough to meet people who would throw out the programme in favour of the poem.

★

There was a time when to say 'poetry makes nothing happen' was reckoned heresy or treason. Today it is worth reversing the terms. Nothing *makes* poetry happen. Programmes least of all.

★

More than a decade ago, I conceived the idea of a poem which, by its sheer insistence on a particular subject, would create a feeling in the reader that this ostensible subject must be a red herring and that the real theme must lie elsewhere. There would be no sign-posts to the real theme, beyond the writer's suspicious enthusiasm for the *ostensible* theme. The reader would simply be unnerved into interpretation.

I wrote the poem, but in the end it was I who lost my nerve and pointed up the moral. The plan had failed.

★

Ten years later I happened upon a subject which, it struck me, was intensely attractive poetically. And since the source of attraction was certain information which was not generally available or known in England, I felt that the information itself *was* the poem. There was no need of 'treatment', only pure statement.

When the poem was published, it puzzled me by puzzling my friends. Gamma would ask Delta for his theory as to the meaning of the poem, and Delta – taking an obvious short cut – would ask me. If I protested that I knew of no other theme than the ostensible one, I would be smiled at in disbelief. I realised that I had inadvertently succeeded in my old plan after all, but alas I had no concealed motive, no alternative subject up my sleeve. Must the second poem also be accounted a failure?

*

Or is there something wrong with the way we read? Have we lost the taste for subject-matter?

*

Imagine a poem that was so intrinsically interesting that it never occurred to people, when discussing it, to mention treatment, method, tradition, influence, form or any other of the usual critical categories. The only thing people wanted to talk about was the subject. Would not that be, in its way, revolutionary?

*

There might be all kinds of reasons for this intrinsic interest in the subject. It might be, for instance, that there was exclusive information available in the poem. Or a bewitching argument. Or there might be the kind of story which made you want to know what happened next.

*

When we talk of narrative poetry today, are we referring to the kind of story in which you want to know what happens next? I think not. I think that kind of story is deliberately excluded from consideration.

*

At a late-night session in Cambridge, I propound my theory of
the poetry of intrinsic interest, mentioning the possibility of an
intrinsically interesting story. Ah, says one present, that is impos-
sible – The Novel usurped the Narrative Function of Poetry in the
nineteenth century.

*

This reply pleases me. It is a Blocking Move. The Critic has told
me I must not do something. That makes that something instantly
attractive. And anyway, I'm not scared of The Novel. Isn't The
Novel supposed to be dead? Or have I misheard The Critic?

*

After all, it is quite reasonable to suspect that the sentence is incom-
plete and should read: The Novel usurped The Narrative Function
of Poetry in the Nineteenth Century, and the Poem usurped The
Narrative Function of the Novel in the Twentieth Century. We
might conceive 'narrative function' as a kind of Alsace-Lorraine,
forever changing hands, but still, in between wars, producing the
odd bottle of good wine.

*

I hardly think that the distinction between a Martian and a
Narrative school can be with substance. 'We must write stories' is
not a poetic slogan. But to say: 'We may write stories if we want
to' – that is both reasonable and necessary. If each poem emerged
as a confutation of some critical taboo, that would be something.
Not everything. Something.

*

The most profoundly interesting narrative poem I have read
recently is Craig Raine's 'In the Kalahari Desert'. I can remember
vividly the circumstances in which I first read it and the sensation
it gave. Some poets contrive to tell you: 'Whatever happens, you
will not be able to write like this.' From others, the message is:
'This too is possible.' The reason why there are so many imitators

of Raine is that he belongs firmly in the second category. He is generous. He is encouraging.

*

But much misunderstood and misread. He is, primarily, an emotional, an erotic poet. It is perhaps the eroticism which is in advance of his day. When a poet looks at his wife and thinks of a tomato, one may feel that he lacks feeling. But when he further shows that his feeling for tomatoes is more deeply affectionate and more sexually alert than most poets' feelings for their first girl-friends, one is obliged to think again. Obliged *to feel* again.

*

If a tomato approached me to ask whether a night out with Mr Raine was advisable, I should be torn between loyalty to Mrs Raine and a natural feeling that tomatoes are entitled to a good time.

*

Empson's remark that 'It is the two / Most exquisite surfaces of knowledge can / Get clap (the other is the eye)' might have been intended as a warning to this delightful writer. The eye is his great erogenous zone. Such promiscuous organs can expect the consequences.

*

Clap may be a risk for a Martian, but all art carries its own level of risk. An English church still displays the bridal veil of an unfortunate young campanologist. She had wanted to participate in the traditional peal at the climax of her own wedding service, but the bell went into a spin, whisked her up to the roof, strangled her with her veil and, an instant later, deposited her at the feet of the groom. To die for your art is something. To die for an art which involves the playing of a single note at the appropriate moment – that kind of dedication is almost Japanese.

*

If we cannot be Martian, we might at least aspire to being Japanese.

42 *from* Babylonish Dialects *and* The Sylko Bandit
Craig Raine

1. How do we think? Consider Nabokov on the stream of consciousness in *Ulysses*: 'it exaggerates the verbal side of thought. Man thinks not always in words but also in images, whereas the stream of consciousness presupposes a flow of words that can be notated: it is difficult, however, to believe that Bloom was continually talking to himself.'

2. How do I refute Nabokov? By saying this is true, but only because we are not always thinking while we are conscious? By offering up Wordsworth on his couch, in vacant or in pensive mood?

3. What about the other mental phenomena which inhabit Wordsworth's vacancy – the dreams, the emotions, those daffodils? They cannot be verbalised, though they undoubtedly exist.

4. I see the current Oxford Professor of Poetry in the street and E.P. Thompson on the train. Both are talking to themselves. They are thinking aloud. If I was closer, I could bathe in their stream of consciousness, hear their words. For a second, I see myself with my trousers rolled up. Is this a thought or a picture?

5. 'How can I tell what I think till I see what I say?' asks E.M. Forster. This implies that all thinking is verbal, that without language we cannot think. This is what happens to Ralph in *Lord of the Flies*: 'he lost himself in a maze of thoughts that were rendered vague by his lack of words to express them.'

6. On the other hand, Forster is also saying that we cannot articulate thought without using language. True. But that still leaves inarticulate thought, Ralph's 'maze of thoughts' in which he is lost.

PR 74:2, 1984

7.   Wittgenstein is masturbating. His mind is continuously occupied for five minutes, shall we say, by a series of obscene pictures – not by the words 'tit' and 'bum'. This is a thought process even though it is unrelated to language.

8.   Music is a language to which we listen in order to experience a distinct penumbra we could not describe. Much poetry initially works in this way, too. 'Genuine poetry,' said Eliot, 'can communicate before it is understood.' A philosopher might retort: 'for people who cannot think, this passes for thought.'

9.   But most of the time, we are at the mercy of language. If we introspect, we see in our minds the words, 'if we introspect'. And surely we can be misled by language, as Wittgenstein explains metaphorically: 'philosophers often behave like little children who scribble marks on a piece of paper at random and then ask the grown-up "What's that?" It happened like this: the grown-up had drawn pictures for the child several times and said: "this is a man", "this is a house", etc. And then the child makes some marks too and asks: "what's *this* then?"'

10.   Often language tells us what to think. Poetry, though, can use language to help us escape this tyranny of language. T.S. Eliot said of Edward Lear's poetry that it was not nonsense but a parody of sense. As readers, we are like Wittgenstein's child, but from deliberate choice. We hear the language and, while we know there is no sense to it, we experience the *sensation* of thought. The mind is Pavlovian: it salivates at the sound of a word, as if there was here real food for thought. The nebulous effect corresponds to something within our minds before we have said what we think.

11.   Poetry written in dialect belongs to the world of non-sense and the world of sense – depending on how familiar you are with the dialect.

12.   All great poetry is written in dialect. This is Johnson on Milton: 'through all his greater works there prevails an uniform peculiarity of *Diction*, a mode and cast of expression which bears little resemblance to that of any other former writer, and which is so far removed from common use, that an unlearned reader, when

he first opens his book, finds himself surprised by a new language...
Of him, at last, may be said what Jonson says of Spenser, that *he
wrote no language*, but has formed what Butler calls a *Babylonish
dialect...*'

13.   It follows that if all great poetry is written in dialect, then it
is all poised between sense and non-sense – which seems unlikely
until you consider, say, Southey's reaction to the 'Ancient Mariner'
('many of the stanzas are laboriously beautiful, but in connection
they are absurd or unintelligible') and Wordsworth's insistence
that new art must create the taste by which it is to be enjoyed.

14.   Most bad poetry is written in the dialect of the previous age.
Some bad poetry is written in the dialect of no particular age – only
the dialect of poetry. But if language dates, no language dates
quicker than the self-consciously timeless, which is already dated.

15.   Wordsworth's dialect, Hopkins's complicated dialect, Frost's
simple American dialect – we have mastered them all. The task is
to invent a new dialect or even dialects.

16.   Why? There are two reasons. We become so familiar with a
dialect that we no longer hear its individuality. Or the dialect
becomes in time more and more difficult: presumably some such
thought is behind A.L. Rowse's scheme to render *Romeo and Juliet*
into modern English.

17.   And there is a further reason. The advantage of dialect is this:
if nonsense poetry can create in us the sensation of thought, then
dialect can create in us different thoughts. Alter the language and
you alter thought. Our ways of thinking are renewed.

18.   Why should we want to do this? Let me quote Wittgenstein
again: 'the idea is worn out by now and no longer usable... Like
silver paper, which can never be quite smoothed out again once it
has been crumpled. Nearly all my ideas are a bit crumpled.' Good:
let us have some uncrumpled ideas, if not some new ones; let us
change the language.

19.   The bonus of dialect is easy to see. 'Wee, sleeket, cowran,
tim'rous beastie' alters our thought, our perception, gives us a

clearer idea of the mouse than standard English. Everything vivid here would cloud at the mere approach of A.L. Rowse.

20.   Hopkins wrote to Robert Bridges that he had been reading *Two Years Before the Mast*: 'all true, but bristling with technicality – seamanship – which I most carefully go over and even enjoy but cannot understand…' This is true of any dialect: we enjoy without at first fully understanding. But what is the nature of the enjoyment? Compare the opening of *The Tempest*: 'Down with the topmast! Yare! lower, lower! Bring her to try with main-course.'

Quite. Shakespeare is bluffing. He is adding spices to his recipe. Neither he nor we may know exactly what they are, but we can taste the tiny, authentic explosions. They give us the sensation of thought by their confident, but ultimately opaque, particularity.

21.   In *Riddley Walker*, Russell Hoban uses language like Molesworth in *Down with Skool*: 'She said, "Its some kynd of thing it aint us but yet its in us. Its looking out thru our eye hoals. May be you dont take no noatis of it only some times. Say you get woak up suddn in the middl of the nite. 1 minim youre a sleap and the nex youre on your feet with a spear in your han. Wel it wernt you put that spear in your han it wer that other thing whats looking out thru your eye hoals. It aint you nor it dont even know your name. Its in us lorn and loan and sheltering how it can."'

One is immediately struck by the way Hoban completely escapes the comedy implicit in the Molesworth idiom, then by how little has been changed – the odd spelling, haphazard punctuation. Yet the effect is enormous: the change in the language has actually changed the thought. The woman is discussing the soul, but much more vividly than if Hoban had confined her to that word. The concept is renewed.

22.   In the same way, MacDiarmid's poem, 'The Bonnie Broukit Bairn', renews our acquaintance with the stars after centuries of stale classical mythologising:

Mars is braw in crammasy,
Venus in a green silk goun…

They are no longer simply stars, but aristocrats in a laird's hall. The metaphor on its own would take us this far, but the dialect brings with it an implicit sense of class awareness: we are underlings of no importance and what is true of the earth is also true of man's place in the universe. Both are fixed systems.

23.   In *The Inheritors*, Golding invents a dialect for his Neanderthal people. Again, the language employed alters our perception of even the simplest things, like a bow and arrow: 'the stick began to grow shorter at both ends. Then it shot to full length again.' Or an echo: 'their words had flown away from them like a flock of birds that circled and multiplied mysteriously.' In both these examples, Golding refuses the easy noun ('he writes in no language') and with it the easy thought. The initial obscurity, the moment of non-sense, puts us in touch with our non-verbal thoughts, or their simulacrum. And even after the necessary translation is effected, the strangeness lingers.

24.   Nothing is more difficult than being open-minded. The mind is a vast country whose borders are closed. We know less than we think about its economy. It is teeming with peasants, productive souls, who are hard-working but mute. There are elections, about which we hear. Language is the prime minister who tells us the results, like a spokesman reading quite confidently from a brief he was handed in the dark, or simply found in his inside pocket.

25.

26.   [...]

27.   [...]

28.

The Sylko Bandit

Sir Walter Raleigh, when they arrested him, had half a million francs on his
back, including a pair of fancy stays.

James Joyce: Ulysses

Something apt to garden,
he does plant those naked boys,
the finest of Holland,
along the length of windowe box.

Were it not for the Buddha,
the whiche he hath acquired
from out of Angkor Wat,
stone melted lobes intact,

he does much resemble a poet,
one that ekes out guilders
in payment for his rented room
hard by the station,

whose terminus of zips
provokes his smile
for that it semes
an ironie writ large...

Yet consider him now,
preparing state cocaine
for guestes, above ten lines,
from the gouverment kiosk:

he is the vnexpected thyng,
who values not those laws
long passed enforcing playnesse
being a smuggler of velvets,

a connoisseur of cloths,
and that despite a good degree,
an Oxford first in drugs,
both divisions of the tripos.

Sick affrayd of sumptuary police,
we do fear his flamboyance
and that fearless way he hath
of strolling to the windowe,

the better there to criticise
some new edition of sylks,
scanning thro them like a scholar.
Small wonder we sweat.

We are vnprepared
for all his compromising giftes
that make us poore,
being ready for something els:

politics, dissent, our bravery.
We did use to practise speeches.
But no man could predict
thys educated laughter,

the grounding in Freud,
learned journals, broken spines,
and a time when cloths
would be cause of betrayal.

He much resembles a psycholeech
in that he vnderstandes
the threat that we fele
from fire appliances

whiche do press them into corners,
darkly, like spies, on each flight
of the stairs. He knoweth our fear
whiche is affrayd of the concierge,

her talkative needles,
their whispered mors code.
We love him. We hate him.
He is too rich to trust.

No matter if we will or no,
the telephone is in our hand,
waking the 'ragge-trade',
asleep in playn-clothes.

Taffeta, grosgraine, bullion,
velvet, satin and chiffon,
samite, sylk and chenille:
it is time at last

to practise betrayal,
like one that recites
from a favourite poem,
slowly, with love,

yet heareth only thys,
the squash court in the heart,
and reads a verdict
in the railway lines...

twenty year with temperatures.

43

Blue
Penelope Shuttle

Out of the blue,
that bundle of fur and blood,
glimpsed flinchingly
as we step quickly by,
what is it,
lying on the path?
Not a rabbit, but a hare.
Lying on the path, torn to red ribbons,
beneath the blue sky.
I walk on. I cannot pick it up,
the remains of the carcass.
The sky is all blue, reciting itself to itself.
Gifts come out of the blue, (and other things).
Is it time to give back what we thought was ours?
The blue awakens and leans back on haunches
like an animal. It is the blueness
of knowing how to come out of the blue.
And of using what it knows.
The path goes on until the very edge.
    Beyond is sea and sky, unblemished blue.
    The hare in its bondage of blood,
    that is what blue has not forgotten.
    But I've forgotten too much that was a sacrifice,
    and am lessened by that.

PR 73:1, 1983

& *from* **From Ulster with Love**
    Peter McDonald

It has always been clear enough that the critical boom in Ulster poetry, which began in the seventies and has never really died down, was a far from unmixed blessing; for the poets themselves, the opportunity to write for a large audience has brought with it the problems of having to satisfy the demand for a public, responsible voice of the kind proper to war-poets. Of course, the responsibility game is one that can be played profitably: full-blown mythologising, as in *North* or *The Rough Field*, is only one approach; there are also Paulin's rasping, strident Ulsterisms, Mahon's self-conscious cosmopolitan exile or Muldoon's oblique parables, all of these leading back to the ever-fertile dilemma of Being A Poet From Northern Ireland. Michael Longley's poetry doesn't fit into this scheme quite so easily, and that is almost certainly one of the reasons why he has been given vague praise for the integrity of his craftsmanship, his accomplishment as a 'nature-' or 'love-' poet, but too little real attention as an artist whose work is 'responsible', not in any self-congratulating or grandiose way, but in its commitment to a precise and controlled language that need not raise its voice to be serious.

    [...]

If Longley isn't an Ulster Poet in the commercial sense, he is at least a poet of the first order whose work couldn't have been written in any other environment than that of Northern Ireland. Comparisons with Heaney are bound to be made, but wrongly, for Heaney is working in a different direction, towards a vatic rhetoric that can, like Yeats's, quarrel with itself, while Longley has chosen a demanding exactitude of response to environment, memory and expert experience, which tends to move away from a public voice. *Poems 1963–1983* fully vindicates Longley's practice, and shows its poet to be not only a fine technician (certainly the most accomplished of his generation) but also a writer whose work never exploits or exaggerates the truth. This may well be seen in the end as an exemplary achievement, and many of the poems here as among the best to have come from Britain since the war, even if they never did spark a critical boom of their own.

Poems 1963–1983, by Michael Longley (Macmillan).

PR 74:4, 1985

& *from* 'I Would Say I Was a Happy Man': W.S. Graham interviewed by John Haffenden

[...]

W.S. GRAHAM   A poem has to be a pleasure. The remembrance of a poem, even it you don't have it word by word, is a lovely thing. All good poems are entertaining.

JOHN HAFFENDEN   *In one poem you speak of words as being 'an aside from the monstrous'. What do you mean by that?*

W.S. GRAHAM   As one of the many reasons to be living this life – that is, as a poet – one creates a place which happens simultaneously with writing, a place to hide from the monstrous. You don't make a paradise, but you make a place at that time where you can feel more truly *in*. Now that is one of the reasons why one writes poetry. The opposite of that could be: 'I want to describe something exactly' (which maybe Marianne Moore might have said, but I doubt it). You make a world for yourself at the time, not suggesting that you are side-stepping reality. That I really believe in, I've said it in my poetry in various ways.

[...]

JOHN HAFFENDEN   *There is also a sense in which you're speaking across a void to your reader.*

W.S. GRAHAM   Of course it is an attempt to communicate from one aloneness to another; one has to try to steer language, to make something that will come across. Let me read you a bit. This is me speaking about how difficult it is to judge what the poem is going out as... it is difficult to judge if one is only using one's own nostalgia... or whether it's going to work for other people. It's called 'Approaches to How They Behave':

1

What does it matter if the words
I choose, in the order I choose them in,
Go out into a silence I know
Nothing about, there to be let

In and entertained and charmed
Out of their master's orders? And yet
I would like to see where they go
And how without me they behave.

2

Speaking is difficult and one tries
To be exact and yet not to
Exact the prime intention to death.
On the other hand the appearance of things
Must not be made to mean another
Thing. It is a kind of triumph
To see them and to put them down
As what they are. The inadequacy
Of the living, animal language drives
Us all to metaphor and an attempt
To organize the spaces we think
We have made occur between the words.

[...]

Interviewed at home in Madron, Cornwall, on the occasion of the publication of
his *Collected Poems 1942–1977* (Faber, 1979).

44 England
John Fuller

Falling towards the map is a controlled illusion,
The text scrolled to the cursor. It is England down there,
Tilted like a display. It is a living space
    Screened for observation,
A gravity-haunted logo, a significant shape
    From which there is no escape.

The shires are whitened with snow, old ploughing
Turned to Aztec friezes and museum crochet.
Between the rafters of weather and the granite flags
    Is a simulated surface
Of plot and portion that we only ever know
    As landscape from below.

It implicates our wish to be welcomed, our resolve
To enter the dull story and to make it remarkable,
To order the memory like a WAAF croupier
    Pushing her heroes across
Inches that are clouds and tiny villages recalling
    Our fear of falling.

At the heart of England we are pursuer and pursued,
Where frozen footprints are the history of that hunt
And towns we think we never visited are like
    Both past and future,
Tremendously distinguished in the willed notation
    Of our imagination.

PR 76:1 & 2, 1986

At the heart of England the drivers are silently crawling
Bumper to bumper, the exits sealed off, the route
A duty to some present but long-forgotten intention
      And the lights are flashing
As if to warn us to keep to the dogged pace
      Of a non-competitive race.

At the heart of England we listen to old stories
With an amusement that guarantees their lack of any power
To direct our attention to what they may be saying
      And off we stolidly stump
Past the gingerbread cathedral and the factory blur
      To the scenery we prefer.

There the eye is of course directed upwards
As paths respect the mossy boulders and outcrop
Of the heights that induce their steady winding and climbing
      Until some point is reached
Where we see the heartland sprawled as in a lap,
      Comatose, half-map.

For the most part they are nibbled humps or great ledges
Swathed in rolling mist like experimental theatre:
It suits us to shade the eyes, to stare for coasts.
      From that isolation
On either side adventurous streams agree
      To part and find the sea.

We never join them. They are unjoinable.
And there is nothing much in the end to be done
Except to return either the way we came
      Or to find some other route,
Which with a monument or some woody confusion
      Maintains the illusion.

And time itself is like this, an elder dimension
Whose fondness for a particular country may turn
At a stroke to a sly or bullying disregard,
    Who knows that place is never
The involving predicate that something meant
    Simply an accident.

And time is after all where we truly belong,
Its present moments less comfortable than sofas
And the presences scattered on tables before them
    That say: 'We are England.
This memory. This book. This headline. And all the things
    That such belonging brings.'

As the very first move is the very first mistake,
Even the king's pawn, the dry kiss, the sinister
Lunge of the baby's toes like Johnson leaving
    The room when all has been said,
As what we are today depends on what we have been
    And all that we have seen,

As the bell while it rings has not ceased to summon us
Though we lose count of the strokes, as one match
Added to the whole becomes the Tower of London
    And we come to the end of the chapter,
As what we are today depends on what we are up to
    And all that we try to do,

As fingers reach where fruit must be before they know
The fruit is there, as the deafening tapes babble of love
And mothers not long out of childhood stitch shrouds
    At the cradle, as our star
Will give us a short grace when it finally disappears
    And we know the prediction of tears,

As we find ourselves again in places that make us happy
And like bar-haunting actors on tour forget our cues,
As we rise in drowning with Greek cries of discovery,
    As we scribble our lucky numbers
And believe the oracle so that the hair lifts from our head
    As we shiver down in bed,

As time itself is unable to build its little Durham
Against anointed oblivion, and we are acknowledged
Its fool servitors, bearing enormous covered dishes
    Into the hungry hall
Where we overhear the talk, seditious, immensely grand
    That we hardly understand,

So we are left at last with only the hopeless instant,
The newborn innocent or wandering dressing-gowned victim
For whom the past must be a fable or abandoned
    Like an exhausted quarry,
For whom the future is that breath beyond the breath
    Taken at the moment of death,

So we are left in the thick of all our extended pleasures,
Hearing in the distance the popping guns moving over
England, and saying quietly, one to another:
    'Something is running for cover,
Something has nowhere to hide out there and likely as not
    Something is being shot,

'Such as the refined whiskery fox, left to die
As a gangster dies, arguing with balletic rhetoric
That when in the paleness of dawn the certainty of pain
    Is fully recognized
There will be no reasoning with it, no arguing at all,
    And we shall lie where we fall.'

& CRITICAL FEATURE
English Identities

from Twenty Ways of Saying Happy Birthday
Mick Imlah

[...] Harry Chambers once admitted to Larkin an intention to write a thesis about him. The reply, 'My God, Harry, you make me feel half-dead already' is an objection which [Anthony] Thwaite is glad to forestall:

> [*Larkin at Sixty*] is of course diffuse and patchy, not definitive: this is not *The Life and Letters of Larkin*, a book already part-way to completion by Dr Jake Balokowsky, and waiting only for its subject's demise.

[...]

Larkin may or may not produce more poems, but he will certainly read this book, and it is interesting to observe the effect of this on some of the contributors. The quality of Kingsley Amis's relationship with the poet makes him quite at ease, and his recollection of their undergraduate experience is unforced, funny, and in places fascinating. But this was the boisterous Larkin at twenty, not at all the essentially private man that others have to animate. This privacy is so generously respected that when George Hartley makes the simple observation of Larkin's personae – even of his personae – that they are 'outside all the main emotional entanglements of most people's lives – love, marriage, children', the editor feels obliged to supply this gloss:

> The fact that he has never married and has no children doesn't entail ignorance of, or contempt for, the institution or its usual result. As for love, 'that much-mentioned brilliance', even to feel outside it one must know what it is; and he does.

There is a comparable over-reaction to the embarrassment that Larkin's politics might cause some of the contributors; Robert Conquest's dissociation of Larkin from the Nazis, whom he calls with sudden and disconcerting alliteration 'the swastika swine', is surely unnecessary.

But eruptions of self-consciousness are bound to occur in a book of this nature. The most successful contributors convey Larkin invisibly;

others seem more concerned to tell us or Larkin something about them-
selves. His publishers, George Hartley and Charles Monteith, are both in
the first category, partly because they include extracts from private
letters. The advice to Monteith on how to promote *All What Jazz* is a fine
rebuke to those who are beginning to overrate this underrated volume:
'Treat it like a book by T.S. Eliot on all-in wrestling.' Some professional
writers are less able than these two to contain themselves. Douglas
Dunn's piece is really about his own career in librarianship, and his prose
is unsuitably inflated. The myth of his not being able to count, for
example, is not made interesting by a pleased flourish of prefixes; 'all
seemed to be there to elicit the exposure of my innumeracy'. Alan
Bennett's idea for a birthday present, 'that sound, part sigh, part affirma-
tion, that I heard once in Zion Chapel, Settle, in Yorkshire, after I'd read
"MCMXIV"', fulfils the book's purpose exactly, so it's all the stranger that
he should spend two pages questioning that purpose – and surely the
matter of what to call 'Mr Larkin' is not as vexing as he pretends.

Harry Chambers, who recounts with curious and endearing simplicity
each of his six meetings with Larkin, discovers by natural tact what to call
him. After initial diffidence and circumlocution ('the man who once sent
Eddie Condon a fan-letter') he moves sensibly to call the man we read,
Larkin, and the man he meets and talks with, Philip. Unfortunately, the
system is not proof against the inspired mischief of the type-setter, who
grants Chambers, on the fifth meeting, an unlikely intimacy with 'Phildi
himself'.

What will please us, and Larkin, most in this volume? Those who will
never meet him may appreciate Harry Chambers' flustered awe at their
second encounter, on a train: 'When I had recovered sufficiently from
the shock to be able to wave *The Whitsun Weddings* at him, he beckoned
me to join him and I nearly forgot to ask for my copy to be inscribed when
I had to get out at Doncaster.' Has even Larkin written a phrase which
conveys so sad a knowledge of one's place as – 'I had to get out at
Doncaster'? […]

Larkin at Sixty, edited by Anthony Thwaite (Faber).

from Larkin's England
Philip Hobsbaum

Philip Larkin made the first decisive alteration to the poetic landscape since Eliot's cab-horses steaming under the gas-lamps. Poets before him tended to superimpose their images of urban life on a half-imagined, half-recollected notion of pastoral England. This meant that what purported to be description was essentially satire. The urban poetry of Eliot, of Auden, even of Betjeman, is a poetry of rejection. It shows in their imagery, which is fixed and belittling, moving towards the mode of catalogue when towns are in question:

> The showers beat
> On broken blinds and chimney-pots,
> And at the corner of the street
> A lonely cab-horse steams and stamps.
>
> And then the lighting of the lamps.
> Eliot, 'Preludes'

> The falling leaves know it, the children,
> At play on the fuming alkali-tip
> Or by the flooded football ground, know it –
> This is the dragon's day, the devourer's.
> Auden, 'Easter, 1929'

In Larkin, however apparently squalid the subject, the images are presented affirmatively, or at any rate with an implied sense of release. It is this context that makes 'The Whitsun Weddings' so poignant. The bachelor does not stay in his buttoned-up railway carriage. He leans out, to watch the primal energies developing:

> The fathers with broad belts under their suits
> And seamy foreheads; mothers loud and fat;
> An uncle shouting smut; and then the perms,
> The nylon gloves and jewellery – substitutes,
> The lemons, mauves, and olive-ochres that
>
> Marked off the girls unreally from the rest.

These are the sacraments in action; this is life going on. But it would not be alive without the living quality of Larkin's verse.

PR 76:1 & 2, 1986

'The Whitsun Weddings' begins with an evocation of the city outskirts which has a push and lift that energizes what, in the hands of a lesser poet, could have been mere urban squalor:

> We ran
> Behind the backs of houses, crossed a street
> Of blinding windscreens, smelt the fish-dock; thence
> The river's level drifting breadth began.
> Where sky and Lincolnshire and water meet.

This is not background but a prime constituent of the poem. Among many other matters, the poem is a run through England, and it reveals, not a satirized landscape, but the context in which most of us spend most of our lives:

> Now fields were building-plots, and poplars cast
> Long shadows over major roads.

The journey is as important as the arrival, and the latter brings us to the metropolis that proves fertile in a firmly urban way:

> spread out in the sun,
> Its postal districts packed like squares of wheat.

The vision is not that of the usurpation of land from some bygone pastoral setting, but rather a peopled city existing in its own right.

Larkin's distinction in this matter can be seen if we follow one of the most discerning of his recent critics, Salem Hassan, and relate 'The Whitsun Weddings' back to its most likely prototype, 'The Metropolitan Railway', by John Betjeman. There is in the latter poem an uneasiness of tone localizable in its facetious inversions and obsolescent poeticization:

> Cancer has killed him. Heart is killing her.
>   The trees are down. An Odeon flashes fire
> Where stood their villa by the murmuring fir.

This can be compared with the fresher eye working in 'The Whitsun Weddings':

> An Odeon went past, a cooling tower,
> And someone running up to bowl.

Betjeman is a satirist who depends for much of his effect upon off-stage nostalgia, while Larkin accepts his environment with an elan that is next door to celebration.

[...]

The properties deployed by Philip Larkin will seem ordinary, or even squalid, only if taken out of context, and the context is not only Larkin's verse but Larkin's England. Seen in the poems themselves, his images have a curious vitality. There is nothing in Larkin's verse so easy as a contrast between present detritus and past nostalgia. His is a description of urban life that owes nothing to a sense of displacement from the countryside.

There is one qualification to be made. In *High Windows* there are signs that Larkin at last began to feel the town was getting on top of him. There is still a sense of release, but at times it transpires perilously close to a death wish. There are some disconcertingly intense images of distance and vacancy; in the title-poem, especially. From the rest of his work, though, Larkin's England remains: brickwork, drainpipes, mortgaged half-built edges. The Larkin-scape will be altered only by a descriptive poet of comparable potency.

from English Equivocation
John Bayley

I like the idea of Englishness in anything, but it has to be a private idea: it should not be given any official or public recognition. Englishness in poetry, like the reaction to poetry itself, is in the end a secret and solitary thing. The time of self-conscious 'Englishness', in art and in public state-ment, at the beginning of this century, was a degenerate time, and vulgarised the concept. There is a taint, even, about the word 'England' in Walter de la Mare's rather beautiful and haunting poem about the sailor who whispers the word when he hears the thrush singing and listens to 'that old noise of seas'. The use of the word requires delicacy, but delicacy itself becomes false when over-emphasised in its context.

There has never, even at that bad time around 1900, been anything 'national' about English poetry in the claustrophobic modern sense. But in the sense that its poetry exists to show what a given language is capable of, English does of course have its special characteristics. [...]

In the context of today's poetry the point could be made by the fairly obvious comparison between two outstanding poets – probably *the* outstanding poets of our immediate English context – Philip Larkin and

Geoffrey Hill. Larkin is an English poet in the sense that Hill is not. In Larkin's world it is the experience that matters, and in Hill's it is the poetry that matters. In the same way one might say that it is the poetry that matters in *The Rape of the Lock*, and the experience which matters in Dr Johnson's poem on the death of Dr Levett. In all these cases the language of poetry is in fact being handled in the same way – how could it be otherwise? – and yet in the case of Larkin, or that of Dr Johnson's poem, that status of poetry is escaped from; the experience and not the poetry is what concentrates us; and it is tempting to say that in the context of language and poetry this feels to be a particularly English experience. Reading Hill, on the other hand, is like going into the Louvre or the Uffizi: we open our guidebooks at once. This is art, and we are to get to know about it in that spirit – an international spirit.

In saying Larkin is 'so English' or 'very English' we must intend to convey something of this kind. The Englishness is not in the subject matter but in the way it conveys itself into our minds, whether in a longish poem like 'Dockery and Son', or a short one like 'As Bad as a Mile'. This is much more English, in our sense, than the obvious way in which poets at the time of Edward Thomas and Walter de la Mare (who wrote the Introduction to Thomas's first *Collected Poems*) thought of Englishness or tried to be English in what they wrote. When Thomas asks 'you English words' to choose him, because they are 'light as dreams, tough as oak, precious as gold', the effect now is not only dated but a bit embarrassing, like another poet's injunction to 'take of English earth as much, as either hand may rightly clutch'.

What is really English in Thomas is the way he discovered himself as a poet by escaping from the poetryness of poetry, and that was largely inspired by his relation with an American – Robert Frost. It is Thomas's syntax, not his sentiments, or his subject matter, which is English in the way I have been trying to convey, the way that makes him close to Larkin. 'Adlestrop' is rather too 'English' a poem, as regards its build-up of an atmosphere and what it is saying, but its language and sentence structure is English in the other, what we can today call the Larkinian, sense. Henry James, in a characteristic phrase, referred to 'the fathomless depths of English equivocation'. It is a phrase that in its context is full of admiration, and suggests much of what is interior and 'inside' in the poetry of Thomas, as in that of Housman, or of Larkin: something sardonic, solitary, personal, and very compelling. 'Adlestrop' is anthologised because of its success in being non-poetic but wholly memorable, because of its quaint English place-name, its implicit praise of the changeless English countryside through which the express makes it rapid ephemeral way, its haunting evocation of bird-song in the English shires making a quiet evening still more tranquil. But it is also, and more compellingly, a poem about Thomas's inner life, and sadness, and wry secret satisfactions. The feeling here is that only in a poem would such an English poet be so forthcoming, however equivocally, and reveal so much of his inner being.

Both the directness and the disguise are part of the Englishness, and this is where Thomas is different even from Frost, and from what he referred to with affectionate respect, in a letter to his American poet friend, as Frost's 'north of Bostonism'. Thomas makes it clear that he has been inspired by 'north of Bostonism', and by a vision of how he could transpose it into an English context, with scenes like that of an English shepherd seen by the poet on the hill, and each looking back on the other. But, as so often happens with inspiration, Thomas's poems in fact turned out quite different, quite different from Frost's tone and craft and calculating New England personality. At bottom they resemble these no more than they do those of Thomas's own fellow countrymen poets, Georgians or quasi-Georgians, who wrote their verses in celebration of an English atmosphere. Thomas can do this too, just as Larkin can, but in both cases the real Englishness is something quite different, a way of being the self conveyed by a way of being the language. T.S. Eliot is as capable of English equivocation as anyone – while gravely praising the classic spirit, and the idea of impersonal tradition, he in fact produced his best poetry, just as Thomas did, as a form of self-concealment and of self-discovery. As an English poet he is much more like Thomas than he is like Frost.

Hardy observed in a poem that he might be remembered as a man who 'used to notice such things', and gives some memorable examples of things which he used to notice. Larkin dryly remarked that he might equally well have written a poem about a man who used to notice nothing at all. Hardy, as the various biographies have showed, depended upon not noticing what was going on around him at home; and one can enjoy even in the poem a faint equivocal awareness of this. The concentration his muse depended on was linked with an equal capacity to seal himself off, and he knew this too, as is shown by 'The Self Unseeing', and the scene of the swallows circling above the river Stour, while the poet ignores in watching them the human scene behind his back. This knowledge only half declared, like the self secretively declared, is as English in Thomas as it is in Hardy. In 'Adlestrop' the directness of rural description, and the pleasure in it, which goes into Thomas's more ordinary poems, and which inspired his minor imitators like Edmund Blunden, is equivocated by the humour of the poem, and its use of memory as a key to what is precise and exact, taken out of time. There is nothing quaint or delightful about the inner poem in 'Adlestrop'. It is full of the sadness of things, and of Thomas's closeness to it, and the minute of the blackbird's song is as precise about this sadness as it is about the nature of the song itself – the birds answering each others' call into the distance, seeming to accentuate the feel of timeless stillness and also, like the wind in the new house, fore-telling what can not be foreseen, what is always ending and beginning again. From the single sentence word 'Yes.' which begins it (and which I prefer to R. George Thomas's choice of a comma in his meticulously edited edition) 'Adlestrop' is a deeply serious and personal poem masquerading as a light and obvious one – what might be thought of as a specially English procedure.

from The Politics of English Verse
Tom Paulin

[...]

Together, Arnold and Eliot ensured that the magic of monarchy and superstition permeated English literary criticism and education like a syrupy drug. Fortunately, the work of Christopher Hill challenges the bland, unhistorical, insidiously tendentious readings of Milton which have been dominant until recently, and in time it may be generally acknowledged that Milton is no more a non-political writer than Joyce was – or Dante, or Virgil.

One of the dogmas of the ahistorical school of literary criticism is the belief that political commitment necessarily damages a poem. Thus poets tend to be praised for their liberal open-mindedness, their freedom from the constricting dictates of ideology. As Douglas Bush has shown, Cleanth Brooks transforms Marvell's 'Horatian Ode' into an expression of modern uncommitted liberalism. Yet the two greatest political poems in English – *Paradise Lost* and *Absalom and Achitophel* – are works of the committed imagination. Milton was a republican, a regicide, the official propagandist of the English parliament, Dryden became a monarchist and a Tory after the Restoration. Their political beliefs are fundamental to their poems and our reading is enriched by a knowledge of those beliefs and an under-standing of the social experience which helped to form them (I say 'helped' because in the end we accede to a political position by an act of faith – Milton's essential faith was love of liberty, Dryden's love of order).

In the Western democracies it is still possible for many readers, students and teachers of literature to share the view that poems exist in a timeless vacuum or a soundproof museum, and that poets are gifted with an ability to hold themselves above history, rather like skylarks or weather satellites. However, in some societies – particularly totalitarian ones – history is a more or less inescapable condition. In those cold, closed societies a liberal belief in the separation of the public from the private life is not possible. Nor is it possible to believe that a poet may permit himself only an occasional interest in politics, or adopt a position which in the West would be termed 'purely aesthetic and non-political'. The ironic gravity and absence of hope in poets such as Zbigniew Herbert, Rózewicz and Holub, remind us that in Eastern Europe the poet has a responsibility both to art and to society, and that this responsibility is single and indivisible. The poet, in Joyce's special use of the term, is the 'conscience' of his or her society. Pasternak on Hamlet, Herbert on Fortinbras, Holub on the illusion that 'Hamlet will be saved and that an extra act will be added', all remind us that in certain societies to write poetry is to act socially, not to turn one's back on contingency. Here, symbols are deployed like ciphers in a secret code – the dissident Hamlet becomes an honorary citizen of the Eastern Bloc. He is the intellectual and poet figure whose presence in a poem always implies the existence of the usurping tyrant, Claudius, who smuggled poison into the garden and caused the Fall. To initiate the analogy is almost to ghost the rumour that Stalin had Lenin poisoned.

The actor-Hamlet's nervousness is Pasternak's fear that by speaking out directly like Mandelstam he will join him in the Gulag. But in this exposed, public confrontation with the tyrant it is Hamlet alone who will die. And it was partly by adopting an 'antic' disposition that Pasternak survived the great purges and lived to translate *Hamlet*. Like Shakespeare, Pasternak saw 'art tongue-tied by authority' and by pretending to be merely voluble, eccentric, a harmless cloud-treader, he earned Stalin's protection. No one would blame him – Nadezdha Mandelstam never did – for in a sense he made a reality of the illusion 'that Hamlet will be saved'.

[...]

And sometimes a political poem does not make an obviously ideological statement – 'To Penshurst', for example, conceals its politics behind a series of apparently innocent and 'natural' images.

Almost invariably, though, a political poem is a public poem, and it often begins in a direct response to a current event, just as a pamphlet or a piece of journalism springs from and addresses a particular historical moment. For example, in March 1681, the Whigs introduced the Third Exclusion Bill which was designed to safeguard liberty by preventing James Stuart, the Duke of York, succeeding Charles II. Charles dissolved parliament (he had already removed it to royalist Oxford), and in July he imprisoned the Whig leader, Shaftesbury, in the Tower on a charge of high treason. Dryden was both historiographer-royal and Poet Laureate, and he supported Charles in a prose-pamphlet, *His Majesties Declaration Defended*, and then in *Absalom and Achitophel* which was published in mid-November and is said to have been undertaken at the King's request. The poem was published as a pamphlet and it aimed to prejudice Shaftesbury's trial at the end of the month. Like Auden's 'Spain' – also first published as a pamphlet – Dryden's poem was generated by the hurry of contemporary political events. It is in no sense disinterested or trans-cendental of society – quite the reverse, in fact, for it aimed to bring Shaftesbury to the scaffold. Politically, it is a brilliant dirty trick, an inspired piece of black propaganda; aesthetically, it is a great masterpiece. But no one should call it 'pure'. The writer who prompts a judge, a jury, and an executioner is necessarily guilty, and although Shaftesbury managed to escape to Holland, that distinguished libertarian is now only a faint presence in the historical memory. He has melted into Dryden's fiction, a fiction that invests him with something of the engaging *élan* of Shakespeare's Richard III – a dramatic character whose historical accu-racy Josephine Tey and others have challenged.

Yeats's couplet on the poet's impurity, his responsibility for political violence, is a well-rubbed quotation, though few critics have tried to follow up the question, 'And did that play of mine send out / Certain men the English shot?' by placing the writings in their immediate social context. This is partly because literary history is almost a lost art and partly because many literary critics have no interest in biography or in history proper [...].

Yeats was an intensely political writer and his frequent sneers at politi-cians, journalists and other 'groundlings' are part of his consistent deviousness, his influential habit of first affirming that art and politics are hostile opposites and then managing to slip through the barrier, a naked politician disguised as an aesthete. It is a self-confessed circus-act which appears to have fooled many spectators into believing the poet was somehow above the vulgarities of politics. This element of populism, cruelty and calculated circus-like improvisation is an important characteristic of Yeats's work and I would guess that Samuel Beckett had the great ringmaster in mind when he created Pozzo in *Waiting for Godot*. Yeats belongs, though, to a separate Irish tradition of political verse; while the English tradition has three strands, the Monarchist, the Puritan-Republican and the Popular.

Despite T.S. Eliot's influence on the shape of English literary history, the monarchist tradition is not the major type of political verse in England. It is important, but not omnipotent as its supporters would have us believe. Although Spenser is a Protestant prophet, his poetry has been commonly aligned with that mystic patriotism, belief in social hierarchy and reverence for institutions 'sprong out from English race' which characterise monarchism, but when Spenser looks forward to the 'new Hierusalem' and identifies the English as God's 'chosen people', he is expressing radical Protestant beliefs which were held by Milton and the English republicans. Spenser's historical placing long before the Civil War enables him apparently to span both the Protestant and the monarchist traditions; but for Milton there was no doubt that 'our sage and serious poet Spenser' was fully committed to the puritan cause.

In present-day England – as opposed to Britain – the Monarchist tradition is represented by Geoffrey Hill, Charles Tomlinson, Donald Davie. The Puritan-Republican tradition is represented by Tony Harrison (Davie has roots in this tradition but his conversion to the Church of England effectively severed them). The Monarchist tradition is costive and self-conscious these days – as any reader of *PN Review* will note. Ted Hughes has brought some of the energy of the popular, vernacular tradition to the gamey corridors of Buck House, to an apparently rival tradition, but I dislike his English tribalism. Crow in Ermine worries me.

The popular tradition, which seemed to be almost extinct in England, has recently been revived, most conspicuously by a number of poets writing in Westindian. This type of political verse began long ago in the complaints and rebellions of the common people against those in authority. It shapes itself in anonymous ballads, popular songs, broadsheets, nursery rhymes like 'Gunpowder Plot Day', and its visceral energies can be felt in both Kipling and Yeats. It is the groundbase, the deep tidal pull, which underlies much political verse written in 'higher' or more 'official' modes. Often it can be witty, tough, idealistic, and resolute with a sense of egalitarian integrity:

> I mean the ploughman,
> I mean the plain true man,
> I mean the handcraftman.

This rich proletarian tradition looks to the pre-lapsarian Adam and Eve as ideal images of a just society, and these primal figures were invoked by John Ball in the text of the revolutionary sermon he preached at Blackheath in 1381. Adam delving, Eve spinning – the image became a radical, republican commonplace and it was invoked frequently during the 1640s. In *Vox Plebis*, a work ascribed to the Leveller, John Lilburne, we read: 'For as God created every man free in Adam: so by nature are all alike freemen born.' The image of free Adam – an image often used pejoratively by episcopalians – passes from Milton and Marvell in the seventeenth century to Clough in the nineteenth, and Clough's ironic, half-admiring reference to 'Democracy upon New Zealand' in *The Bothie of Tober-Na-Vuolich* is a late version of the ideal puritan commonwealth whose failure Milton probes in *Paradise Lost*.

One of the masterpieces in this tradition is John Clare's 'The Fallen Elm', a bitter and tender elegy which speaks for a dying social class – the agricultural labourers who were displaced by the enclosure acts. Like Jonson's 'To Penshurst', Clare's poem is conservative in its sacral sense of the value of tradition, and it gains enormously from Ann Tibbie's restoration of Clare's original orthography:

> The common heath became the spoilers prey
> The rabbit had not where to make his den
> & labours only cow was drove away
> No matter – wrong was right & right was wrong
> & freedoms bawl was sanction to the song
> – Such was thy ruin music making elm
> The rights of freedom was to injure thine

Like a Luddite pamphlet, Clare's poem seems to rise up from a vast, anonymous historical experience, and we can see that experience expressing itself actively in this United English oath which E.P. Thompson cites in *The Making of the English Working Class*:

> In a ful Presence of God. I a.b. doo swear not to abey the Cornall but the... Peapell. Not the officers but the Committey of United Inglashmen... and to assist with arms as fare as lise in my power to astablish a Republican Government in this Country and others and to asist the french on ther Landing to free this Contray.

The Irish accent of the oath is a reminder of the close links between radical movements in these islands, and it is significant that the English Chartist poet, Ebenezer Elliott, should echo Burns in 'Drone v. Worker'.

It seems likely that Browning's 'The Lost Leader' is spoken by a Chartist, and the poem's lithe dactyllic rhythms are shared by many Irish rebel songs. Again, this poem was inspired by a particular occasion – Wordsworth's acceptance of the laureateship on 4 April, 1843. The speaker of the poem voices the feeling that Wordsworth has betrayed 'us' – i.e. the working class. Browning had a nonconformist background and was a convinced Liberal (see, for example, the uncollected sonnet 'Why I am a Liberal'). He was briefly a student at University College and his poems show traces of Bentham's philosophy, and they also manifest a distinctively Protestant fascination with the workings of the individual conscience. It is possible to discern in Browning's numerous portraits of Renaissance egotists both a traditional Protestant and libertarian obsession with the power of Italian Catholicism and a topical criticism of the individualistic ethos of Victorian England. Like Arnold in *Culture and Anarchy*, Browning is voicing – though less directly – an unease with the *laissez-faire* philosophy of 'doing as one likes'. In this he resembles Clough who was deeply interested in political economy and hostile to an unbridled capitalist ethic.

And the Popular tradition is kicking again. Those poets who write in Westindian are advancing the English language, banging new cadences out of – or off of – that naked thew and sinew Hopkins loved. Tony Harrison's use of Yorkshire vernacular and his version of the Mystery plays align him also with the Popular tradition. I'm worried by his use of the sonnet form and by his standard metric but I admire the *Mysteries* very much. It's great to have the good Lord speaking Yorkshire.

[…] Like Tony Harrison I do not cherish the memory of Daniel Jones, the inventor of RP. I cherish these lines, though, from Heaney's 'Broagh':

> that last
> *gh* the strangers found
> difficult to manage.

Here the guttural muse, the accent of the provincial margins – of vast buried populations – moves in on what Matthew Arnold termed 'the tradition of the liquid diction'. When Linton Kwesi Johnson says 'war' he says 'warr' – I've heard the same pronunciation in the North of Ireland. I hope to hear it articulated more and more – only the word – for language belongs to the province of social life, as Clausewitz said of the act of war.

Some of this material appears in the introduction to the *Faber Book of Political Verse* (1986).

45

from Broken Windows or Thinking Aloud
Louis MacNeice

1

I am taking the liberty of thinking aloud – this is more for my own satisfaction than for yours. Being a reader, you want something crystal and perfect – lucidly self-consistent. Being a writer, I want to get rid of a burden.

You need not be afraid I am going in for self-flagellation, for washing my own dirty linen in public. Some of my colleagues have gone all humble; I consider that a mistake. There is a time for writers to be humble; this is their time to be arrogant.

A member of a giggling and twitching intelligentsia? Yes, no doubt I was one, perhaps am still. But it is better to giggle and twitch than to be a stock or a stone, and an intelligentsia – however decadent or 'bourgeois' – is something much finer than the TUC or the Stock Exchange or London Society.

The Marxist obsession encouraged us to crawl, to pretend ourselves cogs in a machine or part of the pattern in the lino. This pretence of humility was morbid – it was like Colonel Lawrence effacing himself in the Tank Corps. Now, with a war on, we need not be so anxious for self-effacement, we can leave that job to the bombs. This is our time to be arrogant.

Especially with people about like Lord Elton – writing off the intellect as fast as they can write.

Not that my primary concern at the moment is writing. Whoso at the moment saveth his art shall lose it.

The War has thrown us back upon life – us and our writing too. But we were less alive than our art because more negative. What we have done we need not recant; the trouble was what we were, but what we were has gone – or as good as.

In the first flush of this change the writer must beware of a lie –

of denouncing his past work as well as his past self. There are saps like Archibald MacLeish who think that art can be negative, destructive. Assuming that the present world-crisis has cancelled out Eliot and Hemingway. This is both nonsense and an insult.

The 'message' of a work of art may appear to be defeatist, negative, nihilist; the work of art itself is always *positive*. A poem in praise of suicide is an act of homage to life.

But different circumstances change the 'message' – the content – and so the method – the style. I notice myself that my two old methods – reportage and lyric – are ceasing to suit me. And I notice I have lost my nostalgia, am no longer worried by the passage of time.

Am ready to jettison the past – that is, my personal past. The general and historical Past remains printed in eternity; will remain monumental even if all the monuments go – all its outward and visible signs.

Let them all go if they must. Take out your razor and shave away the houses; shave away the soil and the sub-soil. If the human animal remains, it remains – an animal and human; instincts, ideals, remain.

An asylum is not freedom and a man's best house is humanity. We had got this concept of freedom all wrong; comfort and security were blinkers.

Freedom must be re-assessed. Because it is reappearing. And God must be re-assessed whether he exists or not. For, whether he exists or not, God is reappearing too. And, as for the human race, it must be reassessed.

In case it is disappearing.

[...]

This previously unpublished handwritten essay was dated c. 1940–1 by E.R. Dodds, MacNeice's first Literary Executor. It was brought to the attention of *Poetry Review* by Edna Longley.

& Memories of Rothwell House
Anthony Thwaite

Reading the obituaries of Terence Tiller in January, I was suddenly reminded how few survivors there now are of the old BBC Radio Features Department. Laurence Gilliam (head of the department for so many years), Douglas Cleverdon, Francis ('Jack') Dillon, Bob Pocock, Christopher Sykes, Rayner Heppenstall, Joe Burroughs, Louis MacNeice – all are dead.

It was MacNeice I got to know best. When I was first 'attached' to the department, as a so-called General Trainee, MacNeice was away on a television secondment, I think; but he and I shared an office for most of the period from the late summer of 1958 until I left to become literary editor of the *Listener* in February 1962. Laurence Gilliam's wry amusement at being landed with yet another poet showed itself: 'You're a poet, aren't you?' he asked me when I presented myself. (I had published one book of poems, the year before.) 'You'd better share with Louis – he's one too.'

Of course I had known MacNeice's poems since I first began reading poetry voluntarily in my middle teens, but I had never met him. I had heard him read, in 1953 or 1954, to the university English Club at Oxford, and chiefly remember his nasal, skirling, menacing reading of 'Bagpipe Music'; and I had seen him once in the George (that favourite BBC pub of the 1940s and 1950s, close to Broadcasting House), standing quizzically and aloofly in what looked like raffish company. Now, in 1958, to be thrust into extended and enforced proximity with him seemed an awkward apotheosis.

There is no doubt that at several levels I was, to begin with, in awe of him, a literary lion. For one thing, there was the age gap: he had published his first book, *Blind Fireworks*, the year before I was born. He was as famous as Auden. His face – lean, handsome, long-nosed, faintly disdainful – was familiar, even in such places as *Picture Post*. I had written about him, in a primer-like book of criticism I had published in Japan when I was twenty-six, just before leaving Tokyo University to join the BBC. Would he think of me as some tiresome youthful sprig or prig, forced into his unwilling company by Laurence Gilliam?

When it came to it, he seemed – if not exactly fulsomely welcoming – abstractedly genial. A routine quickly established itself. Being the new boy, I turned up at Rothwell House (the offices of Features Department) at 9.30 or earlier, keen to get on with my programmes. Louis generally arrived at about 11.30, coughing and wheezing over a cigarette. He would shuffle his papers, scribble a few notes, and at about noon would gesture with his head towards the window: 'Going to the Stag?' The Stag lay diagonally opposite Rothwell House in New Cavendish Street. The company was mixed: Features Department staff, car-dealers and 'rag-trade' people from Great Portland Street and its environs, and always some who were drawn into the Features orbit – R.D. Smith from Drama (sometimes with his wife, Olivia Manning), usually surrounded by actors and actresses eager to be hired by the bonhomous Reggie; and a succession of writers who had been commissioned by Features to do something or other, or who it was hoped might do something or other, including Samuel Beckett, Robert Graves, Patrick Kavanagh, Muriel Spark. Once, astonishingly, someone had brought William Burroughs. He stood there in the Stag, silent, chain-smoking, haggard, in a grubby white raincoat, like a commercial traveller fallen on hard times.

At about 1 o'clock or a little later, there would be a general move towards the George, just down Great Portland Street. Both in the Stag and in the George, Louis's usual stance was one of embattled gregariousness, at the centre of a group without dominating it, yet in no way peripheral. He was not a chatterer, though he enjoyed gossip and contributed to it. In the George there would often be talkative specimens of the London Irish, and with them – as with others – what Louis most enjoyed was dissections of what had been going on at Twickenham or Wimbledon. He was an avid and knowledgeable follower of rugby football and tennis.

There was literary gossip too, but nothing I would call a serious literary discussion. I remember standing in the George one lunchtime in early 1963 (I must have come over from the *Listener* in Marylebone High Street), talking with Louis and others, when Douglas Cleverdon suddenly arrived and told us that Sylvia Plath had been found dead, gassed, that morning. No one else there, I think, had known her, except for Douglas and me. I was shocked; though I hadn't known her well, we had met and talked at parties, I had broadcast her poems, and indeed she had chosen and presented a programme of her poems for me in Features Department. Someone in the group made a joking or disparaging remark about 'women poets'; but before I could say anything, Louis rounded on the man and told him to shut up: 'Can't you see the man's upset, and rightly too?'

Louis's contempt could be wounding. One morning, as we sat at our facing desks in Rothwell House, I'd noticed him scribbling away in pencil (he always used pencil), gazing out of the window, scribbling again. Later, in the Stag, I asked him whether he'd been writing a poem. He fixed me with his most disdainful, supercilious camel look and said, 'Have you nothing better to do than watch what I'm up to of a morning?' Another time, in the George, when I was fairly drunk and therefore insolent, I remarked: 'Louis, I've often wondered why you've got that long line down one side of your face and not down the other.' To which he replied: 'And *I've* often wondered why *you* have no lines on *your* face *at all.*'

But he could be kind even to bores. I was once visited at Rothwell by a couple of Japanese academics who had translated *Finnegans Wake,* or something almost as unlikely. When they heard that I shared the room with Louis MacNeice, they were excessively eager to meet him. We ran him to ground in the Stag, where (after an initial recoil of horror) he went out of his way to be friendly and attentive to these rather boring and absurd men.

Most of the Features Department work we did was entirely separate. Louis's greatest days as a writer for Features were long over: *Christopher Columbus, The Dark Tower,* his and E.L. Stahl's version of Goethe's *Faust.* Indeed, in the late 1950s and early 1960s, Features was having to fight hard, under Gilliam, to hold its corner. But Louis sporadically turned his hand to whatever came up, whether it was work written by him (*They Met on Good Friday, The Administrator*), handling features or plays written by other people, or producing poetry programmes. The enterprise that professionally brought us closest together was a dozen specially commissioned verse translations from the *Odyssey.* Louis was responsible for carving up the epic into twelve manageable consecutive thirty-minute episodes: as producer, I commissioned the translators (among them Rex Warner, Terence Tiller, Ted Hughes, Donald Davie, Alistair Elliot, Patric Dickinson, MacNeice and myself) and rehearsed the actors who spoke the results. Louis was a proper 'classic' (ex-university lecturer in Greek at Birmingham and London), I was not; but we worked well together, Louis approving of and enjoying the extraordinary variety of styles of translation, from Ted Hughes's muscular measures to Donald Davie's eccentric but convincing rendering into demotic West Riding.

But they were dying days at Features. The BBC hierarchy brought in a consultancy team from outside to investigate the department. After the *Odyssey,* Louis went on to a part-time contract. The investigators confronted him. 'We see, Mr MacNeice, that during the past six months you have produced only one programme. Can you tell us what you were doing the rest of that time?' Louis's reply became legendary: 'Thinking.'

Early in 1962 I took the vacant job of literary editor of the *Listener,* still under the umbrella of the BBC, but a desertion from Features. Laurence Gilliam thought I was crazy: 'You're joining a branch line. In a few years you could be running Features.' I published Louis's poems there, used him as a reviewer (books on Homer, Spenser, Yeats, the Edda), and saw him in pubs and at parties.

One of my last memories is of sitting with him in the ML one afternoon. (The ML was at that time a sepulchral drinking club in Little Portland Street, open in the yawning hours between 3.00 p.m. and 5.30 p.m., when all the pubs were closed.) It must have been fairly early in 1963, because Louis had given me the typescript of what was to be *The Burning Perch*, his last book. He was about to deliver to Faber & Faber, and asked me to suggest titles for this collection. I plumped very hard for *Funeral Games* (the last two words of his poem 'Sports Page'), but Louis opined that this title would kill the book stone dead. He inclined towards something to do with Pyres – *Pyres and Journeys*, *Pyres and Staircases*, *Pyres and Corners*, *Pyres and Margins*: he jotted these down on a bit of paper I still have. He also wanted to talk about the new *Oxford Book of Twentieth-Century Verse* which he'd been asked to edit. (The job was later taken up by Philip Larkin after MacNeice's death.) He wanted to begin with Hardy and Housman, and then the bulk of the book would give solid prominence to Yeats, Eliot, Lawrence, Muir, Graves, Owen, and Auden. He was not at all sure about Edith Sitwell, and put a large question-mark against her name.

It was soon after this ML meeting that he asked me whether I would agree to be his literary executor in a new will he was having drawn up. E.R. Dodds, he said, was old, and bound to die before him, and so he wanted someone younger. He said he had thought about Ted Hughes and myself, but had decided that I was 'more businesslike'. I felt flattered, and just a little resentful too, because 'businesslike' could be interpreted as 'boring'. Anyway, I said yes. But Louis died before the new will had been properly executed; and of course Dodds long outlived Louis, and made a very fine job of editing both the *Collected Poems* and the fragmentary autobiography, *The Strings are False*.

I was driving round Suffolk on holiday with my wife in September 1963 when I had a message to telephone Stella Hillier, the chief administrative officer of Features. She told me Louis had died, suddenly, of pneumonia. Auden gave the address at his memorial service in All Souls, Langham Place. The whole of Features Department was there: most of us were ushers. Within a year, Laurence Gilliam died, the efficiency men moved in, and the department was quickly wound up.

46

What We Lost
Eavan Boland

It is a winter afternoon.
The hills are frozen. Light is failing.
The distance is a crystal earshot.
A woman is mending her linen in her kitchen.

She is a countrywoman.
Behind her cupboard doors she hangs sprigged,
stove-dried lavender in muslin.
Her letters and mementoes and memories

are packeted in satin at the back with
gaberdine and worsted and
the cambric she has made into bodices;
the good tobacco silk for Sunday Mass.

She is sewing in the kitchen.
The sugar-feel of flax is in her hands.
Dusk. And the candles brought in then.
One by one. And the quiet sweat of wax.

There is a child at her side.
The tea is poured, the stitching put down.
The child grows still, sensing something of importance.
The woman settles and begins her story.

Believe it, what we lost here in this room
on this veiled evening:
The woman finishes. The story ends.
The child, who is my mother, gets up, moves away.

PR 79:3, 1989

In the winter air, unheard, unshared,
the moment happens, hangs fire, leads nowhere.
The light will fail and the room darken,
the child fall asleep and the story be forgotten.

The fields are dark already.
The frail connections have been made and are broken.
The dumb-show of legend has become language,
is becoming silence and who will know that once

words were possibilities and disappointments,
were scented closets filled with love-letters
and memories and lavender hemmed into muslin,
stored in sachets, aired in bed-linen;

and travelled silks and the tones of cotton
tautened into bodices, subtly shaped by breathing;
were the rooms of childhood with their griefless peace,
their hands and whispers, their candles weeping brightly.

47

Unfinished Business
Primo Levi

Sir, starting next month,
Please accept my resignation
And, if necessary, find a replacement for me.
I leave a lot of uncompleted work,
Either from laziness or practical problems.
I should have said something to someone,
But no longer know what or to whom. I have forgotten.
I should have given something away, too:
A word of wisdom, a gift, a kiss.
I've put it off from one day to the next. Forgive me.
I'll take care of it in the short time that's left.
I have, I fear, neglected important clients.
I should have visited
Far-away cities, islands, deserted lands;
You'll have to cross them off the program
Or entrust them to my successor's care.
I should have planted trees and haven't done it,
Built myself a house,
Perhaps not beautiful but conforming to a plan.
Above all, dear sir, I had in mind
A marvellous book that would have
Revealed innumerable secrets,
Alleviated pain and fear,
Dissolved doubts, given to many people
The boon of tears and laughter.
You'll find the outline in my drawer,
In back, with the unfinished business.
I haven't had time to see it through. Too bad.
It would have been a fundamental work.

April 19, 1981

Translated by Ruth Feldman.

PR 78:1, 1988

48

Sextet
Joseph Brodsky

I

An eyelid is twitching. From the open mouth
gushes silence. The cities of Europe mount
each other at railroad stations. A pleasant odor
of soap tells the dweller of jungles of the approaching foe.
Wherever you set your sole or toe,
the world map develops blank spots, grows balder.

A palate goes dry. The traveller feels a thirst.
Children, to whom the worst
should be done, fill the air with their shrieks. An eyelid twitches
all the time. As for columns, from
the thick of them someone always emerges. Even in your sweet
dream
even with your eyes shut, you see human features.

And it wells up in your throat like barf:
'Give me ink and paper and, as for yourself,
scram!' And an eyelid is twitching. Odd, funereal
whinings – as though someone's praying upstairs – poison the
daily grind.
The monstrosity of what's happening in your mind
makes unfamiliar premises look familiar.

II

Sometimes in a desert you hear a voice. You fetch
a camera in order to catch the face.
But – too dark. Sit down then, release your hearing
to the southern lilt of a small monkey who
left her palm tree but, having no leisure to
become a human, went straight to whoring.

PR 76:3, 1986

Better sail by steamer, horizon's ant,
taking part in geography, in blueness, and
not in history, this dry land's scabies.
Better trek across Greenland on skis and camp
among the icebergs, among the plump
walruses as they bathe their babies.

The alphabet won't allow your trip's goal to be
ever forgotten, that famed point B.
There a crow caws hard trying to play the raven,
there a black sheep bleats, rye is choked with weeds;
there the top brass, like furriers, shear out bits
of the map's faded pelt so that they look even.

III

For thirty-six years I've stared at fire.
An eyelid is twitching. Both palms perspire:
the cop leaves the room with your papers. Angst. Built to calm it,
an obelisk, against its will, recedes
in a cloud, amidst bright seeds,
like an immobile comet.

Night. With your hair quite gone, you still dine alone,
being your own master, your own pawn.
The kipper lies across a headline about striking rickshaws
or a berserk volcano's burps –
God knows where, in other words –
flitting its tail over 'The New Restrictions'.

I comprehend only the buzz of flies,
in the Eastern bazaars! On the sidewalk, flat
on his back, the traveller strains his sinews,
catching the air with his busted gills.
  In the afterlife, the pain that kills
  here, no doubt continues.

IV

'Where's that?' asks the nephew, toying with his stray locks.
And fingering brown mountain folds. 'Here', pokes
the niece. In the depths of the garden, yellow
swings creak softly. The table dwarfs a bouquet
of violets. The sun's splattering the parquet
floor. From the drawing room float twangs of a cello.

At night, a plateau absorbs moonshine.
A boulder shepherds its elephantine shadow.
A brook's silver change is spending
itself in a gully. Clutched sheets in a room elude
their milky/swarthy/abandoned nude –
an anonymous painful painting.

In spring, labor-ants build their muddy coops;
rooks show up; so do creatures with other groups
of blood; a fresh leaf shelters
verging shame of two branches. In autumn, a skyhawk keeps
counting villages' chicklets; and the sahib's
white jacket is dangling from the servant's shoulders.

V

Was the word ever uttered? And then – if yes –
in what language? And where? And how much ice
should be thrown into a glass to halt a Titanic
of thought? Does the whole recall the neat shape of parts?
Would a botanist, suddenly facing birds
in an aquarium, panic?

Now let us imagine an absolute emptiness.
A place without time. The air per se. In this,
in that, and in the third direction – pure, simple, pallid
air. A mecca of it: oxygen, nitrogen. In which
there's really nothing except for the rapid twitch-
ing of a lonely eyelid.

These are the notes of a naturalist. The naughts
on nature's own list. Stained with flowerpots.
A tear falls in a vacuum without acceleration.
The last of hotbed neuroses, hearing the
faint buzzing of Time's tsetse,
I smell increasingly of isolation.

VI

And I dread my petals' joining the crowned knot
of fire! Most resolutely not!
Oh, but to know the place for the first, the second,
and the umpteenth time! When everything comes to light,
when you hear or utter the jewels like
'When I was in the Army' or 'Change the record!'

Petulant is the soul begging mercy from
an invisible or dilated frame.
Still, if it comes to the point where the blue acrylic
dappled with cirrus suggests the Lord,
say, 'Give me strength to sustain the hurt',
and learn it by heart like a decent lyric.

When you are no more, unlike the rest,
the latter may think of themselves as blessed
with the place so much safer thanks to the big withdrawal
of what your conscience indeed amassed.
And a fish that prophetically shines with rust
will splash in a pond and repeat your oval.

Translated by the author; this poem first appeared in the *New Yorker*.

49

from Address to the Global Forum of Spiritual and Parliamentary Leaders on Human Survival

James E. Lovelock

My father was born in 1873 on the Berkshire downs near Wantage, some fifteen miles from Oxford. He was that kind of countryman who felt himself to be part of the natural world. For him there were no weeds, pests, or vermin; everything alive was, in his view, there for a purpose. He had an immense respect for trees and referred to them as the noblest form of plant life.

With this in mind I would like to make trees the theme of my address today. To start with; imagine that you are in a grove of giant redwood trees on the coast of California and that you are standing on the stump of a tree that has just been felled. When standing it was a vast tree weighing over two thousand tons and over one hundred metres tall, a spire of lignin and cellulose, a tree that started life over two thousand years ago.

A strange thing about this tree is that during its life nearly all of it was dead wood. As a tree grows there is just a thin skin of living tissue around the circumference, the wood inside is dead, as is the bark that protects the delicate tissue. More than 97 per cent of the tree we stand on was dead before it was cut down.

Now in this way a tree is very like the Earth itself. Around the circumference on the surface of the Earth is a thin skin of living tissue of which both the trees and we humans are a part. The rocks beneath our feet are like the wood and the air above is like the bark. Both are dead matter, but the air and the rocks, like the wood and the bark, are either the direct products of life or have been greatly modified by its presence. Is it possible that the Earth is alive like the tree?

It was the view from space about twenty years ago, that showed us how beautiful and how seemly was our planet when seen in its entirety. The Earth was also seen from space in invisible wavelengths through the sensors of scientific instruments and their view

PR 80:1, 1990

made some of us re-examine our theories about the nature of the Earth. It led my colleague and friend Lynn Margulis and I, to propose that the Earth itself was indeed in some ways alive like the tree, alive at least to the extent that it could regulate its climate and chemical composition. We called the idea Gaia after the old name for the Earth.

A tree is in many ways a living model of the Earth. Indeed some single trees of the tropical forests are almost complete ecosystems in themselves. They shelter a vast range of species from microbes to large animals, to say nothing of numerous plants growing on their branches. Those tropical trees are nearly as self-sufficient as the Earth, they recycle almost all the nutritious elements within their canopy, and with the other trees, sustain the climate and the composition of the forest.

My view of the Earth sees a self-sustaining system named Gaia like one of those forest trees. Although some of my colleagues in science are beginning to take it seriously as a theory to test, most mainstream scientists prefer to see the Earth as just a ball of rock moistened by the oceans, a piece of planetary real estate that we have inherited. In their view, we, and the rest of life, are just passengers. Life may have altered the environment, or have coevolved with it, as by putting oxygen in the air, but they see this as no more than the act of passengers who, when on a long sea voyage, may decorate their cabins.

If mainstream science is right and the Earth is like this, then to survive it might not matter what we do; so long as we do not foul the Earth so much as to hazard ourselves and our crops and livestock.

But what if instead the Earth is a vast living organism? In such a living system species are expendable. If a species, such as humans, adversely affects the environment, then in time it will be eliminated with no more pity than is shown by the micro-brain of an intercontinental ballistic missile on course to its target. If the Earth is like this, then to survive we face the hard task of reintegrating creation. Of learning again to be part of the Earth and not separate from it. If we choose to go this way the change of heart and mind needed will be great and it will include also the reintegration of religion and science.

In Newton's time he was able to say 'Theology is the queen of the sciences.' I happen to think that, although science has progressed vastly since Newton it has also moved a long way in the wrong direction. Scientists had to reject the bad side of medieval religion: superstition, dogmatism, and intolerance. Unfortunately, as with most revolutionaries, we scientists merely exchanged one set of dogma for another. What we threw out was soul.

The life of a scientist used to be that of a natural philosopher – closely in touch with the real world. It was a life both deeply sensuous and deeply religious, truly in touch with the world. You see, curiosity is the principal motivation of the natural philosopher, and curiosity also is an intimate part of the process of loving. Being curious about and getting to know a person or the natural world leads to a loving relationship.

I sometimes wonder if the loss of soul from science could be the result of sensory deprivation? A consequence of the fact that 95 per cent of us now live in cities. How can you love the living world if you can no longer hear bird song through the noise of traffic, or smell the sweetness of fresh air? How can we wonder about God and the Universe if we never see the stars because of the city lights? If you think this to be exaggeration, think back to when you last lay in a meadow in the sunshine and smelt the fragrant thyme and heard and saw the larks soaring and singing. Think back to the last night you looked up into the deep blue black of a sky clear enough to see the Milky Way, the congregation of stars, our galaxy.

The attraction of the city is seductive. Socrates said, two thousand years ago, that nothing of interest happened outside its walls. But city life, the soap opera that never ends, reinforces and strengthens the heresy of humanism, that narcissistic belief that nothing important happens that is not a human interest.

City living corrupts, it gives a false sense of priority over environmental hazards. We become inordinately obsessed about personal mortality, especially about death from cancer. Most citizens when asked, list nuclear radiation and ozone depletion as the most serious environmental hazards. They tend to ignore the consequences of greenhouse-gas accumulation, agricultural excess and forest clearance. Yet in fact these less personal hazards can kill just as certainly. Sadly we are the witnesses of the disintegration of creation without realising that we are the cause.

The humid tropics are both a habitat for humans and in the heartland of Gaia. That habitat is being removed at a ruthless pace. Yet in the first world we try to justify the preservation of tropical forests on the feeble grounds that they are the home of rare species of plants and animals, even of plants containing drugs that could cure cancer. They may do. But they offer so much more than this. Through their capacity to evaporate vast volumes of water vapour the forests serve to keep their region cool and moist by wearing a sunshade of white reflecting clouds and by bringing the rain that sustains them. Their replacement by crude cattle farming could precipitate a disaster for the billions of the poor in the third world. Imagine the human suffering, the guilt and the political consequences of a Sahel drought throughout the tropics. To say nothing of the secondary climatic consequences here in the temperate regions.

[...]

I have spoken as the representative, the shop steward, of the bacteria and the less attractive forms of life. My constituency is also all life other than humans. I have done so because there are so many who speak for people but few who speak for these others.

[...]

50

Man and Boy
Seamus Heaney

I

'Catch the old one first',
(My father's joke was also old, and heavy
And predictable). 'Then the young ones
Will all follow, and Bob's your uncle'.

On slow bright river evenings, the sweet time
Made him afraid we'd take too much for granted
And so our spirits must be lightly checked.

Blessed be down-to-earth! Blessed be highs!
Blessed be the detachment of dumb love
In that broad-backed, low-set man
Who feared debt all his life, but now and then
Could make a splash like the salmon he said was
'As big as a wee pork pig by the sound of it'.

II

In earshot of the pool where that salmon jumped
Back through its own unheard concentric soundwaves
A mower leans forever on his scythe.

He has mown himself to the centre of the field
And stands in a final perfect ring
Of sunlit stubble.

'Go and tell your father', the mower says
(He said it to my father who told me)
'I have it mowed as clean as a new sixpence'.

PR 81:1, 1991

My father is a barefoot boy with news,
Running at eye-level with weeds and stooks
On the afternoon of his own father's death.

The open, black half of the half-door waits.
I feel much heat and hurry in the air.
I feel his legs and quick heels far away

And strange as my own – when he will piggyback me
At a great height, light-headed and thin-boned,
Like a witless elder rescued from the fire.

51   Avant de Quitter Ces Lieux
John Ashbery

They watch the blue snow.
It is the fifth act in someone else's life,
but here, on Midway Island, reefs and shoals interfere
with that notion. That nothing so compact
as the idea of a season is to be allowed
is the note, for today at least. It is Tuesday morning.
They sing a duet of farewell
to their little table, and to themselves as they were
when they sat at it. Noon intersects with fat birds,
the rhythm of dishes in the cupboard. My love,
he seems to say, is this the way it is for you? Then we shall have
                                                to leave

these shabby surroundings for others, but first
I want to plant a kiss like a star
on your forehead. The ships are knocking together at the quayside,

PR 81:4, 1991–2

the lanions struck, there is more moving
than we were intended for, as we clear out,
nodding to the caryatids we pass. Perhaps they will sing to us.

But in a summer house somewhere in Russia
a clematis soaks up the heat. One can think without breathing
of the blue snow that invades the fields, a curse some obscure
                                                      ancestor
once let fall and now it's the custom, duly serenaded each season
before the apples rust
and the idea of winter takes over, to be followed in short order
                                                      by the real thing.
If all of us could lead lives of razoring things out of the newspaper,
filing them on pincushions… but no. There is the father
and morning to be dealt with, and after that the students arrive.
The rhythm is broken up among them.
That was a cold year, but not
the last. It will be remembered.

Why is it you always ask me this, and this:
is there no question behind the arras of how we now meet
seconding each other's projects, our emotions? Or is that too weak
as a question, though strong enough as an affirmation, so that
                                                      we again go out
from each other. One shades one's eyes automatically, though
                                                      the sky
is dark. 'We have no place to go' (the fifteenth
major situation), and if God decrees we like each other, someday
we will meet on a stone up there, and all will not be well,
but that is useful. Great rivers run into each other and graves
have split open, the tyranny of dust plays well, there is
so little to notice. Besides we have always known each other.

Except for that it was automatically the century
before this one. Thus we are made aware of the continuity
of times that were, and time itself is revealed
not as a series of rooms but a single corridor

·

stretching into the truth: an alpine pasture, with a few goats
and, in the distance, a hovel. It is high noon. Dinorah,
who has lost her goat, sings the mad scene for which her life
has been a preparation, sings it out of daylight, out of the
                                                    outcropping
of rock overhead, out of the edelweiss and cowslips.
Now it is the turn of the mountain god
but he refuses to play. The blue snow returns. Shopfronts are
                                                    boarded up.

Still one should never be in a hurry to end, to contrast the ending
with the articulations that have gone before. True, these are
                                                    merely space,
but one in which lives can take on a single and sparing sharpness
that is an education in itself. This is one life
as we thought it over, and there are other songs, some too true
                                                    to mention,
others of little weight, optional, cut from most editions
but waiting silently in place where they are expected.
The story falls, mountains conspire, brooks hesitate,
the storm endures.

52   Poetry Against Absurdity
                 Miroslav Holub

We began to write poetry in war-time, hiding somewhere and
somehow from the German *Arbeitsamt* (labour administration)
and *Totaleinsatz* (forced labour) and from the Allied bombs. The
bombs were one of the few positive and promising features of life,
as were Seifert's love poems.

PR 80:2, 1990

The inner landscape could have been defined as a little corner in Picasso's *Guernica*.

In 1945–6, after the liberation, there was hardly time to draw breath and find one's own way of getting beyond Adorno's pronouncement: After Auschwitz there can't be any poetry. No poetry after Auschwitz. In my view, an alternative statement or programme was: No more words. Just sharp, concrete, viable, bleeding images, partly inherited from the surrealist imagery of the thirties.

Personally, I was attracted by the heritage of Czech 'civilian' poetry, Group 42, and would have liked to write something like Josef Kainar's 'Taxidermist' *(New Myths,* 1946):

...

Bird's guts are wrapped in fat
fat is wiped off on a glass plate

Something is torn off
With two fingers it is torn off
From time to time something crackles in the palm

...

Nevermore will it find the finest branch
To be rocked on it by the beat
Of its tiny heart
In the calm
They took its life away
And the taxidermist
He took away even its death

It will never more burn in the wind

And if I wrote my poem
If I am stuffing the unknown bird...

But before we could identify ourselves with anybody or anything, before the beginner and outsider could catch his breath, there was 1948, which I can best illustrate by personal experience. I had just won the third prize in poetry and the fifth prize for an 'Essay on the Present Moment' in the nationwide students' competition. After days and nights of student street protests against the Communist coup, there was a meeting at the Students' Union Headquarters where we were supposed to receive our prizes. Instead, the leader of the Communist students announced that the Union had just been dissolved and a blind, hysterical sort of *yuro-divy* ('visionary') young man began screaming about his vision of the May Day parade in which we would all march and sing the Russian songs.

At that moment I realized that there is no poetry not only because of Auschwitz, that there are no words, that there is no identity, that we are completely isolated in the crowds of quasi *yurodivy* colleagues, that there is no 'civilian' poetry, no Walt Whitman nor Carl Sandburg, no Group 42, and no programme except to shut up.

So we entered literature by shutting up. By complete silence. By a complete distrust of everybody. It was a perfect lesson in Creative Non-Writing. It was a short-cut to an almost biological feeling of the absurdity of everything, including one's inner self. Wittgenstein's view that 'in the arts it is difficult to say something which would be as good as to say nothing' was pushed to its extreme.

Whatever was published as admissible poetry was in the guise of Russian socialist realism, with a minimal number of personal, private positive deviations.

The mainstream of poetry, rather than any new language, was merely a cover-up of reality, in which opportunities for humans shrank and opportunities for statues expanded.

The statues rose up above the shabby and peeling façades of buildings in which countless Kafka trials took place. In the streets something would run that was later ascertained to be Ionesco's rhinoceroses, and in private something went on that was later defined as waiting for Godot.

Thus quite involuntarily, without the assistance of any sort of literary programme, a perfect situation of inner and outer absurdity was being created, and was created. It was only a question of poetic nature and a question of context as to who would record it and when.

However, one could instinctively feel that 'recording' was not the thing. Literature and art in general are always a counterpoint to the state of affairs. In a tidy society, literature is inclined to get unruly, uncombed, flourishing underground; in a complete mess, literature believes in (and is believed to create) traces of order and seeds of value. In absurd conditions, literature must have a rational grain and programme. What was written on the walls were metaphors, not entire poems. What was to be recorded was the feeling of human responsibility in the overwhelming absurdity, using its images.

As it happened, the official socialist realism was a frank recording of irresponsibility and nihilism and isolation. Looked at from the outside, it was something like the vision of a sentimental romantic bureaucrat. A romantic bureaucrat is himself a Beckettian hero belonging in *Endgame*. Socialist realism was an integral part of general absurdity.

Anything else that happened in literature could not even be named. It was not modernism, nor postmodernism. It was plain self-defence; when you are drowning, you may not care for theoretical, linguistic and literary denotations of your words or bubbles.

Against the vast official nothingness, any kind of minimal personal or group programme was a step forward, in accordance with Kainar's words in 1960: 'A grain of truth is the entire universe.' But the most radical programme in my view was provided by Kolar and Holan: in Holan's case, his poetry from the time when he 'spoke to the wall – and it replied'. In the lyric-epic *Pribehy* (*Episodes*) he achieved a certain magic matter-of-factness, based on the self-reliant fates of his heroes and a drastic counterpointing of image and meaning. As it is in the 'Ode to Joy', which is about a girl burnt alive. As it is in the key line of the poem 'Flight' ('Utek'):

Only when we kneel, we become life-size.

And 'Ode to Joy' starts with a comprehensive statement of the situation:

A sweet summery early evening... Summery, because

summery,

and absurd, because sweet... Everything is light
and everything is elevated and the elephant's dance
   is the most elevated...

and a later poem ('Again') reads:

Without death life is impossible to feel,
with it, life is just thinkable,
and therefore absurd...

Matter-of-factness as the basic defence against emptiness, concreteness as the counterweight to a lie – before our 'poetry of the everyday' – is actually defined in Holan's poem 'Resurrection':

After this life here, we're to be awakened one day
by the terrible screams of trumpets and bugles?
Forgive me, Lord, but I trust
that the beginning and the resurrection of us, the dead,
will be announced by the crowing of a rooster...

We'll lie on for a little longer...
The first one to rise
will be mother... We'll hear her
quietly making the fire
quietly putting the kettle on,
and cozily taking the coffee grinder out of the cupboard.
We'll be at home again.

Holan's magic matter-of-factness was one form of defence against absurdity. In virtually hopeless situations defence of course becomes attack from the outset.

The second radical record, and a decisive and inspirational one, was the poetry of Jiri Kolar. From the poetry of the town he came, in the circumstances of general absurdity, to the mirror. He discovered that authenticity, living everyday authenticity, plain human speech, and the most ordinary human situation of these years were not only poetically viable but also the most telling argument. By conviction. It was poetry as a project and at the same time as testimony. Poetry as an escape from the book to the street, where now and then a rhinoceros would run past.

Kolar himself defined it as 'to be where life is heaviest'. Methodologically important here is what Marco Polo said to Mr A.:[1]

> We have now reached the heart of the country
> In whose terrible frosts live people spangled with eyes
> The nobler the creature
> The more eyes it has
> The more it sees...

Kolar's authenticity reaches its climax in the *Czech Suite* in which the poems are made up only of free verse lines from the letters of Czech artists of the last century, including compulsive scribblers and including the reports of agents appointed to keep artists under surveillance.

For me it is poetry-which-is-more-than poetry, for instance in this quotation from the report of the secret agent Novotny concerning the obtaining of a woman informer among the acquaintances of the Czech writer Bozena Nemcova:

> Guided by the desire to fulfil my mission responsibly
> I found a person
> suitable for confidential service of the given kind
> in a daughter of our corps of discreet informers
> working under the name of Chemist...
> having regard to the level of her education...
> ... and the delicate nature of the assignment
> allow me
> to recommend a monthly salary of A2 of the second grade.

In a situation where almost every Czech writer had behind him, beside or in front of him somebody with the monthly salary of A2 of the second grade, this is poetry of maximal impact and minimal stylization.

In the given context it's impossible to achieve a greater effect.

---

1   One must note that Kolar's Mr A. preceded Herbert's Mr Cogito.

I consider that both Holan's and Kolar's testimony was a poetic act of more than national importance. During the sixties and seventies the concrete situation proved to be a model: the Czech experience was an epitome of the age-old struggle of intellect with codified stupidity.

Nothing we did since the fifties in Czech poetry and its struggle against the absurdity of the social order surpassed the limits defined by Holan and Kolar.

All we were doing was only serving within these limits.

If I may call to mind the years 1969–71 as a repetition of 1948, I see the editor-in-chief of a 'steamrollered' socialist realist publishing house who was explaining to me why my book on E.A. Poe could not come out under my name: 'You know, comrade, it's like catching a cold. If it's not taken care of in time, it has lasting effects.'

According to this poet's conception, a neglected cold was not merely the basic concept of why-and-what for poetry and why-and-what for man, but also Kantian Pure Reason itself. At the time of making this prediction the National Artist didn't have that *yuro-divy* expression. But this demonstrated that the situation was now even worse because here was absurdity in which even the *yurodi-vost* was faked.

And so it ended.

I don't know how successful we are going to appear from the standpoint of later history. But we were certainly not short of proposals.

Translated by Ian and Jarmila Milner. Based on a lecture given at the Conference on Czech Literature 1890–1990, at New York University, March 1990.

53

['Low water']
Paul Celan

Low water. We saw
the balanid, saw
the limpet, saw
the nails on our hands.
No one cut the word for us from our heartwalls.

(Tracks of the shore crab, tomorrow,
crawl furrows, habitat trails, wind-
trace in the grey
silt, fine sand,
coarse sand, that
detached from the walls, with
other testaceous parts, in the
shell deposits.)

One eye, today,
gave it to a second, both,
closed, followed the current to
its shadow, unloaded
their cargo (no one
cut the word for us from our —), shored outward
to the hook of land – a sand bar in front
of a small
unnavigable silence.

'Niedrigwasser' from *Sprachgitter*, 1959. Translated by Michael Hamburger.

54 Word
Aimé Césaire

In between me
and myself,
beyond every star-system,
in my squeezed-shut hands only
the odd gasp of final fever-spasm,
throbs the word
                    I'd have been luckier outside this labyrinth
Longer larger it throbs
in stronger and stronger waves
in the lasso catching me
in the rope hanging me
all the arrows nailing me
with their bitter poison
to the beautiful axis of utterly fresh stars.

It throbs
the very essence of shadow throbs
in wing in throat risking death
the black word
coming out fully-armed from the yell
of a poisonous flower
the black word
all lousy with parasites
the black word
full of traffickers
grieving mothers
crying children
the black word
a sizzling of flesh that burns

PR 96:2, 2006

acrid and leathery
the black word
like the sun which bleeds from the claw
on the pavement of clouds
the black world
like the last laugh born out of innocence
between the tiger's fangs

and as the word sun is a smacking of bullets
as the word night's a taffeta you rip
the black word
                      is heavy you know
with the thunder of a summer
                which takes
                          incredible liberties.

This translation from *Corps perdu* (1949), published in *PR* in 2006, is included here
with the work of Césaire's international peers of the 1990s.

55 *from* The Poet in the Theatre
Derek Walcott

I gotta use words when I talk to you.
T.S. Eliot, *Sweeney Agonistes*

Great tragedies are based on the propulsion of metre as well as of
character; that is, a symmetry of sound as well as of plot. Yet what
we endorse as tragic in contemporary theatre considers these ideas
to be old-fashioned or exhausted, the argument being that our
condition, if it is tragic at all, is one of monodic suffering without
meaning, and since it is without meaning, without any pretext to

PR 80:4, 1990–1

the cathartic, or more pietistically, the sublime. The sublimity that is supposed to satisfy is one of glints and fragments, with echoes rather than statements, with stasis or repetition rather than plot, but we may have arrived at a point where minimalism has become baroque, where despair and its metrically weighed vacuities are the style of our second Elizabethan era; one in which there is an exuberance of emptiness, an enthusiasm for vacuums; where gaps of silence are revered over the articulate.

The trouble is that this reduction has become as rhetorical as the bombast of the first Elizabethans, not because these play-wrights had something to shout about, as presumably their successors do not, but because we accept a thesis which says as determinedly as the imitators of Seneca, that in the modern theatre we must not shout about anything.

There are two great shouts in great modern theatre, but both are silent – one of course is the silent scream of Brecht's Mother Courage over the body of her daughter; the other, without being too specific, but which is part of the body of Samuel Beckett's work, is the gaping mouth of Krapp. Both are invocations, however mute. Yet the refusal to invoke is no different from invocation itself: like prayer paralyzed, poetry gone dumb. Centuries spin backward and stop at another open mouth: the chorus in *Henry V*. 'O, for a muse of fire that would ascend.' Exultant. Optimistic. Zealous. Propelled by direction in history, by purpose in action.

There is also Dr Faustus's 'Lente, lente, curite, noctus equi', which without an O of invocation is not only as despairing as Beckett's, or Brecht's, but superior to it because it propels itself from the spiritual panic – but is also propelled – by metre beyond stasis, shock, remorse or bewilderment, towards a sublime terror. The sublime: you can hear the cackle of Krapp in the wings. You can visualize the irony in the downward parentheses of Mother Courage's grin.

It is the vanity of metropolitan cultures to believe that they alone have the right to pessimism, just as they alone once held the rights to their opposites: elation, delight, conviction and faith; while those corners of the world that are beyond the centre (the heart of metropolitan theatre) in the depressed and rugged areas of cities may contain their own primitive exuberance, that is their 'O's' of joy or of metrical pain, but they are regarded as outside the centre – like the plays of Soyinka. Exuberance in contemporary theatre is permitted only in certain second-rate shapes, such as musicals. There songs can begin with an 'O'.

The idea of vacuity in modern tragedy is like the idea of the existential or the nihilistic: spiritual vanity. The depth of modern contemplation is of staring into the holes, the emptiest 'O' of all. Such vanity lies in the faith that for the tragic poets of the modern theatre, be they absurdists or minimalists, history happens only where it has meaning. And since for such writers history is now meaningless – at least as morality – where history does happen is the only place where modern tragedy can be played. The argument is: give a provincial or a backward joy enough time and it will catch up with metropolitan tragedy. Teach it enough silence, increase such silences, deepen their significance of emptiness, of wordlessness, and language, then action, will evaporate and stasis will admire stasis because we are observing modern history, and if history is meaningless then so is literature and the theatre.

Mallarmé headed towards the silence of the white page; Beckett for the silence of the hole; the hole as the whole. Irony is the furthest point of tragedy in modern theatre. Not true irony, but sarcasm. This sarcasm mocks literature, scuttles the articulate, deepens chasms – on the pretext that human beings cannot or do not really communicate. Therefore poetry itself is the first victim of this cynicism. And by poetry I do not mean the poetic, but the metre of poetry, which is verse. The audience in any centre of theatre – the metropolis – bristles at the idea of verse in the modern theatre, but this is because each member of the audience considers himself or herself the centre; since it has been told that this is where the centre is. While, without any academic urging, without any sense of siege or nostalgic aggression, verse ignores the centre and continues exuberantly in provincial or ghetto theatre, in rap, in rock music, and in that second-rate expression of exuberance – the stage musical.

This theatre is without walls, just as the Greek and Elizabethan theatres were also arenas, however confined. Without walls and therefore without philosophical *cul de sacs*, without literary chronology, and above all with shape – stanzaic, rhythmic shapes, with participation and chorus. No audience can participate in minimalist or absurdist dramas because that would be a violation of their privileged silences. That would in fact be impolite, a violation of silence. We are not allowed to cough or to talk. Yet in spite of the example of Racine we look for the sources of great tragedy, not in the elegant, but in the vulgar, not in privilege, but in popularity, from stories that are known, whose base is, as with the sources of Greek tragic drama, obscene and provincial – or if we prefer, outrageous. The surest base of tragedy is comic, and the closer tragedy gets to comic absurdity, as it does in Oedipus, or Lear, or Othello, the more we are elated at its outrage.

The argument could be that there is comic absurdity in the centre of theatre, and a great deal of vulgarity as well. But my argument is that it is not propelled by the vigour of great comedy, by the momentum of farce. The fate of Oedipus is a dirty joke. The stubbornness of Lear and the jealousy of Othello are comic. But in modern tragedy there is no room for that reversal of laughter and outrage that brings clear and fluent weeping. Pathos touches, tragedy moves. And it may not be possible to achieve great tragedy without that participation which comedy supplies since there is no such thing as half-hearted laughter; since the headlong declination of a clown towards a banana is only the reverse of a tragic fall.

Prose is generally the medium of comedy and of farce with its reversal of reason and order, the deflating of syntax itself. And those alternating scenes of comedy and drama used by Elizabethan playwrights were used to mock, undermine order – in *Henry IV* and *Lear*, to make the metre of the verse, the metre of rule and order crumble indistinguishably so that the prose of *Henry IV* is greater than the bulk of its verse, and the prose of *Lear* is indistinguishable metrically from its verse.

But the basis is vulgar, popular and shared. The dark, locked rooms of modern theatres encourage, with their amplification and intimacy, the idea of the eye as camera, the ear as microphone, the eavesdropping on whispers, our own hesitation, as audience, in violating privacy. It may be absurd to another audience, non-European – Asian for example – not to want to mind other people's business as it works itself out through the panel of the proscenium arch. We buy tickets and feel like privileged voyeurs. Brecht wanted an audience who would talk in the theatre while the play went on; not one that had to eavesdrop in utter silence. Not one that in the chiaroscuro of Rembrandt lighting is invited to confuse their own lives with that of the one allegedly on stage. Not only not to confuse it but to reject it as reality.

[...]

The point I am going after here is that the metre of tragic exchange in the modern theatre is not an academic or nostalgic question but one that has been demonstrated in a naturalistic context; in a sound no different from prose playwrights and with that unity of verse that audibly demonstrates symmetry. We admire the shape of 'Purgatory' as much as we admire its language. We see hovering over its speed, a meteoric arc. Both plays, that is Eliot's *Sweeney*, and Yeats's *Purgatory*, are based on dialect, of course, but not in prose.

[...] The diction in modern poetry in English – that is the private voice, the lyric or narrative poem in England and America – has created a power peculiar to our epoch: a massive advance in verse, equal in tone if not in vocabulary to the Elizabethan – and perhaps going beyond them even in metre, in verse, to a splendid colloquiality:

If it form the one landscape that we, the inconstant ones,
    Are consistently homesick for, this is chiefly
Because it dissolves in water.
                    W.H. Auden

I sat on the Dogona's steps
for the gondolas cost too much that year
                    Ezra Pound

The salesman is an 'it' that stinks. Excuse me.
                    e.e. cummings

I caught a tremendous fish
                            Elizabeth Bishop

Especially when the October wind
                            Dylan Thomas

I sit in one of the dives
                            W.H. Auden

I have met them at the close of day
                            W.B. Yeats

That Whitsun I was late getting away
                            Philip Larkin

These first lines, springing from memory at random vindicate an argument, which is that an immediacy of tone – the tone of dramatic conversation which can vary in pitch from that of a professor as in Auden, to a middle-class employee, as in Larkin, an amateur fisherman as in Bishop, a traveller in Pound; and the others, from Dylan Thomas, e.e. cummings – is dramatic, and by dramatic I mean theatrical, that is they are tonally speakable. They can be said by actors. Here is Auden's brilliant flattering mono-loguist – and by flattering I mean that Auden's brilliance flatters the listener into making us believe that we share his intelligence. It is a tone, deliberate tone, of a benign, didactic, perhaps even boring, don. If it form the one landscape that we the inconstant ones are consistently homesick for, that is chiefly because it dissolves in water. Huh? Oh sure. Yeah. Right.

   [...]

We notice that only in extremities of insanity and a funeral is any metrical – by which again I mean verse – is a memorable tragic line attempted, by which I mean a reaching for memory, for emblematic summary in measured – in fact, interchangeable – rhythms. The lines are like subtitles over the proscenium arch. They glow like neon instructions. And of course they come at the end. They are poetic tragedies written in the rhythms of what is called day-to-day prose: the familiar, the identifiable, the ordinary. But at their highest tragic moments, the prose not only yearns for poetry, but attempts to become it. But trapped in its own familiarity, its ordinariness, it moves towards a kind of heraldic music – towards scansion; in other words toward verse.

On the other hand poetry begins just where these modern tragedies end, so that if one began, not as a flashback, as a beginning – if one began *A Streetcar Named Desire* with 'I have always depended on the kindness of strangers', as a poem might begin, our question would be 'Why? Why have you always depended on the kindness of strangers?' [...]

From the Poetry Book Society's Ronald Duncan Lecture at the Purcell Room, the South Bank Centre, on 29 September 1990.

& *from* Truly, Deeply, Sonorously
E.A. Markham

A book on the art of Derek Walcott is very welcome. Much has been written about aspects of Walcott (the *Select Bibliography* lists twelve interviews with and eleven essays written by the author as well as just under one hundred and fifty 'books and essays on Walcott or substantially referring to his work'). And the work continues to be compelling. So we feel ready for an attempt to bring it all together. There is a need to show how his explorations in various genres have informed one another, and how he brings technical resources to match imaginative risk. There have been essays, naturally, that hint at these things, that tantalize us, and it's very good to see Mervyn Morris, Edward Baugh and other old friends, with an ability to deliver on Walcott, lined up in the Table of Contents.

Though, we can't ignore a careless bit of packaging of the artist: the back cover reproduces the tired line that Walcott is the greatest

living (Rushdie) and best (Brodsky) English language poet today.
We don't doubt this, particularly; we've long agreed with the
Robert Graves observation (was it made in 1964?) that Walcott's
use of English put him, in effect, at the head of the class. But you
must sometimes be vigilant of praise coming from certain quar-
ters. And I'm sure that Seamus Heaney means no malice (I pursue
this because the point is taken up by Mervyn Morris in his essay
on *The Fortunate Traveller*, and the Heaney quote comes from
Morris) when he says: 'Walcott possesses English more deeply and
sonorously than most of the English themselves'. Deep and
sonorous? We might be talking of our favourite Welsh male voice
choir of the sixties. Or the timbre of an actor's voice! Of two other
critics on the subject quoted by Morris, Dennis Donoghue... finds
some 'gorgeous poems' in *The Fortunate Traveller*, but finds, also,
that Walcott's standard English style is 'dangerously high for
nearly every purpose except that of Jacobean tragedy'. And finally,
James Atlas (commenting on Donoghue) tells us that 'the paradox
of a colonial identity is that it both liberates and oppresses, offering
freedom from a dominating tradition, yet robbing the poet of any
natural claim on the language'. And that's the reason, he says, why
Walcott doesn't share the conviction (with other poets and
readers) that eloquence is no longer possible. (Does either the
Tony Harrison of *V* or the John Ashbery of *Flow Chart* know that
eloquence is no longer possible?) Does Walcott really feel, despite
all he's said to the contrary, that he's got no natural claim to the
language? Does he still need to be 'praised' for writing well in
English?

In his Introduction Stewart Brown rightly seeks to locate
Walcott in his Caribbean cultural context while not denying that
'his is the extraordinary achievement of an extraordinary man'.
Brown takes us through Walcott's long 'Apprenticeship' (*Twenty-
five Poems, Epitaph for the Young, Poems* and *In a Green Night*
(1948–62)) where he absorbed influences from the world of poetry.
What's surprising here, perhaps, was the range of influence – from
Europe, ancient and modern, from Britain and Ireland, and from
the Americas. What's more he made no apology for this. Looking
back, in 1980, Walcott was to say:

> Young poets should have no individuality. They should be total
> apprentices, if they want to be masters. If you get a chance to
> paint a knuckle on a painting by Leonardo then you say 'Thank
> God!' and you just paint a knuckle as well as you can.

What's pleasing here is the lack of defensiveness about learning
your trade. Note, also, that poetry isn't the only art form for the
poet to learn from. This might be one pointer to the scale of
Walcott's ambition – no juvenile notions that originality consists
in demonstrating surface *difference*. This brings to mind an
Anthony Burgess aside – he was writing about the novel – that all
original works of art represent the end of a creative phase rather
than a beginning. Imagine Walcott knowing that in his teens!

[...]

The Art of Derek Walcott, edited by Stewart Brown (Seren).

& *from* Terry Eagleton in conversation with James Wood

[...]

JAMES WOOD *As well as writing books of critical theory, you review poetry in
London papers and in journals such as this one. But these languages – the theo-
retical and the journalistic – are very different. You've spent much of your career,
for instance, poking fun at the easy assumptions and amateurishness of journal-
istic, or 'liberal humanist' critical language. What do you have to suspend,
politically or intellectually or theoretically, in order to review poetry, and what
does this suspension mean for the status of your theory?*

TERRY EAGLETON I'm aware that my poetry reviewing and my theoret-
ical work don't often go together. There are some practical reasons for
this – space and so on. But I think your point is fair, and I think the most
searching test of my political and theoretical position would probably lie
in poetry. After all, Marxism shouldn't always be given an easy ride by
working on Mrs Gaskell or Balzac.

PR 82:1, 1992

I've always tried to write in a variety of voices – I've roughly alternated a heavy theoretical with a more popular work. There's, to my mind, a shameful reluctance to try and compromise on the part of radical critics and theorists. There are those who think that any popularization is bound to be vulgarization. That I very much reject...

JAMES WOOD   *But my point was that, in fact, your poetry reviews are not a popularization of your critical position so much as an evasion – something entirely different. When you review, you use an aesthetic of which much contemporary theory, your own included, is dismissive: you have to use the old fashioned, consensual terms such as realistic/unrealistic, coherent/incoherent, and so on. You have to say if you think a poem 'works' or not, you have to evaluate, to judge something as successful or unsuccessful...*

TERRY EAGLETON   Well, I think it's almost *ultra-leftist* of you to imagine that a Marxist critic would share no language in common with others – we do! And as far as the value question is involved, I've never had a problem with that. I think that there was a time in the seventies and early eighties – the high point of a certain kind of theory – when the value question was put in brackets. But I think that's changed. Evaluation, after all, is part of social existence, and there's no reason why literary evaluation shouldn't be part of that. The question is: what are the conditions for evaluation, what are the grounds? That is a properly theoretical issue of some difficulty, and it's not one you can properly pursue in a short review. So yes, one has to suspend something. One makes the standard adjudications, within, more or less, the standard terms, but in the corner of one's mind one is questioning those very terms and foundations.

JAMES WOOD   *One aspect of this poetry and theory dilemma that interests me is this: at various moments in the literary history of this century, one can see that poetry and fairly specialized, poetry-based criticism have needed each other. In the twenties, I.A. Richards working on T.S. Eliot poems, and Eliot, in several places, quoting Richards; in the forties and fifties, the New Criticism working on poems that were being written with precisely this kind of criticism in mind. There was a mutuality. But poetry and theory seem further apart today than they have ever been.*

TERRY EAGLETON   Maybe fiction and theory are a bit closer. Theory and poetry are very far apart, and one might say that they were constituted to be so. Poetry as we have it, as a *category*, was actually constituted to exclude the political, the discursive, the analytical, and so on. I've always found the people most resistant to theory to be poets – jealously guarding their interiority, which is not be invaded or violated by concepts. I was once in the unenviable position of being, with Fredric Jameson, the only theorist at a conference of some three hundred poets in the States, and we were nearly lynched... As long as poetry goes on being defined as the sensuous particular then you set it up from the outset as something that excludes theory. I think there is the fear on the part of poets that theory is soulless, and there's a seed of truth in that. Theory has a necessary soullessness about it, because of its particular rigorous operations, its particular strategies. But as far as I'm concerned the business of theory is to be soulless about matters which in the end are very soulful.

JAMES WOOD *Why should a poet be interested in theory? What does it have to offer the poet?*

TERRY EAGLETON I always think here of the relationship between the Russian formalists and poets like Mayakovsky, where for a very interesting, if ephemeral historical moment, you had an actual two-way traffic. For a moment, the critic saw himself in a kind of linguistic laboratory which could then serve the practitioner; and later, there was Brecht as artist and Walter Benjamin as critical theorist. Of course, you could say that there were urgent political reasons why that relation should be established. Our political situation is very different. An analogy might be less between poetry and theory than between poetry and politics – treating politics as a theory of abstraction, of enquiry, a sceptical and systemizing discourse, yet one which also is about the deepest realities, as I think the best Marxist criticism is. Rephrase the question and ask what a Heaney or a Mahon can learn from political debate. The answer is a hell of a lot, and they have. Not that it necessarily enters directly into the poetry, but it provides a continuous subtext.

JAMES WOOD *Perhaps we might turn to something that particularly interests me. As you well know, criticism, in the last sixty years, has been busily building itself up as a pseudo-science. Each new development is hailed as a tightening of the available critical language, as a new rigour, a new closeness to the text. Marxist and contemporary post-structuralist theory is notorious in this respect – the word 'rigorous' is never off its lips. Your own work, at various points, has proposed a new 'science' of reading the text. The goal seems to be a clearer way of seeing the text, a new proximity, as the old, vague, amateurish ways are thrown off. Often, the old critical terms are seen as mere metaphors masquerading as precision tools. The theorist's first job is to 'demystify' these metaphors, to strip them of their woolly camouflage. All this is fine, except that, paradoxically, theory, with its jargon and specialized terms, is as metaphorical as the old crit-icism! The jargon of contemporary theory seems precise and transparently close to the text only to its own supporters. You speak, in fact, a private, highly metaphorical language, full of 'sites', 'strategies', 'ruptures', 'binarisms', and so on. Does this language really represent a greater precision ?*

TERRY EAGLETON   If there's a broad sense in which all language is metaphorical, then theory is too – it's no criticism of theory to say it's metaphorical within these terms. But I take your point: there is in oper-ation a kind of excessively impressionistic critical language. But there are several things to say here. One is that theory relies on a set of fundamental metaphors – it is always saying 'this is like that'. Another is that there are all kinds of theories, some of which are deliberately 'poetic' and ludic (Derrida is an example), and others which are closer to the text and more transparent. Don't forget also that one of the important questions that theory asks itself is precisely what is the relation between the critical language and the language of the text. If we've got beyond the idea, as I think that we have, that the critical language is just a reflection of the text, or a simple and 'innocent' writing large of the text, then we have to find some way of describing this relationship.

JAMES WOOD   *But often, I have to say, I don't feel that the language of theory is exploring this relationship so much as surrendering to it. I find this particu-larly acute when reading theory on poetry, where one often feels that the old practical criticism, honed now for nearly eighty years, is the best available expli-cator, the best model. I'm thinking, for instance, of Auden's comment that Christopher Ricks was 'exactly the kind of critic every poet dreams of finding'. Could Auden, were he alive, say that about a post-structuralist theorist?*

TERRY EAGLETON   No, probably not. I agree with most of what you say. I wouldn't want to write off practical criticism or close reading of poetry dogmatically. How could one, when confronted with a close reader of, say, Empson's distinction and flexibility? Even the mandarin Paul De Man, towards the end of his life, was talking about how his early, old-fashioned practical criticism classes had shown him things about the working of texts. But I think there is a question of what 'closeness to the text' means. You are talking about a very obvious closeness, and to that extent, all theorists would want to say that they are close readers. What they would want to add, however, is that there are other kinds of close-ness. What is 'closeness'? A meticulous analysis of a particular metaphor, or a very rich understanding of a text's ideological context? Perhaps to talk about 'illuminating' a text is better than talking about 'closeness' – this gives better a sense of lighting up the text from different angles, from behind and underneath and against, as it were, not just face-on.

JAMES WOOD   *Perhaps we could talk for a moment about the vexed question of intention in the literary work. It seems to me that Marxist literary theory, and the post-structuralist theory that has learned so much from it, refuses to talk about intention not because it doesn't exist, but because it's inconvenient. For Marxism, there is power and ideology. Now it seems to me that ideological institutions, structures of power, contradict themselves rather often. The supposedly establishment Oxford University, for instance, has just appointed a bloodthirsty Marxist to be its next Warton Professor of English... I would suggest that such institutions purposefully, intentionally contradict themselves. But Marxism always presents such contradictions as a mere by-product of the status quo endlessly perpetuating itself. In other words, Oxford appoints a Marxist as a professor not because it really wants to, but because ideology as a system, straining to exclude such contradiction from itself, produces such contradictions anyway. It can't help it. Marxist theory approaches the text in the same way: if* The Tempest *is politically radical in places (Caliban's protests at injustice, and so on) this is not because Shakespeare actually intended such a thing, but because it is in the nature of ideology, as broken up by narrative, to produce occasional contradictions. Indeed, it is the theorist's task to seek out these contradictions. The critic reads the text against itself, but the text is still, basically conservative. The text, in the end, is with the ruling classes.*

TERRY EAGLETON   Well, institutions do have intentions – clearly. But these intentions are never pure – they go in a number of different ways. There can be a fissured intentionality: one which is not entirely at one with itself, producing multiple aims. When you talk about *The Tempest,* one can talk about Shakespeare's intentions, but one can also talk about the intentions of *The Tempest* – not seeing it as a given structure, nor reducing it to Shakespeare's head. But then the deconstructive point would be that a text's projects are not self-identical, and this is how contradictions arrive.

JAMES WOOD   *I feel that this re-inscribing of intention at the level of the text – talking about* The Tempest *having intentions – is useful, obviously. It takes proper cognizance of the way texts have their own lives, of the way words have their own weight, independent of a writer's intentions, in a language. But I do think that when intention is politicized, it becomes a way of evading something – a way of evading the fact that people have good intentions, a way of evading the notion of innocent intention. Take Oxford, for instance. Why not accept 'pure' and 'good' intentions, rather than talking about fissured intention and so on?*

TERRY EAGLETON   This is an ethical point?

JAMES WOOD   *Yes, I suppose it is.*

TERRY EAGLETON   Hmmm... (Pause) The ruling class is full of good intentions! (Laughs) I don't think that Marxism has ever doubted that. Actually, it starts from that position – where you talk about justice, equality and so on, we're not impugning your motives, we're asking why the hell this is never realized. Otherwise, you'd end up with the most cynical conspiracy theories. One has to assume a well-intentioned trajectory which gets systematically blocked.

JAMES WOOD   *But surely this doesn't apply to literature, does it?*

TERRY EAGLETON   What would it mean to talk about a writer having good intentions?

JAMES WOOD   *Politically, it would mean to talk about a writer's 'good' political intentions, i.e. radicalism rather than conservatism. But good is defined here as precisely that intention or quality which the Marxist critic won't believe in. Shakespeare's radicalism, for instance.*

TERRY EAGLETON   Clearly, one doesn't want to erase intentionality, because this would lead to enormous problems with the literature of commitment – Brecht and so on. These people had 'good' intentions.

JAMES WOOD   *In the commonsense world in which you review poetry or see a film, don't you regularly invoke the idea of a maker's intention? You say: 'This doesn't work. I can see what he or she is trying to do (i.e. intending) but it isn't successful.'*

TERRY EAGLETON   But why can't one say: 'I can see what the poem is trying to do, but it fails'? This lets the poem have its own life.

JAMES WOOD   *I don't see how this is especially helpful. Can't one have as complex a notion of, say Tom Paulin, as of one of his poems?*

TERRY EAGLETON   When I review a book of poems by Paulin, I haven't got a clue what Paulin is trying to do. I really haven't. I don't find myself asking what this person called Tom Paulin is trying to do. I find myself looking at a text.

JAMES WOOD *But the text reveals, in complex ways obviously, Paulin's intentions. The text did not write this poem, Paulin did. When you review a new book of Heaney's, for instance, you have certain intentions and aims set down in print by Heaney – in interviews, in critical prose and so on. And you may well use those expressed intentions.*

TERRY EAGLETON Yes, I agree, but then the text itself will reform Heaney's intentions.

JAMES WOOD Yes, *but not so absolutely that Heaney's intentions aren't important anymore, not so completely that Heaney just drops out of the picture, and suddenly, only the text is granted intentions.*

TERRY EAGLETON Well, to de-centre the subject, the author, is not to eradicate it.

[…]

56 On Not Remembering Some Lines of a Song
Ciaran Carson

It's the pawl-and-ratchet mechanism
Of one of those antique, whirligig-type, wooden rattles, only
Some of the teeth are missing. Or there's fluff
On the needle of the pick-up, and bursts of steam –
Ampersands, asterisks and glottal stops – puff round
The words, like those signals in the distance
That announce the almost-imminent arrival
Of the train which everyone had given up for lost.

If I'd been you, I wouldn't have started
Off from here, the anxious tourist was informed. He'd come
Prepared for rain, but dusk was streaming

PR 81:2, 1991

Down on the little station, on
His orange oilskins. Over and above the musk
Of creosote and hawthorn, he could just make out
The pipe bands struggling homewards, the skirts
Of clouds obscured by twilit music.

That windblown, martial girn and drone reminded me
I came from the wrong side of the tracks.
The criss-cross meaning of their Black Watch tartan
Was a mystery to me, and I could never fathom
How they synchronized
The swing of their hips, kilts waving like a regiment
Of window-wipers, so the drizzle doesn't fog
Their automatic pilot.

It's coming back in dribs and drabs, for nothing ever
Is forgotten: it's in there somewhere in the memory-bank,
Glimmering in binary notation. I think you have to find
That switch between the *off* and *on*, the split chink
Through which you peer with half an eye
And glimpse the other, time-drenched world.
A jitter of fragmented bird-song, in which the microtones
Are birds, twittering between the staves.

And the demarcation lines of white tape
Drifted into side-streets, tangled up with children's skipping –
Ropes, the hide-and-seek of counting-rhymes.
Evening draws in like a hyphen: the parade
Had ended hours ago
And the Sabbath quiet of that Monday
Had been long implicit in the festival agenda
As the marchers learned to walk again by rote.

The regalia were consigned to the future blue
Where a fancy skywriter lets the message bloom and fluff
And then dissolve before our eyes
Until everything is indecipherable, the blown wisps

Of letters becoming an 'acoustic perfume'. And
The slogan was so perfect, so much
In tune with television jingles, that it seemed to breathe
From everybody's mouths

As if freshly minted there, this squeezed-out root of toothpaste
That bears the tang of aromatic speech. It oozes
From the floodlit shrubbery
Where gypsy moths are whirling in commemorative World War I
Camouflage, describing Celtic dogfights, loop-
The loops and tangents. For everything blooms out of season:
Surely the children had anticipated all of this, these frosty nights
As they chanted stories from the gabbled alphabet of stars.

57 Phrase Book
Jo Shapcott

I'm standing here inside my skin,
which will do for a Human Remains Pouch
for the moment. Look down there (up here).
Quickly. Slowly. This is my own front room

where I'm lost in the action, live from a war,
on screen. I am an Englishwoman, I don't understand you.
What's the matter? You are right. You are wrong.
Things are going well (badly). Am I disturbing you?

PR 82:2, 1992

TV is showing bliss as taught to pilots:
Blend, Low silhouette, Irregular shape, Small,
Secluded. (Please write it down. Please speak slowly.)
Bliss is how it was in this very room

when I raised my body to his mouth,
when he even balanced me in the air,
or at least I thought so and yes the pilots say
yes they have caught it through the Side-Looking

Airborne Radar, and through the J-Stars.
I am expecting a gentleman (a young gentleman,
two gentlemen, some gentlemen). Please send him
(them) up at once. This is really beautiful.

Yes, they have seen us, the pilots, in the Kill Box
on their screens, and played the routine for
getting us Stealthed, that is, Cleansed, to you and me,
Taken Out. They know how to move into a single room

like that, to send in with Pinpoint Accuracy, a hundred Harms.
I have two cases and a cardboard box. There is another
bag there. I cannot open my case – look out
the lock is broken. Have I done enough?

Bliss the pilots say is for evasion
and escape. What's love in all this debris?
Just one person pounding another into dust,
into dust. I do not know the word for it yet.

Where is the British Consulate? Please explain.
What does it mean? What must I do? Where
can I find? What have I done? I have done
nothing. Let me pass please. I am an Englishwoman.

58

All Souls' Night
R.S. Thomas

Outside a surfeit of 'planes.
Inside the hunger of the departed
to come back. 'Ah, erstwhile humans
would you make your mistakes
over again? In life, as in love,
the second time round is
no better.'
                    I confront their expressions
in the embers, on grey walls:
faces among the stones watching
me to see if this night
of all nights I will make sacrifice
to the spirits of hearth and of
roof-tree, pouring a libation.

'Stay where you are' I implore.
'This is no world for escaped beings
to make their way back into.
The well that you took your pails
to is polluted. At the centre
of the mind's labyrinth the machine howls
for the sacrifice of the affections;
vocabulary has on a soft collar
but the tamed words are not to be trusted.
As long as the flames hum, making
their honey, better to look in
upon truth's comb than to
take off as we do upon fixed wings
for depollinated horizons.'

PR 83:2, 1993

59
After Marina Tsvetaeva

A Word Before Sleep
Wendy Cope

Life tells us lies, inimitably,
Beyond all expectations, outdoing other liars.
You know, when all your veins are trembling,
You recognise it – life!

It is as if you're lying in a field of rye,
In ringing blueness, falling heat (and so what if it's lies
You're lying in), the sound of bees through honeysuckle.
Rejoice. You have been called.

No, don't reproach me, my dear friend –
Our souls are easily bewitched.
Already, now, my head is entering a dream.
Why did you sing?

Your quietnesses are a clean, white book,
Your 'yeses', savage clay.
I bend my head towards them, quietly.
The palm of my hand – life.

8 June 1922

Translated from a poem by Marina Tsvetaeva, using a literal translation from
Russian by Gerard Smith. Tsvetaeva composed this after reading Boris
Pasternak's book *My Sister Life*. Later she wrote to him: 'It was summer then, and
I had my own balcony in Berlin. Stones, heat, your green book on my knee (I am
sitting on the floor) – at that time I lived by it for ten days.'

In Praise of Aphrodite
Kathleen Jamie

These are wicked days. The very gods
are brought low, folding their wings
like gulls or cushie-doos

white and rain-grey. No honeyed quaich
transforms your sweat;
your low mouth's crowded

where kingdoms flutter,
stoop, take sup from your hands,
your breasts rounded as clouds.

Every flower of the cliff,
saxifrage, thrift, witch-wife:
shows your face. Your body of stone

rising, always rising armless
from the foam, whence we crawl
through salt, sweat, the white spume.

23 October 1921

Quaich: a shallow, two-handled cup.

60
Gwyneth Lewis
The Hedge

With hindsight, of course, I can see that the hedge
was never my cleverest idea
and that bottles of vodka are better not wedged

like fruit in its branches, to counter the fears
and the shakes in the morning on the way to work.
Looking back, I can see how I pushed it too far

when I'd stop in the lay-by for a little lurk
before plunging my torso in, shoulder high
to the hedgerow's merciful root-and-branch murk

till I'd felt out my flattie and could drink in the dry
and regain my composure with the cuckoo-spit.
Then, with growing wonder, I'd watch the fungi,

lovely as coral in the aqueous light.
Lovely, that is, till that terrible day
when the hedge was empty. Weakened by fright

I leant in much deeper to feel out which way
the bottle had rolled and, cursing my luck
(and hearing already what my bosses would say

about my being caught in this rural ruck)
I started to panic, so I tussled and heaved
and tried to stand upright, but found I was stuck.

I struggled still harder, but you'd scarcely believe
the strength in a hedge that has set its mind
on holding a person in its vice of leaves

PR 83:2, 1993

and this one was proving a real bind.
With a massive effort, I took the full strain
and tore up the hedgerow, which I flicked up behind

me, heavy and formal as a wedding train.
I turned and saw, to my embarrassment,
that I'd pulled up a county with my new-found mane,

which was still round my shoulders, with its telltale scent
of loam and detritus, while trunk roads and streams
hung off me like ribbons. It felt magnificent:

minerals hidden in unworked seams
shone like silver in my churned up trail.
I had brooches of newly built housing schemes

and sequins of coruscating shale;
power lines crackled as they changed their course
and woodsmoke covered my face like a veil.

Only then did I feel the first pangs of remorse.
Still, nobody'd noticed so, quickly, I knelt
took hold of the landscape, folded and forced

it up to a chignon which I tied with my belt.
It stayed there, precarious. The occasional spray
of blackthorn worked loose, but I quickly rebuilt

the ropey construction and tucked it away.
Since then I've become quite hard to approach:
I chew mints to cover the smell of decay

which is with me always. Food tastes of beech
and I find that I have to concentrate
on just holding the hairstyle since it's started to itch

and the people inside it are restless of late.
Still, my tresses have won me a kind of renown
for flair and I find my hair titillates

certain men who want me to take it down
in front of them, slowly. But with deepening dread
I'm watching my old self being overgrown

while scruples rustle like quadrupeds,
stoat-eyed, sharp-toothed in my tangled roots
(it's so hard to be human with a hedge on your head!).

Watch me. Any day now I'll be bearing fruit,
sweet hips that glint like pinpricks of blood
and my dry land drowning will look quite cute

to those who've never fallen foul of wood.
But on bad days now I see nothing but hedge,
my world crazed by the branches of should,

for I've lost all centre, have become an edge
and though I wear my pearls like dew
I feel that I've paid for my sacrilege

as I wish for my autumn with its broader view.
But for now I submit. With me it will die,
this narrowness, this slowly closing eye.

61

Mrs Aesop
Carol Ann Duffy

By Christ, he could bore for Purgatory. He was small,
didn't prepossess. So he tried to impress. *Dead men,*
Mrs Aesop, he'd say, *tell no tales.* Well, let me tell you now
that the bird in his hand shat on his sleeve,
never mind the two worth less in the bush. Tedious.

Going out was worst. He'd stand at our gate, look, then leap;
scour the hedgerows for a shy mouse, the fields
for a sly fox, the sky for one particular swallow
that couldn't make a summer. The jackdaw, according to him,
envied the eagle. Donkeys would, on the whole, prefer to be lions.

On one appalling evening stroll, we passed an old hare
snoozing in a ditch – he stopped and made a note –
and then, about a mile further on, a tortoise, somebody's pet,
creeping, slow as marriage, up the road. *Slow*
but certain, Mrs Aesop, wins the race. Asshole.

What race? What sour grapes? What silk purse,
sow's ear, dog in the manger, what big fish? Some days
I could barely keep awake as the story droned on
towards the moral of itself. *Action, Mrs A., speaks louder*
than words. And that's another thing, the sex

was diabolical. I gave him a fable one night
about a little cock that wouldn't crow, a razor-sharp axe
with a heart blacker than the pot that called the kettle.
I'll cut off your tail, all right, I said, *to save my face.*
That shut him up. I laughed last, longest.

PR 84:3, 1994

&   *from* **Storm Warnings:**
     Adrienne Rich in conversation with Sarah Maguire

[…]

Women poets of my generation are all writing in the wake of Adrienne Rich, consciously or not, simply because she's changed our agenda, extended our paradigms; just as we are all writing in the wake of feminism, whatever our politics; it's the *Zeitgeist* we can't breathe outside. What Adrienne Rich has done for us, particularly in her early essays such as 'When We Dead Awaken: Writing as Re-Vision' published in 1971, is to address the issues of how it is possible to be a woman and a poet without being viewed as exceptional, as a surrogate man. Never before have so many women been writing – and publishing – so much poetry as they are nowadays (just think what it was like merely a decade ago). […]

In May [1994] she came over to London to promote her new book of essays, *What is Found There: Notebooks on Poetry and Politics*, through an extensive reading tour. We spent two hours talking together, focusing largely on the shifts her poetry has undergone during her long and distinguished career.

[…]

Of her second book, *The Diamond Cutters*, Adrienne Rich said, 'It's a very bad book for the most part I think – it feels very derivative to me and like a tremendous effort. A lot of that had to do with this first manuscript being chosen by Auden and published by the Yale University Press. I had no idea what to do with that. It was an identity I couldn't grasp – that of published poet. I thought of myself still as an apprentice poet – and I was – and I should have been. Then at that point I married, and my first child was born when the second book was in proof. This has something to do with both the cautiousness of that book, and the fact that I realised that I had to break out of this formal mode of doing things. Life had gotten really messy and anarchic. Domesticity never seemed safe to me – it seemed very dangerous!'

It took Adrienne Rich eight years to find a way of getting out of the mode of writing which characterises these first two books – a period in which she gave birth to three sons (in 1955, '57 and '59). As she said, 'When you really aren't getting enough sleep, creativity suffers. However, I did write during those years. I would get up in the middle of the night with a child and write a few lines, so I ended up with all these scraps, and that was what eventually I realised was the long poem called "Snapshots of a Daughter-in-Law". I began to see the possibility that what I had were not just fragments, but that they were the fragments of something bigger. Then finally I remember numbering them, as if they belonged to something larger.

'By then I was reading a lot of poets whom I had not read, or whom I hadn't read attentively before, such as William Carlos Williams. I had met Denise Levertov, which was a very important connection for me to make because she was entirely involved with the Black Mountain poets, with Creeley and Duncan and Olson and others, and she was also a woman, and she was also the mother of a son, in a marriage – and so this was like a tremendous opening up of possibilities for me, I mean just that combination. In a certain way we were both token women in our different poetic geographies but we of course didn't realise that at the time! But we did talk about what it was like to have a child and to try to write.

'Until the book *Snapshots of a Daughter-in-Law* came out [in 1963] I had been rather a darling of the poetry reviewers and had been doing just nicely; but then there were grumbles and remarks about my having sacrificed beauty, about the jaggedness of the lines, about my abandonment of music. (Although, of course, I don't think I've ever abandoned music – it's a different music, a more complex music. I much prefer the longer line, the looseness of it. I think it's more difficult. You can write iambic pentameters endlessly and, at least in sound, go on repeating yourself. I think that's why people like Williams wanted to smash the iamb: they felt this confinement was deleterious to poetry.) But when *Snapshots* came out, the same critics who had loved me were not so sure – they slapped my wrists and said that I should go back to what I did so beautifully. That was very disconcerting. And what was more disconcerting was they accused me of being political – which I had no idea I was being! And of being at the same time too personal. It was the poem "Snapshots of a Daughter in Law" that was seen as personal and bitter. I was working in a certain sense unconsciously in that book. I was doing what I felt I had to do. And so I had to go back and think, "What am I doing here?"

'I think it's notable that, although in a lot of the poems in *Necessities of Life* [published in 1966] I went on doing certain similar things [to the work in *Snapshots*], those poems are much more obliquely personal, and a lot of them are about death. I really was thinking, "I can't go back to what I used to do; if what I'm doing now, and feel I must do, is increasingly going to alienate me as a poet, then what do I have?" I felt very despairing during the time those poems were written.'

I asked Adrienne Rich what her relationship with Robert Lowell was during that time. 'I had already begun to feel the necessity to write differently, to write a different kind of poem when *Life Studies* came out [in 1959] so the book seemed to me to be further confirmation of that. At the time I had material which was personal, which in no way was I going to put into poems directly in the way that Lowell was putting his own private life into poetry. But the *structure* of some of those poems was what I was able to get a lot from. It was the combination of personal life with the historical sense, that was the thing that was very, very important to me about Lowell.'

I also asked Adrienne Rich about her contact with Sylvia Plath who, for years, secretly regarded Rich as her 'arch-rival', the woman poet whom she most admired – and envied for her talent and success.

'Sylvia was always very nice to me. I didn't have the feeling that she was jealous of me. Of course, at that point everyone saw Ted as The Poet. We all knew that she was writing poetry, but his book *The Hawk in the Rain* had just come out in the States. I must have seen some of her poetry written after she came back here in little magazines or anthologies. But it wasn't until after her death when the posthumous work was published in the States that anyone seemed to have any idea of her significance. It was a shock. I remember Lowell taking me out to lunch and he was armed with this copy of *Encounter* and there was a whole bunch of her posthumous work in there including some of the bee poems – and they were absolutely dazzling.

'I was teaching by then [the mid-sixties] and I was running into women students who were cultists of Plath who assumed that the poetry drew its energy from the destructive urge. I kept trying to say in this flattening way that when someone has a gift for language like that it can be applied to any kind of experience. The fact that some of these poems seemed to be pointing toward death doesn't mean that they couldn't point in other directions had other things been different. The energy in that poetry is incredible. Sylvia Plath is not a confessional poet. That term has done so much to diminish poetry in a certain way and to diminish some of the most striking and promising poetry too, because it's like you name it and you kill it – you drive a pin through the butterfly as you name it.

'I'm not crazy about this term postmodernism because it seems to me to mean too many things to too many people at this point (rather like feminism!) but in a way her poetry seems to me to be a kind of postmodern breakthrough. I think that it's very quintessentially a woman's poetry with a lot of female physicality in it. It's unabashedly in a woman's voice. You never feel that she's trying to sound like an honorary man and at the same time it has a kind of impersonality too. Something in the poetry is held.'

[…]

& *from* Sylvia Plath's Word Games
Anne Stevenson

[…]

I was first alerted to the amount of T.S. Eliot Plath incorporated into her writing by a not-very-complimentary review. *Bitter Fame*, wrote the reviewer, culpably failed to connect an abandoned title for Plath's first book of poems with Eliot's *Ash Wednesday*. True enough, 'The Devil of the Stairs' comes from part III of Eliot's poem: 'At the first turning of the second stair / I turned and saw below / The same shape twisted on the banister / Under the vapour in the fetid air / Struggling with the devil of the stairs…'

At around the same time (1958–9) Plath also considered borrowing a phrase from Eliot's *Four Quartets* and using it as the title of a short story. The story was finally called 'The Daughters of Blossom Street'. 'The Earth Our Hospital', however, initially struck the author as appropriate – taken from Eliot's lyric for Good Friday (*East Coker* part IV): 'The whole earth is our hospital / Endowed by the ruined millionaire' Since 'million-aire' crops up in 'Stopped Dead' as well as (rather exaggeratedly) in a good many of Plath's letters and journals, it is possible that Eliot helped to furnish her mind with the word – along with other Plathic familiars: the surgeon, the nurse, Adam, metal wires (nerves), fever, roses, flames and the Eucharistic blood and flesh of Eliot's hymn. Very likely Sylvia Plath knew part IV of *East Coker* by heart.

In it, Eliot's 'wounded surgeon', a figure of Christ, operates on the body of Christainity lying 'distempered' under his 'bleeding hands'. The second stanza introduces a 'a dying nurse' whose care it is to keep Christianity's disease instrumental to its health, reminding us of 'Adam's curse' and insisting that 'to be restored, our sickness must grow worse'. It is at this point the famous lines about 'the earth our hospital' occur, 'endowed by the ruined millionaire'– that is, by a God bankrupt in the world he created, who ordains that 'if we do well' we will die (and thus be saved) of the 'absolute paternal care' that has given us life. Finally, two paradoxical stanzas reassert the palingenetic myth at the heart of the Christian mystery. It is striking how Plath-like Eliot's succession of images is:

> The chill ascends from feet to knees,
> The *fever* sings in *mental wires*.
> If to be warmed, then I must freeze
> And quake in frigid purgatorial *fires*
> Of which the *flame is roses*, and the *smoke is briars*

Plathian words are italicised. For Plath's burning roses, see also George Macdonald's children's tale, *The Princess and the Goblin*. For briars, read hooks. Eliot continues:

> The *dripping blood* our only drink,
> The *bloody flesh* our only food...

Of course we can't single out Eliot's hymn, in its unmistakable Christian context, as the only source of Plath's imagery. Roses and – or as – flames, usually with sexual implications, run all though the Western poetic tradition, as Plath well knew. Yet, though not specifically Christian, the terms of Plath's death-and-resurrection myth hardly eschewed Christian iconography. Remember how often she had recourse to the 'Communion tablet' – even while rejecting it. If you trace the Communion wafer through her work, you soon see that it stands for a whole class of words having to do with eating (accepting) as likewise and significantly for its opposite, revulsion (rejecting). In 'Medusa', for example:

> Who do you think you are?
> A Communion wafer? Blubbery Mary?

Later, she cried out in 'Totem', 'Let us eat it like Plato's afterbirth, / Let us eat it like Christ...' (Christ, here, must be Plato's afterbirth); and, in 'Mystic', 'What is the remedy? / The pill of the Communion tablet...?'

'Adam's curse' would have been familiar to Plath from Yeats as well as Eliot – as in 'Side of green Adam' in 'Purdah'. See also 'mud... / Thick, red and slipping. It is Adam's side' in 'Getting There'. Ted Hughes says Plath knew that the name Adam means 'red earth', so it's pretty certain she consciously made a connection between the biblical reference and the blood-coloured Devon soil from which Eve/Plath in 'Getting There' is being (re)born. Indeed, there was no reason why this poet should not make use of every bit of mytho-poetical language she could lay her hands on. Eliot believed that to bring other poets back to life was one of the perennial tasks of modern criticism. Even a comparatively early poem such as 'The Stones' can be considered, in one of its aspects, as a comment on and criticism of Eliot that brings a she-Christ back to life in a questioning, perhaps even sceptical frame of reference.

> Love is the uniform of my *bald nurse*,
> [skull of the risen god/goddess]
> Love is the bone and sinew of my *curse*
> [Adam's/Eve's fall]
> The vase, reconstructed, houses
> The *elusive rose*...
> [redemption through love]
> > (my italics)

Plath, of course, was recounting her own emergence from spiritual death and purgatorial suffering. It would have been natural for her to feminise and adapt the older poet's rituals for the ceremony of her rebirth. In her last poem, 'Edge', the rose recurs, together with the bald nurse-moon, but here the flower is killed by the skull-like moon's crackling blacks (its eye-and-mouth sockets) that, despite poetry and its healing 'blood jet', are dragging the poet for ever out of the rose garden:

> She has folded
>
> Them [her children] back into her body as petals
> Of a rose close when the garden
>
> Stiffens and odors bleed
> From the sweet, deep throats of the night flower.
>
> The moon has nothing to be sad about,
> Staring from her hood of bone.
>
> She is used to this sort of thing.
> Her blacks crackle and drag.

'The Bee Meeting', too, makes undercover reference to Eliot. Here is the 'sacred grove' transformed into a garden rank with hawthorn that 'etherizes' its children (as in that famous line from 'Prufrock') followed by a passage describing ordinary neighbours and bee-keepers as ritually attired priests or celebrants. Simultaneously, they are robed patients gathered in expectation of a surgeon who will perform a vital yet almost certainly fatal operation:

> They are leading me to the shorn grove, the circle of hives
> Is it the hawthorn that smells so sick?
> The barren body of hawthorn, etherizing its children.
> Is it some operation that is taking place?
> It is the surgeon my neighbors are waiting for.
> This apparition in a green helmet,
> Shining gloves and white suit...

Ted Hughes testifies that Plath everywhere combined Eliot's sacrificial myths with those of D.H. Lawrence, whose fable 'The Man Who Died' had made a powerful impression upon her when she was at Cambridge. 'I was the woman who died', she wrote in August 1953, referring to Lawrence's resurrected, sexual Christ cum Osiris, 'and I came in touch through Sassoon [a former lover] with that flaming of life, that resolute fury of existence...'

In the pre-*Ariel* poems, Eliot's rhythm and diction tended to overlay Lawrence's thematic matter. (Though it could be argued, too, that Plath's more plaintive *Ariel*'s voice to some extent echoes Lawrence's in his last poems.) Not only did Plath in 'The Bee Meeting' snip bits from Eliot's vocabulary; she adopted, in the interrogative mood, the very syntax and sounds of 'Prufrock', mixing it with echoes from the vegetation ceremony in *East Coker*. Listen to the short i combined with s and t that spikes the rhetorical questions in 'The Bee Meeting': *is it, is it?* straight out of 'Prufrock': 'Oh, do not ask, "what is it?" / Let us go and make our visit'. Further examples of hissing noises are rife in Plath's mockery (perhaps) of Eliot's portentousness in her poem 'A Birthday Present'.

> What *is this*, behind this veil, *is it* ugly, *is it* beautiful?
> *It is* shimmering, *has it* breasts, *has it* edges?
>
> ... '*Is this* the one I am to appear for,
> *Is this* the elect one, the one with black eye-pits and a scar?'

>   (my italics)

'A Birthday Present', indeed, seems an absolute present to the feminists amongst us, who will correctly read it as an attack on the entire patriarchal tradition. Lies, lies, lies, the poem cries, like the rest of history.

How cleverly, though, Plath plays with her pastiche of Eliot's tone. I take 'it' in this poem to stand for some terrible sacrificial truth hidden in the veils of social orthodoxy (present giving). The conclusion recasts Eliot's Christian myth in Plath's characteristically iconoclastic mould. Veils and shroudings are among her recurrent images, habitual distress-signals belonging to the Plathian code.

> Only let down the veil, the veil, the veil.
> If it were death
> I would admire the deep gravity of it, its timeless eyes.
> I would know you were serious…

The way in which Plath used signs and sounds to suggest connections she liked to make with literary tradition – even when she attacked it – was brought to my attention by an English scholar, Mrs C.G. Richmond. To be fair, Mrs Richmond, not I, should be presenting a paper on Sylvia Plath's word games, for Mrs Richmond – who first studied Plath as a mature student about twenty years ago – believes that all Plath's poems were constructed according to a system encoded in their texts, a cryptic game based on Roget's *Thesaurus* that, given persistence and a gift for detection, can be discovered by any devotee patient enough to follow a trail of deliberately laid clues. I'm not sure I go along with all Mrs Richmond's ideas, but they are certainly interesting. She suggests, for instance, that Plath often used sounds to suggest names for fictional characters. Disguises for Eliot would include 'Elly Higgenbottom' and 'Elaine' in *The Bell Jar*, 'Ella Mason and her Eleven Cats', 'Ellen' in 'The Baby Sitters', 'Ellen' in the short story 'Day of Success' and 'Nellie Meehan' in the story 'All the Dead Dears'. Recurrent in Plath's writing are sounds such as *el*, *eli*, *li*, *lee*; i.e. embellish, bell, smell, delicate, sleep – all cryptograms for Eliot.

Well, perhaps. Plath did admire James Joyce, and many of her early poems are indeed cleverly executed Joycian exercises. Later poems, however, give evidence that her borrowings were more straightforward. The opening of 'Poem for a Birthday', written at Yaddo in 1959, echoes, for example, one of Eliot's 'Choruses from "The Rock"'. Here is Plath's 'Who?':

> The month of flowering's finished. The fruit's in,
> Eaten or rotten. I am all mouth.
> October's the month for storage.

And here is Eliot's second 'Chorus':

> Of all that was done in the past, you eat the fruit, either rotten or ripe.
> And the Church must be forever building, and always decaying, and
> > always being restored.

It's hard not to conclude that Plath has taken Eliot's Christian symbol
literally and used 'fruit' as a building block in her own mythology. 'All
mouth' in the same sequence we know was borrowed from Jung, while
the structural 'feel' of the poem shadows Theodore Roethke's 'The Lost
Son', which Plath read seemingly for the first time at Yaddo that autumn.

Whatever her debt to Eliot and Roethke, 'Poem for a Birthday' surely
represents Plath's first serious attempt to transmute her experience of
madness and the 'death' and 'rebirth' that followed her 1953 suicide
attempt into art. And clearly, as a work of art, the seven-part sequence
exemplifies the modernist practice of piecing together a text out of
copious borrowings from the culture's word-hoard. Plath also, of course,
added to the mix some goodly chunks of her own. Defoe's dragon-like
disease-carrying monsters of infected breath from *A Journal of the Plague
Year* become inhabitants of the vast lake of dreams Plath invokes in *Johnny
Panic and the Bible of Dreams* – and that dream lake, as Ted Hughes
confirms, was an actual nightmare Plath experienced in terrifying detail.

Sometimes Sylvia Plath's almost perfect memory got in her way. In
her Journal of 1959, for example, she complained of remembering too
much. 'Lines occur to me and stop dead: "The tiger lily's spotted throat".
And then it is an echo of Eliot's "The tiger in the tiger pit" to the syllable
and the consonance.' True enough, Eliot's 'Lines for an Old Man' begins
'The tiger in the tiger pit / Is not more irritable than I, / The whipping
tail is not more still, / Than when I smell the enemy / Writhing in the
essential blood / or dangling from the friendly tree...' Light verse?
Nevertheless, Eliot's black joke puts in a prior claim, not only for Plath's
tiger, but for the gigantic class of words she associated with blood; as also
for her (partly) Tarot-inspired hanging man, and her madness. Like all
modern poets, she confronted the aggravating, sometimes insuperable
problem of writing in a tradition in which almost every word is a hand-
me-down.

[...]

62

Four Ages
Ted Hughes

Metamorphoses, Book I

And the first age was gold.
Without laws, without law's enforcers,
This age understood and obeyed
What had created it.
Listening deeply, man kept faith with the source.

None dreaded judgement.
For no table of crimes measured out
The degrees of torture allotted
Between dismissal and death.
No plaintiff
Prayed in panic to the tyrant's puppet.
Undefended, all felt safe and were happy.

Then the great conifers
Ruffled at home on the high hills.
They had no premonition of the axe
Hurtling towards them on its parabola.
Or of the shipyards. Or of what other lands
They would glimpse from the lift of the ocean swell.
No man had crossed salt water.

Cities had not dug themselves in
Between deep moats, guarded by towers.
No sword had bitten its own
Reflection in the shield. No trumpets
Magnified the battle-cries
Of lions and bulls
Out through the mouth-holes in helmets.

Men needed no weapons.
Nations loved one another.

And the earth, unbroken by plough or by hoe,
Piled the table high. Mankind
Was content to gather the abundance
Of whatever ripened.
Blackberry or strawberry, mushroom or truffle,
Every kind of nut, figs, apples, cherries,
Apricots and pears, and, ankle deep,
Acorns under the tree of the Thunderer.
Spring weather, the airs of spring,
All year long brought blossom.
The unworked earth
Whitened beneath the bowed wealth of the corn.
Rivers of milk mingled with rivers of nectar.
And out of the black oak oozed amber honey.

After Jove had castrated Saturn,
Under the new reign the Age of Silver –
(Lower than the Gold, but better
Than the coming age of Brass) –
Fell into four seasons.

Now, as never before,
All colour burnt out of it, the air
Wavered into flame. Or icicles
Strummed in the wind that made them.
Not in a cave, not in a half-snug thicket.
Not behind a windbreak of wattles,
For the first time
Man crouched under a roof, at a fire.
Now every single grain
Had to be planted
By hand, in a furrow
That had been opened in earth by groaning oxen.

After this, third in order,
The Age of Brass
Brought a brazen people,
Souls fashioned on the same anvil
As the blades their hands snatched up
Before they cooled. But still
Mankind listened deeply
To the harmony of the whole creation,
And aligned
Every action to the greater order
And not
To the blind opportunity of the moment.

Last comes the Age of Iron.
And the day of Evil dawns.
Modesty
Truth
Loyalty
Go up like a mist – a morning sigh off a graveyard.

Snakes, tricks, plots come hurrying
Out of their dens in the atom.
Violence is an extrapolation
Of the cutting edge
Into the orbit of the smile.
Now comes the love of gain – a new god
Made out of the shadow
Of all the others. A god who grins
From the roots of the eye-teeth.

Now sails bulged and the cordage cracked
In winds that still bewildered the pilots.
And the long trunks of trees
That had never shifted in their lives
From some mountain fastness
Leapt in their coffins
From wavetop to wavetop
Then out over the rim of the unknown.

Meanwhile the ground, formerly free to all
As the air or sunlight,
Was portioned by surveyors into patches,
Between boundary markers, fences, ditches.
Earth's natural plenty no longer sufficed.

Man tore open the earth, and rummaged in her bowels.
Precious ores the Creator had concealed
As close to hell as possible
Were dug up – a new drug
For the criminal. So now iron comes
With its cruel ideas. And gold
With crueller. Combined, they bring war –
War, insatiable for the one,
With bloody hands employing the other.
Now man lives only by plunder. The guest
Is booty for the host. The bride's father,
Her heirloom, is a windfall piggybank
For the groom to shatter. Brothers
Who ought to love each other
Prefer to loathe. The husband longs
To bury his wife and she him.
Stepmothers, for the sake of their stepsons,
Study poisons. And sons grieve
Over their father's obdurate good health.
The inward ear, attuned to the Creator,
Is underfoot like a dog's turd. Astraea,
The Virgin
Of Justice – the incorruptible
Last of the immortals
Abandons the blood-fouled earth.

from Critics and Essayists (Seamus Heaney, Helen Vendler and Eavan Boland)
Donald Davie

[... In] *The Redress of Poetry*, Seamus Heaney, [...] more frankly than ever before, relates these pieces – on Marlowe, on John Clare and Brian Merriman, on Hugh MacDiarmid and Dylan Thomas, on Yeats and Larkin and Elizabeth Bishop – to a change that many have noticed in his own poetry. It is a change – so someone has wittily said – from Caliban to Ariel, from a poetry that is of the earth earthy to a poetry that is more rarefied and for many readers more elusive. His poems have become, in a word, more transcendental; he knows this, it is a deliberate move, and here he tries to vindicate it. No longer content faithfully to mirror reality as he experiences it, he now seeks to redress that reality, to deliver in poetry something to set against the manifest imbalances in the actuality that we all experience and suffer from. The politics of Northern Ireland is one, but only one, of the instigations that has prompted this new departure. Whereas, Heaney assures us, most people north and south of the border yearn for a harmonious Ireland, they have come to recognise that the harmony cannot be attained by constitutional – still less, by military – means; it remains crucial that the imaginary outcome be kept in mind, and only poetry can ensure that, giving in that way redress. We are not used to having poetry given such a strained and elevated role; and there's an obvious danger that, unless Heaney picks his words very carefully, he can seem to be making of poetry only wishful thinking. He does pick his words with care; and so those who know and love him for his jokey and winning ways on the platform will find a certain chill descend. For Seamus at the podium is a beguiling character, whereas Seamus at the typewriter is a great deal sterner and more demanding – as he has to be, given the unfashionable and really quite abstruse task that he has set himself.

    Helen Vendler, Heaney's friend and Harvard colleague, also writes with authority, though of a different kind. Her reviews in *The New Yorker* and *The New York Review of Books* and similarly influential magazines are widely, and I guess rightly, taken to carry more weight than any others by other hands in the States. And again we must be grateful that she, as a scholar, finds so much time to spare for the humble task of reviewing new collections as they appear. I've particular reason to be grateful, since apart from Heaney I'm the only non-American poet to be considered in her *Soul Says*. This is a notable act of friendship and kindness on her part; for she is quite certain that the only poetry on which she can speak with confidence is American poetry. To a British reader this erects certain barriers; for American reviewing is a great deal more kindly and indulgent, on the surface, than what we are used to from home-grown reviewers, whose tart and peremptory verdicts are seldom backed up by as much patient reading as Vendler gives to every poet she writes about. All the same, the barrier remains.

Vendler says roundly: 'The poets about whom I have written in the essays in this book are poets whom I admire.' This is heart-warming (and Heaney, incidentally, could have said the same). But the critical function is only half performed when the critic refuses to consider poets to whom he has given a thumbs-down. It is the negative verdicts that give substance and quality to the appeals for applause. A critic is meant to be that – critical. And a British reader, whatever his or her gender or racial affiliation, is likely to feel that in her tributes to Rita Dove, to Lucie Brock-Broido and Jorie Graham, Vendler has overlooked certain rudimentary considerations concerning verse-form. In case this objection should seem sexist or racist (or both), consider how Vendler deals with the white Southerner, Dave Smith. Smith has published five volumes of poems, along with a *Selected Poems*. Enough, one would have thought, for at least an interim judgement. But no! Smith's claim on us, it seems, is still all promise, not performance: 'What this Jacob will write when his wrestling with the angel of death finds its dawn is beyond conjecture.' This is hardly the language of judicious evaluation. The truth is that Vendler, a Bostonian, finds the American South as much a foreign country as any European country, including Britain. The nearest she gets to a judgement is when she writes: 'The southern-gothic themes – family, memory, fear, fate, sex, violence – remain, but the hope of forming them into structures of either historical intelligibility or philosophical consolation is becoming ever more precarious.'

A sufficiently conclusive judgement, one might think; but no, Vendler drives on through several more pages, impelled as it seems only by the victorious Yankee's guilt towards the vanquished Confederacy. One honours the generosity of that attempt to make amends, but what does it have to do with a cool judgement of poems, whether written above or below the Mason-Dixon Line? This is only one instance of how a British reader is implicated, without his knowing it, into a specifically intra-

American debate. Helen Vendler, who is a scholar of George Herbert, quarrels with Heaney's account of that English poet. But both of them, Vendler the American and more plainly Heaney the Irishman, hear George Herbert's voice (which both of them venerate) as the voice of the colonising power which both of them, as ex-colonials, have ultimately to repudiate. But Herbert spoke out of, and spoke for, a pre-imperial England which had not yet acquired an empire nor yet dreamed of acquiring one. Serene equanimity (not easily attained, as Heaney knows and demonstrates) had nothing to do with imperial aggrandisement or imperial destiny. Moreover, the Anglican Christianity to which Herbert vowed himself was in his day a new-fangled and still precarious compromise between Rome and Geneva. His composure therefore was specifically religious, not to be rendered down or argued away in sociopolitical terms. Both Heaney and Vendler are rightly contemptuous of such reductive readings of the poetic masterpieces of our common past; and yet, properly sceptical as both of them are of such ideological misreadings, they are infected by them, as we all are.

For instance we are all of us – men and women alike – affected by the ideology that we call feminism. I call it an ideology, because that is how it must appear to a man of my age; but I recognise that in intention, and increasingly for younger readers in fact, the feminist movement is altogether more than that. It is, or it has been, an earthquake: a movement indeed! In my lifetime I have felt the ground move under my feet, and it is moving still, so that the landscape I grew up in has changed irreversibly even as I have walked over it. I don't like that, I resent it quite bitterly. In poetry, which I have made the business of my life, the present century has caused enough tormenting perturbations, without my having to take on board the possibility that through the centuries one half of the human-race has victimised the other half. Because these are my feelings (which I am trying only to explain, not to justify), I am the wrong person to review Eavan Boland's *Object Lessons*. Not that she writes as a committed feminist, any longer.

Indeed, some more militant women may scorn her as one who has betrayed the cause and given up on the struggle. But that is what one means by calling feminism an earthquake; it is not, if it ever was, a cause, still less a 'school'. It has defined, and is still incalculably moulding, the mental landscape that we move in, whether we consider poetry or anything else. It is near the end of her book that Eavan Boland declares: 'As a younger poet I had discovered that feminism had wonderful strengths as a critique and almost none as an aesthetic.' That is roundly said, and I wish it had been said on an earlier page, for saying things 'roundly' isn't Boland's way. Her procedures are quite deliberately circuitous and repetitious. *Object Lessons* is neither the clear narrative of a life, her own; nor is it a sequence of essays, but rather an interlinked chain of meditations. These are not pretentious, nor are they written in jargon; we are being confided in, and that is attractive. And yet I'm not sure I know what to do with her confidences. Heaney and Vendler take me through landscapes where for the most part I can keep my feet; but the feminist earthquake has produced a sort of lunar landscape where I come up against concepts which Boland seems to think I shall understand whereas I understand them only cloudily and uncertainly. This is odd because the physical setting is mostly Dublin, a city that I know quite well and remember fondly. Moreover, though neither title nor subtitle uses the word 'Irish', I can readily, from memories of Irish literary life, recognise that the woman poet in Ireland faces more obstacles than her sisters in the UK and the US have to cope with. For in the country of Kathleen na Houlihan, women are celebrated in poems and rhetoric, but they are not expected to compose the poems and orations, unless they can summon up a man's voice, thus denying their own corporeal being. That is the bind that Eavan Boland has found herself in, and she struggles in it without either self-pity or facile indignation.

The Redress of Poetry: Oxford Lectures, by Seamus Heaney (Faber); *Soul Says: On Recent Poetry*, by Helen Vendler (Belknap Press); *Object Lessons: The Life of the Woman and the Poet in Our Time*, by Eavan Boland (Carcanet).

63

The Painter as an Old Man
Thom Gunn

> Vulnerable because
> naked because
> his own model.

Muscled and veined, not
a bad old body
for an old man.
The face vulnerable too,
its loosened folds
huddled against
the earlier outline: beneath
the assertion of nose
still riding the ruins
you observe the down-
turned mouth: and
above it,
the assessing glare
which might be read as
I've got the goods on you
asshole and I'll expose you.

The flat palette knife
in his right hand, and
the square palette itself
held low in the other
like a shield,
he faces off
the only appearance
reality has and makes it
doubly his. He
looks into
his own eyes
or it might be yours
amd his attack on the goods
repeats the riddle
or it might be
answers it:
       Out of the eater
            came forth meat
      and out of the strong
            came forth sweetness.

64

Prudence
Czesław Miłosz

Carefully, carefully.
The sun in the angle of a wall and pigeons are cooing.

School excursions carry little banners, ice cream sticks and green
                                                                dragons.
On the piazzas women selling flowers shake off drops of water
from bunches of peonies they take from buckets.

Carefully, carefully.
Blond loaves of bread lie on the shelves of a bakery, their scent
                                                fills the narrow street.
A girl in a yellow blouse and a boy in a black sweater watch the
                                                receding streetcar tracks.
A small pleasure boat moves on the river, majestic, under the
                                                                clouds.

Carefully. Carefully, Memory is wrong.
In spite of memory let us honor the earth.

That was all a dream, heavy, that leaves defects in the labyrinths
                                                of the dull body.

And the one who had the dream keeps still, so that nothing
                                disturbs the ceremony of bows and smiles.

For suddenly it will flare, burst and disintegrate to demonstrate
that it was not real.

Translated by the author and Leonard Nathan.

PR 85:2, 1995.

65 Lucretian
Peter Reading

[Only pain, not oblivion, hurts.]
   Since the mind, like the body, is mortal,
death doesn't matter a toss.
   When the brain and the carcass are severed,
we, who shall then be nothing,
   can be troubled by nothing at all.

If we have ever existed
   in any previous state,
we *now* know nothing about it;
   so, when we snuff it, we won't
feel deprived of the present.

If, after death, there were dearth,
   then the mind would have to be present
to experience deprivation;
   but death, which denies the existence
of thought, exempts us from this.

One who no longer *is*
   can't suffer – is merely the same
as one who has never been.

   In sleep, neither mind nor body
feels itself 'absent' or craves life.
   Extend this repose to eternity –
no sense of loss can obtain.

PR 85:1, 1995

Prolonging life doesn't reduce
   the duration of death, for the time
after departure is infinite –
   non-being lasts just as long
for those who expire today
   as it does for defunct Eolithics.

66 Grief
C.K. Williams

Dossie Williams 1914–1995

1

Gone now, after the days of desperate, unconscious gasping, the
               reflexive staying alive,
tumorous lungs, tumorous blood, ruined, tumorous liver
               demanding to live, to go on,
even the innocent bladder, its tenuous, dull golden coin in the
               slack translucent bag,
gone now, after the months of scanning, medication, nausea,
               hair loss and weight loss;
remission, partial remission, gratitude, hope, lost hope, anxiety,
               anger, confusion,
the hours and days of everyday life, something like life but only
               as dying is like life;
gone the quiet at the end of dying, the mouth caught agape on
               its last bite at a breath,
bare skull with its babylike growth of new hair thrown back to
               open the terrified larynx;
the flesh given way but still of the world, lost but still in the
               world with the living;

PR 86:2, 1996

my hand on her face, on her brow, the sphere of her skull, her
                  arm, thin, flaccid, wasted;
gone, yet of us and with us, a person, not yet mere dream or
                  imagination, then, gone, wholly,
under the earth, cold earth, cold grasses, cold winter wind,
                  freezing eternity, cold, forever.

2

Is this grief? Tears took me, then ceased; the wish to die, too,
                  may have fled through me,
but not more than with any moment's despair, the old, surging
                  wish to be freed, finished.
I feel pain, pain for her fear, pain for her having to know she was
                  going, though we must;
pain for the pain of my daughter and son, for my wife whose
                  despair for her mother returned;
pain for all human beings who know they will go and still go as
                  though they knew nothing,
even pain for myself, my incomprehension, my fear of so many
                  stories never begun now never ending.
But still, is this grief: waking too early, tiring too quickly,
                  distracted, impatient, abrupt,
but still waking, still acting, thinking, working; is this what grief
                  is, is this sorrow enough?
I go to the mirror: someone who might have once felt something
                  merely regards me,
eyes telling nothing, mouth saying nothing, nothing reflected
                  but the things of the world,
nothing told not of any week's, no, already ten days now, any
                  ten days' normal doings.
Shouldn't the face evidence anguish, shouldn't its love and loss
                  and sadness be revealed?
Ineffable, vague, elusive, uncertain, distracted: shouldn't grief
                  have a form of its own,
and shouldn't mind know past its moment of vague, uncertain
                  distraction the sureness of sorrow;

shouldn't soul flinch as we're taught proper souls are supposed
                                                    to, in reverence and fear?
Shouldn't grief be pure, perfect, complete, reshaping the world
                                                    in itself, in grief for itself?

3

Eighty, dying, in bed, tubes in her chest, my mother puts on her
                                                    morning make up;
the broad, deft strokes of foundation, the blended-in rouge,
                                                    powder, eye shadow, lipstick;
that concentration with which you must gaze at yourself, that
                                                    ravenous, unfaltering focus.
Grief for my mother, for whatever she thought her face had to
                                                    be, to be made every morning;
grief for my mother-in-law in her last declining, destroying
                                                    dementia, getting it wrong,
the thick ropes of rouge, garish green paint on her lips; mad,
                                                    misplaced slash of mascara;
grief for all women's faces, applied, created, trying to manifest
                                                    what the soul seeks to be,
grief for the faces of all human beings, our own faces telling us so
                                                    much and no more,
offering pain to all who behold them, but which when they turn
                                                    to themselves, petrify, pose.
Grief for the faces of adults who must gaze in their eyes deeply
                                                    so as not to glimpse death,
and grief for the young who see only their own relentless and
                                                    grievous longing for love.
Grief for my own eyes that try to seek truth, even of pain, of
                                                    grief; but find only approximation.

4

My face beneath your face, face of grief, countenance of loss,
                                                    fear, final, irrevocable extinction;
matrix laid upon matrix, mystery on mystery, guise upon guise,
                                                    semblance, effigy, likeness.
O, to put the face of grief on in the morning; the tinting,
                                                    smoothing, shining and shaping;

and at the end of the day, to remove it, detach it, emerge from
the sorrowful mask.
Stripped now of its raiment, the mouth, caught in its last labored
breath finds last resolution,
all the flesh now, stripped of its guises, moves towards its place
in the peace of the earth.
Grief for the earth, accepting the grief of the flesh and the grief of
our grieving forever;
grief for the flesh and the body and face, for the eyes that can see
only into the world,
and the mind that can only think and feel what the world gives it
to think and to feel;
grief for the mind gone, the flesh gone, the imperfect pain that
must stay for its moment;
and grief for the moment, its partial beauties, attachments,
affections, all severed, all torn.

67 A Poppy
Michael Longley

When millions march into the mincing machine
An image in Homer picks out the individual
Tommy and the doughboy in his doughboy helmet:
'Lolling to one side like a poppy in a garden
Weighed down by its seed capsule and rainwater,
His head drooped under the heavy, crestfallen
Helmet' (an image Virgil steals – *lasso papavera*
Collo – and so do I), and so Gorgythion dies,
And the poppy that sheds its flower-heads in a day
Grows in one summer four hundred more, which means
Two thousand petals overlapping as though to make
A cape for the corn-goddess or a soldier's soul.

PR 87:4, 1997–8

68
FEATURE
Ruth and Harry Fainlight

The Same
Ruth Fainlight

The same wound you made
now you want to cure –
yet when the torn and bloody
tissues, soothed, begin to mend
you tear the scarf-skin off once more.

The same dagger, thrust
into my flesh, you use
to trim new bandages –
then rip away the half-formed scar.
And healing hurts the most of all.

The same gentle words
and acts – or cruel, cruel.
Which is worse to bear?
The tape reverses, but still spools
the same tales of love and war.

['The moon shows through']
Harry Fainlight

The moon shows through as if
The earth began to see its breath;
Moths stirring from
The chilly ankle shallows.

Such stillness now as if each tree
Were a gate left standing open,
Or AUTUMN were the name
Of an Egyptian god.

PR 87:1, 1997 & PR 68:2, 1978

& *from* Pick Me Flowers for Vietnam
Ian Hamilton in conversation with Gregory LeStage

[...]

IAN HAMILTON   In general, I think there is this continual process of action and reaction throughout the development of poetry. Al Alvarez examined this [in his essay, 'Beyond the Gentility Principle'] with the notion of 'negative feedback'. Eliot wrote about it a lot. You expect poetry of any given epoch to be in a quarrelsome relationship with the epoch that preceded it.

I think I could have probably predicted – and perhaps even did – the Martian phenomenon that came after the kind of stuff I was encouraging in *The Review* and *The New Review*. When I was arguing, as a reviewer and critic, for Lowell and company, I was arguing for a kind of poetry of intense personal experience, a kind of lyric poetry based in individual experience. This excluded the fanciful, the inventive, the narrative. It excluded lots of things, in fact. It got narrower and narrower and narrower in its focus; too narrow in the end. Of poets like Auden and Wallace Stevens, we would have said, 'Oh, they're *thinking* poets; they're *inventing* poets; they're poets who make up things. They're not poets who write out of the sort of visceral intensities we're concerned with.' So, you could have predicted that the next thing would be a resurgence of Auden and Stevens, and I think that Martianism came out of that. Then you might have predicted the resurgence of narrative or political poetry. The gulf between the idea of poetry as intensely personal and the idea of poetry as a political instrument had become vast. Political poetry had been taken over by the Liverpool Poets or Pop poets or Beat poets. They're the people who wrote sloganeering verse about Vietnam and other hot issues. That wasn't the kind of thing we did. If we were to write about Vietnam, it would have to do with going into some field and picking a flower that would somehow faintly remind us of a look or a gesture that distantly might hint of a war in Southeast Asia. But the poem would be about walking in the field. We were very against overtly political poetry. So, you could have predicted that there would have been a sort of coming together of this political role for poetry and non-Pop poetry. You'd get someone like Heaney, for example, whose training is in what you might call 'mainstream', or 'traditional', poetry, but with him you have a political location and situation in Ireland.

GREGORY LESTAGE   *You have written that Heaney was a pivotal figure in shifting poetry from the residual confessioneering left over from the sixties to a resurgence of the impersonal, or anti-personal. He re-introduced 'bardic anonymity', which allows him to address deeply-felt cultural and intensely political issues, such as the mythic and the Troubles, with all of the power and none of the whinging.*

IAN HAMILTON   Exactly. You can't say that he's introverted, self-obsessed, subjective, or narrow because he's got The Subject. And having The Subject gives him the confidence to 'put on the airs', as it were. I don't mean that unkindly at all. Having put on the poetic airs, he can speak in an authoritative poetic voice. I think that one of the legacies of The Movement, which destroyed the poet's bardic self-confidence, was to rob the poet of a sense of his own possible centrality and authoritativeness. Overwhelmingly, their message was that *the poet mustn't take himself too seriously.* So then you got me and my peers, who were prepared to take our 'selves' seriously, but were not prepared to promote or to send those seriously perceived 'selves' out into the world to comment authoritatively about things in which we had no expertise, i.e. society, politics, etc. It always seemed slightly bogus to us to assume authority over issues in those realms. Some authority was ceded as a result of the Movement enterprise because it said, 'you can't write with authority'; you can't write like Auden. In the thirties, Auden had this marvellous authority in writing about 'necessary murder' and about Spain. You simply couldn't have written that way about Vietnam.

GREGORY LESTAGE   *In the early seventies, you mediated a symposium in* The Review *entitled 'The State of Poetry', taking the measure of poetry and poets of that time. What might be the key in such a symposium today?*

IAN HAMILTON   I'm a bit out of touch really, but what I see around I don't feel greatly in sympathy with, I must say. I am not sure that those poets who are considered popular now should be proposed as poets to be admired. I don't even know that I would define this period at all. I do feel that poetry's become more of a rag bag – more inclusive, more shapeless, more chatty, more discursive, more of a receptacle for amusing observations. I think that poetry should begin with the kind of intensity and focus and craftsmanship that insists on every line being perfect. Most of what is out there today isn't really poetry. Is the 'New Gen' really about poetry? It might be a form of writing that is engaging and sharp and entertaining, but it is not poetry. It's important to make these distinctions:

every line doesn't count, every word hasn't been chosen carefully, it doesn't have any structure; there's no reason why this line is broken and that line is not. What we see today is more what poetry *is not* than what it *is*. This is what I am continually struck by. You call *this* poetry? I think it's something, but I don't think it's poetry.

GREGORY LESTAGE *Your critical persona is detached, avoids camps and schools, and stands back and considers issues of poetry in and out of their own contexts, each with their own strengths and weaknesses. It's a kind of criticism of equilibria. However, one senses a set of standards for poetry.*

IAN HAMILTON I think the idea that poetry is still hard to do – that there are some rules – is very important. You can play around with the rules, but you don't just throw it all out. I think that this tendency has to be resisted, particularly in an age of informality. There has to be a way of insisting on form, or directing the attention towards form without finding oneself in that 'why isn't it rhyming, why isn't it scanning' position. Everything must be ventured in poetry and criticism from an informed position. I think that the reason I studied a book like Lowell's *Life Studies* was that the whole of that tradition could be heard at the back of this seemingly free verse. There is the essential noise of iambic pentameter running under it all. It sounded relaxed, like talk or prose, but you could always hear the rules he was breaking. You could always see the structures he was departing from. I heard and saw it less in Berryman. I always thought there was something slightly fraudulent about Berryman, I must say.

[...]

GREGORY LESTAGE *As an anthologist and magazine editor, you are conscious of the significance of your function in the formation and preservation of the poetic tradition. In the* Oxford Companion to Twentieth Century Poetry *(1994), for instance, you state: 'It isn't true that "if it's good it will survive"; someone, somewhere has to keep saying that it's good.' Can you elaborate on this?*

IAN HAMILTON I believe what I wrote. This is why one would do anthologies or edit poetry magazines. Because cultural memories are short, they need to be jogged. As an editor or anthologist, you can both shape the future and protect the past. Best of all, your work can show where the links are, where the continuities are between the past and future.

GREGORY LESTAGE *In the preface to* Poems Since 1990, *you declared that 'anthologies [...] should either be representative or personal'. Are today's anthologists fulfilling their responsibilities to poetry?*

IAN HAMILTON   Today, I think that many anthologies are published chiefly to woo an audience, which they do by finding the lowest common denominator. They sell short the idea that poetry can be and should be difficult and complex. To be able to translate the difficulty and complexity into something meaningful, you must have read other poetry. This allows you to see the merits because you can hear the echoes of and references to other poems. In other words, most poems of the past and most poems of the immediate past have been written by people who have read a lot of poetry – they've got a lot of poetry into their heads. Today, I think that many poems are being written by people who have no poetry in their heads. They don't know where their work came from. Maybe they spin off from the Pop scene, maybe they spin off from journalism, maybe they spin off from television, but they don't emerge from or have the support of the poetic tradition of which they are largely ignorant. And so you get bad readers. Bad readers produce bad writers, and *vice versa*. They don't know where they are when you present them with a poem by Hardy or Frost. They're not prepared for the immediate sense of difficulty or strangeness because they have no background in poetry. If it doesn't hit them in the face or make them laugh, it has no value to them. This is the lowest common denominator.

Those who publish anthologies today are worried about making their audiences 'comfortable'. That's the depressing thing about poetry readings, too. Everybody has to throw in a poem that makes people laugh so that everyone can relax and cough and shift around in their seat. So, every hack on the circuit will know that you have to have a poem that makes people laugh. There is something odious about this, about the fact that you have to say, 'Okay, I'll read something a little lighter now', and they all perk up, and you throw them some piece of doggerel, and they all laugh, and then you get back to the grim business of zapping them with your serious subject matter.

GREGORY LESTAGE   *You have not been afraid of producing an anthology based on personal taste. You did so with* Poems Since 1900 *and inform the reader of the fact in the preface. You choose poems within the tradition that you supported when you were editor of* The Review. *You like poetry of 'intelligent criticism', poetry that is short, 'concrete', and has 'a purchase on matter'.*

IAN HAMILTON   The people who have read that book – and there aren't that many – usually like it quite a lot because the poems in it aren't obscure. Also, it follows the lyric tradition through, giving it consistency. It is partisan in terms of the poems and poets chosen, leaving a lot of room for argument. But such arguments are necessary. If someone asked me, 'What should I read?', I would still give them that book. If you're going to engage in the criticism of poetry, you have to be polemical. You have to give that sense of where you are by expressing what you think things *should* be like, who you think has been neglected in the past, which direction you would like poetry to take. In doing so, there are enemies that should be headed off and destroyed: 'Here come some narrative poets: let's stop them in their tracks. Here come some Pop Liverpool poets: let's stop them.' The defensive posture, I think, came out of some strange sense of duty to the poets of the past.

[...] Lowell had this wonderful idea about heart-break poetry, which is always treading a tightrope, teetering above sentimentality without falling into it. It dares to get that close. That's been my aim. The concomitant fear is of sentimentality, of toppling over. [...]

& *from* The State of the Language: On Irish English
Dennis O'Driscoll

Languages, like people, operate at optimum efficiency within a degree or so of the average temperature. When writers deviate too much from the linguistic equivalent of 98.4° – the normal spoken language of their time and place – the results can be feverish or hypothermic. The English spoken in Ireland is not exactly noted for being cool; indeed, the danger for Irish writers is that they will live up to the expectations of foreign audiences by producing a kind of coal-effect literature, artificially heated to the required blaze of extravagance and colour.

Because one's language comes as naturally to one's larynx as air to one's lungs, it is difficult to analyse it with detachment. Our own English is always 'standard' to ourselves. For instance, not until I recently read a commentary on Thomas Kinsella's marvellous poem, 'Hen Woman', did I realise that the word 'shore' (in the context of the poem) would need to be glossed for non-Irish readers as 'a dialect word for a drain-hole covered by a grating'. We all unwittingly shore personal fragments against our ruin.

PR 85:4, 1995–6

I remember sitting in on a discussion between Seamus Heaney and several of his translators at which he remarked that, 'As a poet, you draw a circle around your world; and, within that world, you want to represent things exactly as they were.' He went on to speak of his pleasure, when writing *North*, at having been able to use the word 'coomb' in a way which had currency in no more than about fifteen Ulster parishes. Significantly, the influence on Heaney's language of local dialect, Gaelic and Anglo-Saxon literatures, and the Ulster Scots inheritance – taking him as far as possible from an international Esperanto style– has broadened rather than narrowed his appeal. A homogenised, sterilised version of the language is no substitute for full-cream, textured richness.

The ghost behind much of what is written and spoken in Ireland is the Gaelic language. From Joyce, Yeats, Synge and Flann O'Brien to the work of contemporaries like Michael Hartnett, the impact of Gaelic on style and syntax has been seminal. Seamus Heaney, Thomas Kinsella, John Montague and Brendan Kennelly have absorbed and extended the tradition through translation. Paul Muldoon's first published poems were written in Gaelic, while Eilean Ní Chuilleanáin and Ciaran Carson grew up in Gaelic-speaking households. Derek Mahon's 'Achill', Michael Longley's 'On Hearing Irish Spoken', and their versions of poems by Nuala Ní Dhomhnaill, evince an awareness of the language and its literary hinterland among poets who are not themselves speakers of the language.

[...]

69
from Letters to Edward Thomas
Glyn Maxwell

Dear Edward, just a note to say we're here
And nowhere could be better. And your key
Was where you said it would be, and the air
Is fresh with things you think, while looking kindly

On us intruders. Jenny says let's wait,
You can't be far away, while George of course
Has toppled into every single seat
To find his favourite. Five-to-one it's yours
He'll plump for, but Team Captain of the Cottage
Declares it's not allowed. I've said we're off
On a foraging expedition to the village
And that's where we are now, or soon enough
We shall be. We can't wait to see you, Edward.
We feel as if we have. I mean your home
Was breathing softly when we all invaded,
Not only air but breath, as in the poem
    I treasure that you showed me,
Which clings and flutters in me like a leaf
And falls when I remember how you told me
You couldn't write a poem to save your life!
    Consider that thing done.
Here's just a note to say we've been and gone.

*

Dear Edward, just a note to say your wood
Has summoned us away, as you yourself
Hinted it might. The horde has swooped and fed
And drunk (in George's case three times) your health,
And Rose and Peter wouldn't hear of sleep,
Said it was banished back to Hampstead, swore
No path would go untrodden, and no sheep
Untroubled by us – George said 'And no door
Of any inns unswung!' and so we're gone
A second time, though you'll have no idea
I wrote a first time. Blame the evening sun
For luring us back out. We love it here
And only you are missing. What that does
Is make us lonely. True, for all my chatter.
A beauty-spot will do that. What it has
Is one thing missing. Ask me what's the matter

Anywhere it's beautiful
And there's your answer. Long before it's dark
You'll hear us creatures rolling up the hill
In twos, to be the last into your Ark,
    Or to be told by you
What things we missed, went by, lost, didn't do.

*

[...]

Dear Mr Thomas, now it's been so long
We lost your first name in the meadow grass
At dusk, when on a road we thought was wrong
We started recognising things. Your house
Then viewed us dimly. But you must excuse
The new meander in my messages,
And blame it on the elderflower juice
That George said would be *choice* with sandwiches
And seems so to have been. We all agree
We shall not leave tomorrow if our host
Insists on his invisibility,
And clears the table round us like a ghost
And seems to comment in the silences.
Rose and Peter have to leave, but George
Declares this week is cancelled, or his is.
Or so we can infer from how he snores.
    I tried to start some games
But after walking longer than we've ever
Who's in the mood for folding up the names
Of ones we know in town? Who cares whose lover
    Really cares for whom?
Our heads are bowed and spinning in the room.

*

[...]

To punish you I threw the note away
I wrote you in your kitchen. Now my thanks

Are scribbled among strangers as we sway
Through Hampshire towards town, and the sun blinks
Behind the poplars. Edward Thomas great
Unknowable, omniscient, your cottage
Waits for you: no sign we ever sat
Around your fire, no trace of pie or porridge,
Nor dreg of George's ale remains. No talks
Of ours will last the time you take to light
Your clay, and your first steps will make our walks
As brief and viewless as a shower at night.
There are our heartfelt thanks. We could have haunted
Many houses where we wouldn't see you.
At yours we thought it likely to be granted
Sight or sound, but it was not to be. You
    Were needed in the field,
By hawk or hedge, who knows, their need was greater
Than ours, who wanted names for things revealed
That we should know by now or may ask later.
    And reason not my need,
Who writes what nobody but she will read.

★

Poem to Mr Thomas and Mr Frost,
Created by a dandelion you passed
As you in talk about a stanza crossed
Half Herefordshire, till you sat at last
In silence. I'm the dandelion that saw
Two aspens shake and shed in a quick wind,
And tried to loose her own leaves to the floor
Like they did and did manage in the end
When they were both long gone in the great storm:
One to the west and one to the east, away
Towards the blood-commander in the dawn
And all his soldiers, pink becoming grey.
And you won't see this, if you live as long
As what you sent me: 'As the team's head-brass'

It starts but isn't titled. If I'm wrong
And your great hands one day are holding these
      Dandelion hairs,
The storm would not have come, the trees have kept
Their ground, and through the hearts of all the shires
Would Mr Thomas and Mr Frost have stepped
      And war like a rough sky
Been overlooked in talk, and blown on by.

                              ★

                            [...]

Dear Father Thomas, every Christmas Eve
Good children of the world are quite as shy
As I am to write *Dear* and then believe
For twenty lines our goodness could be why
It's worth our time. Our faith turns to this thread
That shuttles downward while the mischievous
Need nothing but a coalsack by the bed,
And wake to the same carols. Each of us
Is writing, Edward, asking the great space
Below us what is missing still, what gift
Will make us whole again. We fold and place
Our answers in the chimney and are left
These pink embarrassed authors by the fire.
We all talk tommy-rot we understand.
Somebody coughs, politely to inquire
Did they not kick a ball on No Man's Land
      Two years ago? 'That's so',
Smiles Peter, adding: 'Not tonight, I fear.'
And I hear George's voice say: 'Cricket, though,
So Edward gets a knock.' But he's not here,
      George, he's where you are,
Restless tonight like all good children are.

                              ★

                            [...]

Dear Edward, when the war was over, you
Were standing where a wood had been, and though
Nothing was left for you to name or view
You waited till new trees had hidden you.
Then you came home and in a forest called
The Times your name was found, and not among
The officers but in a clearing filled
With verses, yours. Then your new name was sung
With all the old. And children leafing through
And old men staring and their daughters stilled
With admiration, all this happened too,
Or had already by the time you pulled
The book I hide this in from your top shelf
And blew its dust away. The year is what,
1930? '40? Please yourself,
But do remember as you smile and sit
    That everything's foreseen
By a good reader, as I think I am
On David's Day of 1917,
Reaching for blotting-paper. Now's the time
    To fold the work away
And find me on this bleak or brilliant day.

*

[...]

Dear Edward, now there's no one at the end
There's nothing I can't say. Some eight or nine
I have by heart. Your farmer-poet friend
Is flying round the world on a fine line
That starts in you, or grows out from the days
You passed together. England is the same,
Cheering to order, set in its new ways
It thinks are immemorial. The Somme
Has trees beside it but some shovelwork
Will bring the dead to light. There's so much more
I want to say, because the quiet is dark,

And when the writing ends I reach a shore
Beyond which it's so cold and that's what changed,
Edward, on that Easter Monday. You
Were land to me, were England unestranged,
Were what I thought it had amounted to,
    But look at the fields now,
Look eyelessly at them, like the dug men
Still nodding out of Flanders. Tell them how
You walked and how you saw, and how your pen
    Did nothing more than that,
And when it stopped, what you were gazing at.

                *

Dear Edward Thomas, Frost died, I was born.
I am a father and you'd like the names
We gave our girl. I'm writing this at dawn
Where Robert lived, in Amherst, and your poems
I keep by his, his housebrick to your tile.
I teach you to my students, and aloud
I wonder what you would have come to. While
I wonder they look out at a white cloud
And so we pass the time. Perhaps I'll guess
Which one will ask me what they always ask:
Whom do I write for? Anybody? Yes,
You. And I'll walk home in the great dusk
Of Massachusetts that extends away
Far west and north, the ways you meant to go
To save your life. A good end to the day,
That's going to be. It's going to be cool, though,
    I see out in the town,
And start to turn the trees to what the world
Comes flocking here to see: eight shades of brown
Men never saw, and ninety-nine of gold,
    More shades than can have names,
Or names to bring them back when the snow comes.

70

FEATURE
Scottish Identity in the 1990s

from A Different Drummer
Douglas Dunn interviewed by Attila Dösa

[...]

DOUGLAS DUNN   I think I coined the term 'barbarians' in a poetic
context in the mid-1970s when I wrote the first part of my collec-
tion *Barbarians* (1979). Tony Harrison was in the same district of
thought and feeling at the time, and Seamus Heaney also (perhaps
even a little earlier). I used the term to mean the oppositional or
socially and politically hostile aspect of contemporary poetic sensi-
bility, which was shared chiefly by poets of a working-class and/or
non-English origin in the British Isles. A friend of mine calls this
the 'hairy-arsed school of poetry', although how he knows is a bit
of a mystery to me. In much of Central and Eastern Europe, the
same 'opposition' was expressed, but by far less direct means, by
'Aesopian' or semi-secret routes. In the North-West European
Archipelago poetry was capable of a greater directness although it
could be instructive to notice its protective ironies as well.

[...]

'Barbarians', in the poems I wrote around that title and concept,
are those who have otherwise been excluded from High Culture,
but who, by the later part of the twentieth century in the North-
West European Archipelago, come to possess it, very much to the
embarrassment of those who assume that they have inherited and
own the language and its poetic possibilities. Indeed, what you call
'the dynamic of the relationship' is where anything artistic might
happen – or may have done, as this is an aspect of my work which
is now in the past. At the same time it is part of my mind that could
be re-activated if circumstances required it or mind and imagina-
tion conspired to bring it back to me. You seem to indicate a
tension between 'High' Culture and the concerns of 'the people',
and I would agree. I want to be a poet of High Culture but at the

same time I don't want to be disloyal to my native parish, my home, my most immediate people, children, friends.

ATTILA DÖSA   [...] *Is 'Britishness' an appropriate paradigm in reading contemporary Scottish writing, or has it ever been one?*

DOUGLAS DUNN   'Britishness' is a concept that has perplexed me in my adult years. It didn't bother me at all when I was younger. For example, when I was a schoolboy, I was in something called the Sea Cadet Corps. Many weekends were spent at a naval anchorage on the Firth of Clyde, while each summer we spent a fortnight on a ship of the Royal Navy. In my case it was HMS *Diana*, a 'D' class destroyer, based at Loch Foyle at Londonderry in Northern Ireland, from where we sailed to Gibraltar and back with units of the Home Fleet, and HMS *Starling*, a very famous frigate of the Second World War, flagship of Admiral Vian, a great scourge of German U-Boats in its time, but by then a navigational training ship, and in which I sailed from Portsmouth to Randers in Denmark and then back to Harwich. I remember feeling very Royal Navy and very British. That I also felt very Scots didn't come into the equation even if companions called you 'Porridge' or 'Jock' or commented on your accent. You simply spoke back and held your end up. It strikes me that I've been doing the same ever since. I have to consider your question pragmatically and as experienced as that. Poetry doesn't arise from a theory but from what the poet knows in life more than in intellect. Yet I have to admit that a 'British' national identity may well be in question but due – and this is empirical rather than 'historical' in a broad sense as conveyed by Linda Colley's book [*Britons: Forging the Nation 1707– 1837*] – to the puzzlement of English people at the rise of a post-imperial multi-racial society, the erosion inflicted by the Provisional IRA, Ulster Loyalists, and other terrorist factions in Ireland with their adjunct activities on the mainland, the so-called National Party in England with its fascist and Nazi affiliations, and far less to the convictions of the Scottish National Party. Scottish Nationalism is distinguished in Europe for its democratic principles and procedures. It hasn't killed anyone while no one as far as I know has died for its cause in this century unless through stress, overwork, or disappointment. What I'm saying is that the nation-alism with which I'm familiar is benign, and not to be confused with nationalisms elsewhere or their lethal activities.

It's not so much a question of 'Britishness' or 'Britishism' as of the English language. Scotland admits to three languages – English, Scots and Gaelic. The first of these is a *lingua franca*, but with a Scottish accent (although sometimes with an English accent), and it is the language in which I write and speak (with a Scottish accent), although I have a facility to speak in Scots if I feel like it or the social context invites me to do so. I've never been embarrassed by this fact, which I acknowledge, simply, as a fact. But 'Britishness' fails to offer a paradigm to a reading of contemporary Scottish writing. Why? – I believe the reason to be a matter of class politics among Scotland's writers and readers as much as nationalism.

[…]

A debate about Scottishness has been going on for a very long time – ever since the run-up to the Treaty of Union of 1707. I'd just as soon stop talking and do something, but then I feel I don't want to try to be in any way politically 'influential'. There's something in me that resists 'simplifying myself' (as Turgenev put it) in order to be a political activist. It's a debate in which I've played little part other than through whatever's represented in my own writing. Were I to stand on public platforms and say in prose some of the things I've said in verse, then not only would I be paraphrasing my verses, and repeating myself, but I'd be surrendering to a topical force inferior to the art I represent and to which I've dedicated my life. I don't know why – it could be reckless, or feckless – but I feel brave enough to say that.

[…]

Renan (I think) defined a nation as 'a large-scale solidarity'. Clearly, a country needs a nationality and citizenship to stand behind. Also, a country has to be in a position to take responsibility for itself; it shouldn't have to endure secondary status. Part of Scotland's trouble has been the willingness of so many of its people, in all walks of life, to behave as if second-rate or inferior. I don't feel second-rate, and I don't feel inferior. Boasting is not my style, and that's not my game here. Moaning and whingeing are conditions which I loathe and detest. I take full responsibility for my life and its decisions. Scotland is a country and a nationality into which I feel proud to have been born.

[...]

ATTILA DÖSA   *As a poet who began his career in Hull and now is living in Tayport, Fife – always as far from metropolitan centres as possible – you've been sensitive to claims of provincialism and nationalism. Throughout his criticism Robert Crawford is very keen on making the concept of 'provincial' into a 'term of praise'. But, because of its negative undertone, Crawford abandons it for another term, 'identifying poets', in his book of the same title. Thus he establishes a new paradigm for interpreting regional poets, deliberately devolving authority from the centre to what had previously been seen as periphery. [...]*

DOUGLAS DUNN   I now live in Dairsie, smaller even than Tayport, and distant from metropolitan centres. It's a temperamental thing with me – I don't like living in cities, although I enjoy opportunities to visit them from time to time. Much of my writing refers to places and people, which comes naturally to me. Perhaps it's simply part of the apparatus I need in order to express my formal and aesthetic concerns. To try to write poetry at the present time obliges a poet to confront and struggle with a range of technical, formal issues, interwoven through the poet's thematic, emotional and intellectual obsessions. In the act of writing, the substance which a poet tries to shape– like wayward clay on a potter's wheel, handled by an apprentice potter – is both what the poet is trying to say and the technical means by which the poet tries to form the poem. It's hard to take one's mind off either of them, so that criticism which neglects a poet's artistry for the sake of chasing after an idea (no matter how interesting the idea) always seems to me to be incomplete. Or it could just be that a readable, technical criticism is difficult to achieve.

[...]

I work in a university that was founded in 1411/12, and which is recognized as one of the major universities of Europe and perhaps of the world. It's a very well-known university – so I don't feel conscious of being on the periphery except perhaps in an imaginative sense. But I discover within myself the same germ of freedom, style of self-challenge, that I find myself impressed by in a writer like Robert Louis Stevenson. Did Sir Walter Scott feel peripheral? Did Stevenson? Did Robert Burns for that matter? – I suspect Burns's localism to have been a tactic calculated by a powerful intellect simply to make it known that he existed. But I'm glad you see a wider frame of reference in my work. Throughout my writing life I feel I've engaged as much as has been possible for me with European literatures. I've always had to work hard for my living and so I've never enjoyed the leisure or the means to culti-vate some of my interests as much as I would have liked. It annoys me, but my Samoa will always be one of the mind. Besides, in mid-life, I've discovered that I'm a practical man as much as a poet. Or practical-poetic. Or poetic-practical.

[...]

Imagination is crucial to poetry and any other form of literature and art. In his masterpiece novel *Lanark* Alasdair Gray writes of Glasgow as an 'unimagined' city, a city that for many years was somehow (or by and large) avoided by art. Even if there was much interest in art there Glasgow was rarely its subject. All that has changed and I'm convinced it's true of other parts of Scotland as well as of Glasgow. From my own view of my work (which like any other writer's is unreliable) I feel that my '(re)creation' of communal loyalties occurs in some of my poems but in most of my short stories.

[...]

Cabaret McGonagall
W.N. Herbert

Come aa ye dottilt, brain-deid lunks,
ye hibernatin cyber-punks,
gadget-gadjies, comics-geeks,
guys wi perfick rat's physiques,

PR 85:4, 1995–6

fowk wi fuck-aa social skills,
fowk that winnae tak thir pills:
gin ye cannae even pley fuitball
treh thi Cabaret McGonagall.

Thi decor pits a cap oan oorie,
ut's puke-n-flock à la Tandoori;
there's a sculpture made frae canine stools,
there's a robot armadillo drools
when shown a photie o thi Pope,
and a salad spinner cerved fae dope:
gin ye cannae design a piss oan thi wall
treh thi Cabaret McGonagall.

We got: Clangers, Blimpers, gowks in mohair jimpers,
Bangers, Whimpers, cats wi stupit simpers –
Ciamar a thu, how are you, and hoozit gaun pal,
welcome to thi Cabaret Guillaume McGonagall.
We got: Dadaists, badass gits, shits wi RADA voices,
Futurists wi sutured wrists and bygets o James Joyce's –
Bienvenue, wha thi fuck are you, let's drink thi nicht away,
come oan yir own, or oan mi phone, or to thi Cabaret.

Come aa ye bards that cannae scan,
fowk too scared tae get a tan,
come aa ye anxious-chicken tykes
wi stabilisers oan yir bikes,
fowk whas mithers waash thir pants,
fowk wha drink deoderants:
fowk that think they caused thi Fall
like thi Cabaret McGonagall.

Fur aa that's cheesy, static, stale,
this place gaes sae faur aff thi scale
a ony Wigwam Bam-meter
mimesis wad brak thi pentameter;
in oarder tae improve thi species' genes,

ye'll find self-oaperatin guillotines:
bring yir knittin, bring yir shawl
tae thi Cabaret McGonagall.

We got: Berkoffs, jerk-offs, noodles wi nae knickers,
Ubuists, tubes wi zits, poodles dressed as vicars –
Gutenaben Aiberdeen, wilkommen Cumbernauld,
thi dregs o Scoatlan gaither at Chez McGonagall.
We got: mimes in tights, a MacDiarmidite that'iz ainsel
                                                        contradicts,
kelpies, selkies, grown men that think they're Picts –
Buonaserra Oban and Ola! tae aa Strathspey,
come in disguise jist tae despise thi haill damn Cabaret.

Panic-attack Mac is oor DJ,
thi drugs he tuke werr aa Class A,
sae noo he cannae laive thi bog;
thon ambient soond's him layin a log.
Feelin hungry? sook a plook;
thi son o Sawney Bean's oor cook:
gin consumin humans diz not appal
treh thi Bistro de McGonagall.

Waatch Paranoia Pete pit speed
intil auld Flaubert's parrot's feed,
and noo ut's squaakin oot in leids
naebody kens till uts beak bleeds
and when ut faas richt aff uts perch,
Pete gees himsel a boady search:
thi evidence is there fur all
at thi Cabaret McGonagall.

We got: weirdos, beardos, splutniks, fools,
Culdees, bauldies, Trekkies, ghouls –
Airheids fae thi West Coast, steely knives and all,
welcome to thi Hotel Guillaume McGonagall.
We got: Imagists, bigamists, fowk dug up wi beakers,

lit. mag. eds, shit-thir-beds, and fans o thi New Seekers –
Doric loons wi Bothy tunes that ploo yir wits tae clay;
ut's open mike fur ony shite doon at thi Cabaret.

Alpha males ur no allowed
amang this outré-foutery crowd
tho gin they wear thir alphaboots
there's nane o us can keep thum oot,
and damn-aa wimmen care tae visit,
and nane o thum iver seem tae miss it:
gin you suspeck yir dick's too small
treh thi Cabaret McGonagall.

There's dum-dum boys wi wuiden heids
and Myrna Loy is snoggin Steed,
there's wan drunk wearin breeks he's peed –
naw –than's thi Venerable Bede;
in fack than auld scribe smells lyk ten o um,
he's na cheenged 'iz habit i thi last millennium:
gin thi wits ye werr boarn wi hae stertit tae stall
treh thi Cabaret McGonagall.

We got: Loplops and robocops and Perry Comatose,
Cyclops and ZZ Top and fowk that pick thir nose –
Fare-ye-weel and cheery-bye and bonne nuit tae you all,
thi booncirs think we ought tae leave thi Club McGonagall.
But we got: Moptops and bebop bats and Krapp's Last
                                        Tapeworm friends,
Swap-Shop vets and neurocrats, but damn-aa sapiens –
Arrevederchi Rothesay, atque vale tae thi Tay,
Eh wish that Eh hud ne'er set eye upon this Cabaret.

Dottilt: *daft, confused*; oorie: *dirty, tasteless*; gowks: *fools*; ciamar a thu: *how are you
(Gael.)*; kelpies: *river spirits in the shape of horses*; selkies: *seals which can take on human
form*; leids: *languages*; Culdees: *members of the Columban church*; loons: *young men*;
Bothy tunes: *ballads from the rural North-East*; ploo: *plough*; foutery: *excessively fussy*.

Zero
Robert Crawford

Thank you for calling Heatheryhaugh Nuclear Arsenal.
If your main lust is for weapons of mass destruction
Please try our other number in Inverbervie.

On your touchtone phone jab one for details
Of bombs that kill crofters but leave brochs and megaliths standing;
Two for snug dumpsites; three for pre-owned

Atomic oddments with warranties for several years;
Four for rucksacks of fissile material;
Five will patch you through to Glencora Gillanders,

Anthrax buyer for the Loch Ness and Great Glen area;
Six for the Arsenal's renowned in-house distillery;
Seven affords highlights of our unusual safety record,

Reassuring callers we are sited in a remote location,
Though, should you wish to visit, pressing eight provides
Pibrochs from this area of comical natural beauty.

Nine connects you to our twelve-hour emergency helpline
(Not staffed on Sundays, Hogmanay, or New Year's Day).
If this extension is busy, please yell your number

So someone can ring back at a more convenient time.
Thanks again for calling HNA.
Slàinte! Do not press zero.

PR 88:4, 1998–9

71

Syrinx
Amy Clampitt

Like the foghorn that's all lung,
the wind chime that's all percussion,
like the wind itself, that's merely air
in a terrible fret, without so much
as a finger to articulate
what ails it, the aeolian
syrinx, that reed
in the throat of a bird,
when it comes to the shaping of
what we call consonants, is
too imprecise for consensus
about what it even seems to
be saying: is it *o-ka-lee*
or *con-ka-ree,* is it really *jug jug,*
is it *cuckoo* for that matter? –
much less whether a bird's call
means anything in
particular, or at all.

Syntax comes last, there can be
no doubt of it: came last,
can be thought of (is
thought of by some) as a
higher form of expression:
is, in extremity, first to
be jettisoned: as the diva
onstage, all soaring
pectoral breathwork,
takes off, pure vowel
breaking free of the dry,

the merely fricative
husk of the particular, rises
past saying anything, any
more than the wind in
the trees, waves breaking,
or Homer's imploring
Thespesiae iachē:

those vestiges, last hoverings
above the threshold of
the dispossessed of breath.

72 Silhouette
Billy Collins

There is a kind of sweet pointlessness
that can visit at any time,
say this afternoon when I find myself
rustling around in the woods behind the house

and making with my right hand
the head of a duck,
the kind that would cast a silhouetted
profile on a white screen
in a darkened room with a single source of light
if one were in the mood to entertain.

PR 89:2, 1999

But I am outdoors today and this duck
has a wrist for a neck
and fingers for a beak that never stops flapping,
jabbering about some duck topic,
unless I rotate my arm and let him face me.

Then he stops his quacking
and listens to what I have to say,
even cocking his head like a dog
that listens all day to his master speaking
in English or Turkish or Albanian.

There was talk of war this morning
on the radio, and I imagined the treads of tanks
churning over the young trees again
and planes hacking the air to pieces,
but there is nothing I can do about that
except to continue my walk in the woods
conversing with my hand –

so benign an activity that if everyone
did this perhaps there would *be* no wars,
I might say in a speech
to the ladies' auxiliary of the future farmers of America.

And now it is getting to be evening,
a shift from blue to violet
behind the bare staves of trees.
It is also my birthday,
but there is nothing I can do about that either –
cannot control the hands of time
like this hand in the shape of this duck
who peers out of my sleeve
with its beak of fingers, its eye of air.

No – I am doing no harm,
but nor am I doing much good.
Would any bridge span a river?
Would a college of nurses have been founded?
Would one stone be placed on top of another
if people let nothing enter their minds
but the non-existent shadows of ducks?

So the sky darkens as always,
and now I am tripping over the fallen branches –
time to head downhill
toward the one burning light in the house
while the duck continues its agitated talk,
in my pocket now,
excited about his fugitive existence,
awed by his sudden and strange life
as each of us should be, one and all.

But never mind that, I think,
as I grab the young trees with my other hand,
braking my way down,
one boot in front of the other,
ready for my birthday dinner,
my birthday sleep, my crazy birthday dreams.

73

The Holy Show
Les Murray

I was a toddler, wet-combed
with my pants buttoned to my shirt
and there were pink and green lights, pretty
in the day, a Christmas-tree party
up the back of the village store.

I ran towards it, but big sad people
stepped out. They said over me *It's just, like,*
for local kiddies and *but let him join in*;
the kiddies looked frightened
and my parents, caught off guard

one beat behind me, grabbed me up
in the great shame of our poverty
that they talked about to upset themselves.
They were blushing and smiling, cursing me
in low voices *Little bugger bad boy!*

for thinking happy Christmas undivided,
whereas it's all owned, to buy in parcels
and have at home; for still not knowing
you don't make a holy show of your family;
outside it, there's only parry and front.

Once away they angrily softened to
me squalling, because I was their kiddie
and had been right about the holy show
that models how the world should be
and could be, shared glittering in near focus

right out to the Sex frontier.

PR 89:1, 1999

74

Breviary
Zbigniew Herbert

Lord
    I know that my days are numbered
    there are only a few left
    Barely enough in which to gather the sand
    my face will be covered with

    I won't now be able
    to do justice to those who've been wronged
    nor yet to ask the forgiveness
    of all those I have hurt
    because of this my soul is heavy

    my life
    should have been a circle
    it should have ended like a well-composed sonata
    but now I can see exactly
    in the moment before the coda
    broken chords
    misapplied colours and words
    dissonance clatter
    tongues of chaos

    why couldn't
    my life
    have been like ripples over a pond
    rising from infinite depths
    a beginning which grows
    orders itself in grain degree
    fold so as to die quietly
    at your inscrutable knees

Translated by Clive Wilmer and George Gömöri.

PR 89:2, 1999

75

Remember the Ship
John Agard

As citizen
of the English tongue

I say remember
the ship
in citizenship

for language
is the baggage
we bring –

a weight
of words to ground
and give us wing –

as millennial waters
beckon wide

and love's anchor
waiting to be cast

will the ghost of race
become the albatross
we shoot at our cost?

I'm here to navigate –
not flagellate
with a whip of the past

PR 90:1, 2000

for is not each member
of the human race
a ship on two legs

charting life's tidal
rise and fall

as the ship
of the sun
unloads its light

and the ship
of night
its cargo of stars

again I say remember
the ship
in citizenship

and diversity
shall sound its trumpet
outside the bigot's wall

and citizenship shall be
a call
to kinship

that knows
no boundary
of skin

and the heart
offers its wide harbours
for Europe's new voyage

to begin.

76

The Ode not Taken
Tony Harrison

C.T. Thackrah (1799–1833)

Dissecting corpses with Keats at Guy's,
Leeds-born Thackrah, shared the poet's TB.
Cadavers that made Keats poeticise
made Thackrah shun the call of poetry.

Praising the Classics to the *Lit & Phil*,
versed in Greek and Latin, and Eng. Lit.
he scribbled no sonnets on the scribbling mill
but penned descriptions of the scribblers' shit.
Could write hexameters by Virgil's rules,
and parrot Latin epics but he chose
flax-hecklers' fluxes with their 'gruelly' stools:
the shit of Yorkshire operatives, in prose.

But there are pentameters in Thackrah's tract,
the found iambics no prose can destroy,
which want to stop the heart with simple fact:

we do not find old men in this employ

PR 91:3, 2001

77 Chainsaw versus the Pampas Grass
Simon Armitage

It seemed an unlikely match. All winter unplugged,
grinding its teeth in a plastic sleeve, the chainsaw swung
nose-down from a hook in the darkroom
under the hatch in the floor. When offered the can
it knocked back a quarter-pint of engine oil,
and juices ran from its joints and threads,
oozed across the guide-bar and the maker's name,
into the dry links.

From the summerhouse, still holding one last gulp
of last year's heat behind its double doors, and hung
with the weightless wreckage of wasps and flies,
moth-balled in spider's wool...
from there, I trailed the day-glo orange power-line
the length of the lawn and the garden path,
fed it out like powder from a keg, then walked
back to the socket and flicked the switch, then walked again and
coupled
the saw to the flex – clipped them together.
Then dropped the safety catch, and gunned the trigger.

No gearing up or getting to speed, just an instant rage,
the rush of metal lashing out at air, connected to the main.
The chainsaw with its perfect disregard, its mood
to tangle with cloth, or jewellery, or hair.
The chainsaw with its bloody desire, its sweet tooth
for the flesh of the face and the bones underneath,
its grand plan to kick back against nail or knot
and rear up into the brain.
I let it flare, lifted it into the sun

PR 91:1, 2001

and felt the hundred beats per second drumming in its heart,
and felt the drive-wheel gargle in its throat.

The pampas grass with its ludicrous feathers
and plumes. The pampas grass, taking the warmth and light
from cuttings and bulbs, sunning itself,
stealing the show with its footstools, cushions and tufts
and its twelve-foot spears.

This was the sledgehammer taken to crack the nut.
Probably all that was needed here was a good pull or shove,
or a pitchfork to lever it out at its base.
Overkill. I touched the blur of the blade
against the nearmost tip of a reed – it didn't exist.
I dabbed at a stalk that swooned, docked a couple of heads,
dismissed the top third of its canes with a sideways sweep
at shoulder height – this was a game.
I lifted the fringe of undergrowth, carved at the trunk –
plant-juice spat from the pipes and tubes
or dust flew out as I ripped into pockets of dark, secret warmth.

To clear a space to work,
I raked whatever was severed or felled or torn
towards the dead zone under the outhouse wall, to be fired.
Then cut and raked, cut and raked, till what was left
was a flat stump the size of a manhole cover or barrel lid
that wouldn't be dug with a spade or prized from the earth.
Wanting to finish things off, I took up the saw
and drove it vertically downwards into the upper roots,
but the blade became choked with soil or fouled with weeds,
or what was sliced or split somehow closed and mended behind,
like cutting at water or air with a knife.
I poured barbecue fluid into the patch
and threw in a match – it flamed for a minute, smoked
for a minute more, and went out. I left it at that.

In the weeks that came, new shoots like asparagus tips
sprang up from its nest, and by June
it was riding high in its saddle, wearing a new crown.
Corn in Egypt. I looked on
from the upstairs window like the midday moon.

Back below stairs on its hook, the chainsaw seethed.
I left it a year, to work through its man-made dreams,
count back across time
to what grass never knew to forget.
The seamless urge to persist was as far as it got.

78

Egg and Spoon
Hugo Williams

Look out! Look out!
Here come the parents, the mad delivery boys,
holding out to us in spoons
the sum of all they know.

Their eyes pop out of their heads,
they bite their tongues,
in their efforts to place something
infinitely precious in our mouths.

PR 91:1, 2001

79

Letters of the Dead
Wisława Szymborska

We read the letters of the dead like puzzled gods –
gods nevertheless, because we know what happened later.
We know what money wasn't repaid,
the widows who rushed to remarry.
Poor, unseeing dead,
deceived, fallible, toiling in solemn foolery.
We see the signs made behind their backs,
catch the rustle of ripped-up wills.
They sit there before us, ridiculous
as things perched on buttered bread,
or fling themselves after whisked-away hats.
Their bad taste – Napoleon, steam and electricity,
deadly remedies for curable diseases,
the foolish apocalypse of St John,
the false paradise on earth of Jean-Jacques…
Silently, we observe their pawns on the board
– but shifted three squares on.
Everything they foresaw has happened quite differently,
or a little differently – which is the same thing.
The most fervent stare trustingly into our eyes;
by their reckoning, they'll see perfection there.

Translated by Vuyelwa Carlin.

PR 91:3, 2001

80

from Speech! Speech!
Geoffrey Hill

92

Either the thing moves, RAPMASTER, or it
does not. I disclaim spontaneity,
the appearance of which is power. I wíll
match you fake pindaric for trite
violence, evil twin. Here I address
fresh auditors: suppose you have gone the full
distance. Take up – ón líne – the true nature
of this achievement. Prove that you have fixed
the manifold. Dismiss the non-appearance
of peculiar mercies. Presume to examine
the brain in its eclectic cauldron
regarding the Brazen Head.

93

Pardon is incumbent, RAPMASTER, ór it
is nót. On balance I thínk nót. So
get in line, SNÚFF-MAN – with PRINCE OF FEATHERS –
PRATFALL his oppo – mourning Persephone
lost in September tribute, England's daughter.
Hack violence to yourself | brief miracle
confessions overridden. None of these
gifts us self-knowledge: she is beyond it
and you are nowhere | spielers of abuse.
Slów búrn, slów double-táke. The Northampton
MADONNA AND CHILD. She there? Cán it be
the grief matronal? Í shall return to thát.

PR 91:3, 2001

94

Hopefully, RAPMASTER, I can take stock
how best to oút-ráp you. Like Herod
raging in the street-pageants | work the crowd.
Bít short of puff these days. Swíg any óne
elixir to revive the *membrum*. Squeeze
bóth tubes for instant bonding. IT'S HÍS CÁLL.
In the Algarve, places like that, the Brits
are | heroes living as they háve to (*cheers*).
Where áre we? Lourdes? SOME sodding mystery tour.
Whát do you meán | a break? Pisses me off.
Great singer Elton John though. CHRIST
ALMIGHTY – even the buses are kneeling!

95

Politics, RAPMASTER, múst be a part
of oúr conformable mystery, this
twinship of loathing and true commonweal.
As yoú haunt Tudor polity | so Í
re-gaze the gaze of Holbein, my drawn face
a breath, a dust, of chalk-bloom; pettish
client between porch and easel. Skeleton Laureate
was a right rapper: outdance yoú with you shádes
ány dáy, And is góne, Moriscos, hatchet-men,
you would have been | and are. *De
Regno Christi*: breeding up a good and ill,
breaker of Eurostallions.

81

At the Old Powerhouse
Peter Redgrove

Kingston on Thames

A swan stretching
        its neck like a javelin speeds
                a couple of metres
Above the roughened river,
        the stridor of its breath-shaped
                wings like the creaking
Of a supple switch, a whipstock;
        descending further, the swan steps
                across the water in five
Giant strides, in five
        mighty braking steps, settles
                its own foldings
Among the waterfoldings, tucks
        its wings into its armpits, shrugging
                them in, and yachts onward
As a serenely-sailing ornamental waterbird
        reborn out of the turbulent and draughty
                air-voyager;
The river glitters like errant electricity
        and a watermusic floats downstream,
                a jazz funeral no less
With a band and a catafalque and a small black barge
        full of golden instruments;
                the powerhouse draws itself up
To attention like the old soldier
        it is; I expect smoke from the broken
                chimneys, from the colossal

PR 91:2, 2001

Hearth-chambers, but those
                        are swifts coiling on the air
                                        as the music coils
In the air that rushes
                sonorously through
                                the river-doubled
Trumpets and trombones.

82 The Hangar Ghosts
       Pauline Stainer

They come
as the hare dozes
in the dustless air

desultory
in their flying helmets
between huge drums of straw

silent, allspeaking
against the bruiseless blue,
as if the fuselage

        still judders through
        their bone-marrow
        between sorties

        and the sky,
        serious with snow,
        closes behind them.

PR 91:2, 2001

83

Eine Kleine Nachtmusik
Moniza Alvi

after the painting by Dorothea Tanning

You can lock the doors, even
bolt the air, but there's no way
of keeping your daughters in at night.
It doesn't matter how old they are –
three or four, six or seven –
a tornado throws them down the path
and ravishes them.
Stars glint like metal in their hair.
The darkness, fine as artists' ink,
seeps into their nightclothes.
If you follow them down the path –
you turn to stone.

Then long after the midnight hour
the wind flings them back into the hallway
and up onto the landing
with its cracked green paint.
Their blouses open up like curtains
on their narrow, childish chests.

Your daughters grow giant sunflowers
in the gloom.
Their hair streams upwards
thick as cypress trees.

PR 91:1, 2001

84

Big Safe Themes
Paul Farley

You can look all you like but the big safe themes are there
all around, forestalling what you were going to say.
A robust description of a cedarwood cigar box
has grown so big it could now contain Cuba and history.

No refuge in things. They stand at one or two removes
from the big themes: so any warm weather fruit might bring
visiting times and the loved one we begged not to leave
as soon as you sniff at the rind or spit out a pip.

You can start with a washer, a throat pastille, a mouse mat
and watch them move in like the weather. Trying to be brave
ends in tears: I've seen the big safe themes walk all over
incest and morris dancing in their ten-league boots.

Why resist anyway? Bend with the big safe themes.
Let them do what they will and admit that the road you walk
again and again – right down to its screw-thread of blood
in a quivering phlegm – is becoming your big safe theme.

PR 91:1, 2001

& Authentically Excruciating
Sean O'Brien

It is surely a widely shared view among freelance poet-critic-journalist-creative writing tutors of the Anything Legal Considered persuasion that in these evil economic times Hugo Williams's *Freelance* column in the *TLS* is one of the few things that make the whole business of freelancing bearable. Beset (or, worse, not beset) by deadlines, alarmed with threats, blasted by sighs and dismayed by broken editorial promises, the literary scuffler can pause at the outset of an anxious Thursday to reflect that at least he/she has not had to endure Williams's latest bout of – surely completely authentic – excruciation at the hands of financial necessity, cruel chance and his own beguilingly declared incompetence. Thus refreshed, the reader is able to move down the page and face this week's horrors in the NB column, which is Ecclesiastes to Williams's Wodehouse. This must be what they mean by balance.

Who apart from Williams has had to produce a column called 'Out and About in Women's Clothes'? How many others have ended up tutoring a bunch of fraudulent nutters on a Greek island? Even allowing for the endemic horrors of the writing class, who else has had to begin to explain in what ways a Plath-inspired poem beginning 'I am a garden of red and black sausages' leaves something to be desired? Imagine having to convey to a student that despite his conviction that 'the goal with which I started, to open my mind and release the creative energy inside me, has been accomplished', his work gets a C, not a B, never mind an A. Everyone involved in writing will of course have been close to some of this. They will have wished that people would leave their creative energy where it belongs. They will have wished, above all, to be elsewhere, at home, watching television or even (absurd notion) writing a poem. What Williams gives us is the nightmare in its perfected, Platonic form. His role is to suffer on our behalf – a cross between Saint Sebastian, Shelleyblake and Paul Pennyfeather: the patron saint of freelance life.

Reading this selection from several years of Williams's columns, it is soon clear that, unlike virtually all journalism, his stuff really does deserve to be reread. In fact, viewed as an unfolding project rather than the series of desperate last-minute accidents and inspirations Williams claims it to be, it achieves a weird encyclopeadic grandeur. Writer's block; the problem of apparently not working for a living; being distracted by cracks in the living room wall; accepting tasks for which one is not qualified; the time spent on trains; 'questions' at poetry readings; not getting an Arts Council bursary; schools courses at Arvon... The last of these is wincingly accurate:

> TUESDAY: the staggered consultations go gradually out of sync; by the end there are three fractious SAS types with headphones and shag spots sitting on my bed waiting to present their 'character sketch' of a big brother in the Navy before dashing off to the pub.

Exactly. If I were called in to design a hell for whichever pillock was responsible for promulgating the idea that the entire youth of the nation is seething with literary creativity fervently awaiting release, I would send him to teach one of these courses for the duration of eternity, if not longer. Yet, of course, Williams, like everyone else, does turn up in spite of it all. He does the teaching or whatever and he himself, rather than the punter, is the most frequent object of his own disfavour. And this too is true to the life, which often consists of self-sacrifice undertaken in the doomed interests of selfishness.

Freelancing is often howlingly funny. Those countless bores who write the kind of column-from-the-so-called-life which clogs the feature pages of the press could learn a lot from Williams. For example, in this field it isn't the verisimilitude that matters, so much as the quality of the supplier (*pace* a recent contributor to the letters page of the *TLS* on the subject of Tallulah Bankhead). Williams has reached the stage where he is at liberty to write about whatever he pleases – family history, holidays, the doomed youth of the sixties, standing in the wings of *This is Your Life*. It seems fair to suspect that, despite a careful air of unimportance, these cross sections of a life and times will turn out to be useful social history. And in the history of embarrassment, which is Williams's true subject in both verse and prose, he will be seen as one of the great explorers.

Freelancing, by Hugo Williams (Faber).

85

Orpheus
Alan Jenkins

What is life to me without thee?
                              Much the same,
except that I can't hear the great aria
sung by Kathleen Ferrier
and not be filled with longing and with shame,
so uncannily her portrait on the CD cover
resembles you; so uncannily her 1950s perm
brings you back, that first day of term,
waving me on to school. I missed you like a lover
and would have clawed through concrete and earth
to be at home with you, who had to let me go,
who gave me such a sense of my own worth
that I sing with her, as if Orpheus was my name...

*

What is left if thou art dead?
                              My attic flat,
the cat you took such pleasure in, who wonders why
I sit so late, and drink, and do not go to bed
to sleep an hour or so then wake
and soak the pillow for your sake,
who comforts me with purring in her sleep,
the gentle sleep she offers like a gift;
who does not as I do turn over in her head
the knowledge that you died between the night and morning shift,
that as you felt yourself slip
you heaved up the black bitter years that would dry
on your cold dead lips; she does not know that.

*

PR 94:1, 2004

Thy dear lord am I so faithful?
                                              No more or less
than when I bundled you into a wheelchair
in a stained pink hospital quilt
and the dazed smiles of women stranded in the regimen
of sleep and pills, your new friends, were rooting for us
as we struggled to that suburban high street where
you sat for your last wash and perm;
and we came back to their wondering chorus
of 'Ooh, lovely, dear', and you were young again,
touching your new hair, and I was without guilt
and loved you as on that first day of term,
as if I had won you back by this huge success.

86

Another Anniversary
Elaine Feinstein

Today is your birthday. There is cool sunshine.
Fig leaves and roses cover the wooden fence.
What happiness can I wish you in your death?

Here is the garden that I made for us
though you saw only the winter shape
of a weeping crab apple and a bare plum.

It was my offering. And so you received it.
Yet most of what we work at disappears.
Little we worry over has importance.

The greedy and the generous have the same end.
The dead know nothing and we cannot speak with them.
Still, in that silence, let me write: *dear friend*.

PR 95:4, 2005–6

87 Ghazal
Mimi Khalvati

after Hafez

However large earth's garden, mine's enough.
One rose and the shade of a vine's enough.

I don't want more wealth, I don't need more dross.
The grape has its bloom and it shines enough.

Why ask for the moon? The moon's in your cup,
a beggar, a tramp, for whom wine's enough.

Look at the stream as it winds out of sight.
One glance, one glimpse of a chine's enough.

Like the sun in bazaars, streaming in shafts,
any slant on the grand design's enough.

When you're here, my love, what more could I want?
Just mentioning love in a line's enough.

Heaven can wait. To have found, heaven knows,
a bed and a roof so divine's enough.

I've no grounds for complaint. As Hafez says,
isn't a ghazal that he signs enough?

PR 95:1, 2005

88   *from* I Would Softly Tell My Love
John Berger

[...]

Saturday

I'm not sure whether I ever saw Nazim Hikmet. I would swear to
it that I did, but I can't find the circumstantial evidence. I believe
it was in London in 1954. Four years after he had been released
from prison, nine years before his death. He was speaking at a polit-
ical meeting held in Red Lion Square, London. He said a few words
and then he read some poems. Some in English, others in Turkish.
His voice was strong, calm, highly personal and very musical. But
it did not seem to come from his throat – or not from his throat at
that moment. It was as though he had a radio in his breast, which
he switched on and off with one of his large, slightly trembling,
hands. I'm describing it badly because his presence and sincerity
were very obvious. In one of his long poems he describes six people
in Turkey listening in the early 1940s to a symphony by
Shostakovich on the radio. Three of the six people are (like him)
in prison. The broadcast is live; the symphony is being played at
that same moment in Moscow, several thousand kilometres away.
Hearing him read his poems in Red Lion Square, I had the impres-
sion that the words he was saying were also coming from the other
side of the world. Not because they were difficult to understand
(they were not), nor because they were blurred or weary (they
were full of the capacity of endurance), but because they were
being said to somehow triumph over distances and to transcend
endless separations. The here of all his poems is elsewhere.

> In Prague a cart –
> > a one-horse wagon –

PR 95:4, 2005–6

passes the Old Jewish Cemetery.
The cart is full of longing for another city,
I am the driver.[1]

Even when he was sitting on the platform before he got up to speak, you could see he was an unusually large and tall man. It was not for nothing that he was nicknamed 'The tree with blue eyes'. When he did stand up, you had the impression he was also very light, so light that he risked to become airborne.

Perhaps I never did see him, for it would seem unlikely that, at a meeting organised in London by the International Peace Movement, Hikmet would have been tethered to the platform by several guy-ropes so that he should remain earth-bound. Yet that is my clear memory. His words after he pronounced them rose into the sky – it was a meeting outdoors – and his body made as if to follow the words he had written, as they drifted higher and higher above the Square and above the sparks of the one-time trains which had been suppressed three or four years before along Theobald's Road.

You're a mountain village
                    in Anatolia,
you're my city,
                    most beautiful and most unhappy.
You're a cry for help – I mean, you're my country;
      the footsteps running towards you are mine.[2]

[…]

Wednesday

Nazim, I want to describe to you the table on which I'm writing. A white metal garden table, such as one might come across today in the grounds of a *yali* on the Bosphorus. This one is on the covered verandah of a small house in a southeast Paris suburb. This house was built in 1938, one of many houses built here at that time for

1 Nazim Hikmet, *Prague Dawn*, trans. Randy Blasing and Muten Konuk (Persea Books, 1994).
2 *You*, trans. Blasing and Konuk. *Ibid.*

artisans, tradesmen, skilled workers. In 1938 you were in prison. A watch was hanging on a nail above your bed. In the ward above yours three bandits in chains were awaiting their death sentence.

There are always too many papers on this table. Each morning the first thing I do, whilst sipping coffee, is to try to put them back into order. To the right of me there is a plant in a pot which I know you would like. It has very dark leaves. Their undersurface is the colour of damsons; on top the light has *stained* them dark brown. The leaves are grouped in threes, as if they were night butterflies – and they are the same size as butterflies – feeding from the same flower. The plant's own flowers are very small, pink and as innocent as the voices of kids learning a song in a primary school. It's a kind of giant clover. This particular one came from Poland where the plant's name is *Koniczyna*. It was given to me by the mother of a friend who grew it in her garden near the Ukrainian border. She has striking blue eyes and can't stop touching her plants as she walks through the garden or moves around her house, just as some grandmothers can't stop touching their young grandchildren's heads.

> My love, my rose,
> my journey across the Polish plain has begun:
> I'm a small boy happy and amazed
> a small boy
> looking at his first picture book
>   of people
>   animals
>   object, plants.[3]

In story-telling everything depends upon what follows what. And the truest order is seldom obvious. Trial and error. Often many times. This is why a pair of scissors and a reel of Scotch tape are also on the table. The tape is not fitted into one of those gadgets which makes it easy to tear off a length. I have to cut the tape with the scissors. What is hard is finding where the tape ends on the roll, and then unrolling it. I search impatiently, irritably with my finger-

3   'Letter from Poland', trans. Berger.

nails. Consequently, when once I do find the end, I stick it on to the edge of the table, and I let the tape unroll until it touches the floor, then I leave it hanging there.

At times I walk out of the verandah into the adjoining room where I chat or eat or read a newspaper. A few days ago, I was sitting in this room and something caught my eye because it was moving. A minute cascade of twinkling water was falling, rippling, towards the verandah floor near the legs of my empty chair in front of the table. Streams in the Alps begin with no more than a trickle like this.

A reel of Scotch tape stirred by a draught from a window is sometimes enough to move mountains.

Thursday evening

Ten years ago I was standing in front of a building in Istanbul near the Haydar-Pacha Station, where suspects were interrogated by the police. Political prisoners were held and cross-examined, sometimes for weeks, on the top floor. Hikmet was cross-examined there in 1938.

The building was not planned as a jail but as a massive administrative fortress. It appears indestructible and is built of bricks and silence. Prisons, constructed as such, have a sinister, but often also a nervous, make-shift air about them. For example, the prison in Bursa where Hikmet spent ten years was nicknamed 'the stone aeroplane', because of its irregular lay-out. The staid fortress I was looking at by the station in Istanbul had by contrast the confidence and tranquility of a monument to silence.

Whoever is inside here and whatever happens inside here – the building announced in measured tones – will be forgotten, removed from the record, buried in a crevice between Europe and Asia.

It was then that I understood something about his poetry's unique and inevitable strategy: it had to continually overreach its own confinement! Prisoners everywhere have always dreamt of the Great Escape, but Hikmet's poetry did not. His poetry, before it began, placed the prison as a small dot on the map of the world.

The most beautiful sea
              hasn't been crossed yet.
The most beautiful child
              hasn't grown up yet.
Our most beautiful days
              we haven't seen yet.
And the most beautiful words I wanted to tell you
              I haven't said yet.

They've taken us prisoner
they've locked us up:
              me inside the walls,
                you outside.
But that's nothing.
              The worst
is when people – knowingly or not –
carry prison inside themselves...
Most people have been forced to do this,

honest, hard-working good people
who deserve to be loved as much as I love you.[4]

His poetry, like a geometry compass, traced circles, sometimes intimate, sometimes wide and global, with only its sharp point inserted in the prison cell.

    [...]

Friday evening

Sometimes it seems to me that many of the greatest poems of the twentieth century – written by women as well as men – may be the most fraternal ever written. If so this has nothing to do with political slogans. It applies to Rilke who was apolitical; to Borges who was a reactionary; and to Hikmet who was a life-long Communist. Our century was one of unprecedented massacres,

---

4 *9–10pm. Poems*, trans. Blasing and Konuk.

yet the future it imagined (and sometimes fought for) proposed fraternity. Very few earlier centuries made such a proposal.

> These men, Dino,
> who hold tattered shreds of light:
> where are they going
> in this gloom, Dino?
> You, me too:
> we are with them, Dino.
> We too Dino
> have glimpsed the blue sky.[5]

Saturday

Maybe, Nazim, I'm not seeing you this time either. Yet I would swear to it that I am. You are sitting across the table from me on the verandah. Have you ever noticed how the shape of a head often suggests the mode of thinking which habitually goes on inside it?

There are heads which relentlessly indicate speed of calculation. Others which reveal the determined pursuit of old ideas. Many these days betray the incomprehension of continuous loss. Your head – its size and your screwed up blue eyes – suggest to me the coexistence of many worlds with different skies, one within another, inside it; not intimidating, calm, but used to overcrowding.

I want to ask you about the period we're living today. Much of what you believed was happening in history, or believed should happen, has turned out to be illusory. Socialism, as you imagined it, is being built nowhere. Corporate capitalism advances unimpeded – although increasingly contested – and the twin World Trade Towers have been blown up. The overcrowded world grows poorer every year. Where is the blue sky today that you saw with Dino?

Yes, those hopes, you reply, are in tatters, yet what does this really change? Justice is still a one-word prayer, as Ziggy Marley sings in your time now. The whole of history is about hopes being sustained, lost, renewed. And with new hopes come new theories.

5 'On a painting by Abidine, entitled The Long March', trans. Berger.

But for the overcrowded, for those who have little or nothing except, sometimes, courage and love, hope works differently. Hope is then something to bite on, to put between the teeth. Don't forget this. Be realist. With hope between the teeth comes the strength to carry on even when fatigue never lets up, comes the strength, when necessary, to choose not to shout at the wrong moment, comes the strength above all not to howl. A person, with hope between her or his teeth, is a brother or sister who commands respect. Those without hope in the real world are condemned to be alone. The best they can offer is only pity. And whether these hopes between the teeth are fresh or tattered makes little difference when it comes to surviving the nights and imagining a new day.

Do you have any coffee?

I'll make some.

I leave the verandah. When I come back from the kitchen with two cups – and the coffee is Turkish – you have left. On the table, very near where the Scotch tape is stuck, there is a book, open at a poem you wrote in 1962:

If I was a plane tree – I would rest in its shade
If I was a book
I would read, without being bored, on sleepless night
Pencil I would not want to be, even between my own fingers,
If I was door
I would open for the good and shut for the wicked
If I was window, a wide open window, without curtains
I would bring the city into my room
If I was a word
I would call out for the beautiful, the just, the true
If I was word
I would softly tell my love.[6]

6 'Under the Rain', trans. Özen Ozüner and Berger.

89

Fantasia on a Theme of James Wright
Sean O'Brien

There are miners still
In the underground rivers
Of West Moor and Palmersville.

There are guttering cap-lamps bound up in the roots
Where the coal is beginning again.
They are sinking slowly further

In between the shiftless seams,
To black pools in the bed of the world.
In their long home the miners are labouring still –

Gargling dust, going down in good order,
Their black-braided banners aloft,
Into flooding and firedamp, there to inherit

Once more the tiny corridors of the immense estate
They line with prints of Hedley's *Coming Home.*
We hardly hear of them.

There are the faint reports of spent economies,
Explosions in the ocean floor,
The thud of iron doors sealed once for all

On prayers and lamentation,
On pragmatism and the long noyade
Of a class which dreamed itself

PR 95:3, 2005

Immortalized by want if nothing else.
The singing of the dead inside the earth
Is like the friction of great stones, or like the rush

Of water into newly opened darkness. Oh my brothers,
The living will never persuade them
That matters are otherwise, history done.

90   The Glair
Robin Robertson

The slow drag across the sandpaper,
scratching smoke
from the head of the match
again and again until it flares.
Lamplight lies heavy on her breasts,
her flanks; the hand's passage
slow as ceremony, persistent
as a dream unsleeved; the spark
drawn in hard with a catch
of flame: the lumbering storm
and the white bolt, the bright rope, on
and on and on. The albumen. The glair.

PR 95:4, 2005–6

91

Ama et fac quod vis
John Burnside

for Piritta Maavuori

The God of St Paul, who is
no respecter of persons

might just as easily have been
the self

     – that loves what it will
and watches us quicken and fade
with the passing of time

as calmly as we watch our shadows form
and lengthen, with each shift and slant of light.

★

Silencio es argumento levado a cabo por otros methodos.
Ernesto Guevara

What we intend
and what we allow to happen
is anyone's guess.

All week my voice was failing – first husky, then strained,
till it guttered away to a whisper

and disappeared;
           guttered away

PR 95:3, 2005

this morning, when the snow began to fall,
whiting out streets and gardens, muffling the cars,

until it seemed the only good reply
was silence:
                    not

the quiet of dismay,
but what Guevara thought of as the argument
continued – *carried on*

by other means – that cold and salty pact
the body has with things unlike itself

– a snowfall, or a gust of Russian wind,
the evanescence of an upper room
that might be something new, or someone gone

a moment since
                              and how it is transformed
by what it never finds
                                        – no soul; no
shadow:

                              ⋆

Propose what you like;
                                        propose
causality
              the notion of the self
how one thing follows another
in grim succession

it only takes a moment in the wind
to break that argument.

Consider the body: changeable, incomplete,
yet still continuous:

think how it holds the perfect likenesses
of all the former selves that it is not,

how casually it gathers and renews
the forms we have scarcely noticed – winter buds,

a flock of starlings turning on the air,
the bleached grass skirting the lake
                                        or the snake-bark of maples –

and how, on a morning like this, with our everyday lives
suspended
                in these white parentheses

we start again from scratch: the coming night;
the ferry that runs to the island;
                                        the sullen ice;

the shapes we have scarcely noticed, bearing us on
to all we have yet to become
                                to the blank of a future.

                        *

I wake in the dark and the dream evaporates before I can grasp
                                                        the details

– something about a bell, and prints in the snow;
my dream self distinct from the person I seem in waking;

my dream self, bright and light-footed,
a holy, unclouded soul, tracking these prints to the edge of a
                                        sycamore wood –

the details blurring and suddenly melting away
and only a moment's afterlife of joy:
the body a solid again, the mind a distraction,
the net of the slipshod entangling the peregrine heart.

★

In the small hours,
awake and alone,

waiting for snow, or watching the snow as it falls,
from an upper room,

as far as I am from home,
and as strange as I seem,

what could I really prefer
to the weight of the self?

its deftness, on nights like this,
its immutable grace,

the only means I have
of bearing witness?

★

This morning I followed a trail
to the edge of the woods,

then felt the shadow watching as I lost
my nerve:
                    a brightness

slipped behind the rain;
an aftermath
                    of lanolin and dust.

*

Now I look back from the warmth
of a scentless house

with something foreign
cradled in my chest

and wonder that I took its weight
for safety, all those nights I passed untouched

and dreaming,
like a calf lulled in the dark

while something sweet
unfolds along the blade,

lifeblood
                         or rapture
taken for a song.

92

Darling
Jackie Kay

You might forget the exact sound of her voice,
Or how her face looked when sleeping.
You might forget the sound of her quiet weeping
Curled into the shape of a half moon,

When smaller than her self, she seemed already to be leaving
Before she left, when the blossom was on the trees
And the sun was out, and all seemed good in the world.
I held her hand and sang a song from when I was a girl –

Heel y'ho boys, let her go boys
And when I stopped singing she had skipped away,
Already a slip of a girl again, skipping off,
Her heart light, her face almost smiling.

And what I didn't know, or couldn't see then,
Was that she really hadn't gone.
The dead don't go till you do, loved ones.
The dead are still here holding our hands.

PR 96:4, 2006–7

& *from* The Lyric Principle, Part 2: The Sound of Sense[1]
Don Paterson

[...]

Poetry, I think, proceeds not from a selfish but a generous instinct. Whatever inner tensions have been assuaged in our writing, we want to give these things away in the end. To have someone else want your poem for themselves, it must be desirable; to be desirable, it must be – in the broadest sense – beautiful; and for a reader to find it beautiful, it must exhibit some of the symmetry we find in the natural. (By 'symmetry' I don't merely mean 'symmetry of form'.) This last might seem a bit of a leap, though it's as old-school as it comes, of course: it's been a cliché since Plato and Aristotle to say that the reason we find a piece of art satisfying is because it is 'imitative of nature'.[2] I still like to think of a poem as kind of a man-made natural object, our 'best effort', that we quietly slip back into the world, and to which the world can make no serious objection.

Poetry is often compared to music, but most of the comparisons are pretty facile, or plain false. In important one way, however, I think they're closely analogous processes. If we define music as those sustained noises that we consensually agree make satisfying or emotionally meaningful arrangements of sound, when we examine such a noise, and look at the way that one note-event follows another, we find that their sequenced

---

1 Might as well start with a footnote. No, I don't mean quite the same thing as Frost, who used the phrase more generally to describe syntax as well as tone, and the poem as 'talk-song'.

2 The occasional use of the phrase 'organic verse' for 'free verse' is just substituting an error – a pretty stupid one – for a misnomer. In the organic, symmetry is everywhere. Once wholly 'freed' from every aspect of formal patterning, a poem may indeed be 'organic', but only like some kind of diseased amoeba. A better defence of faith-based free verse practice is the Lawrentian argument that it more closely represents the dynamic shape of spontaneous thought; but even this tends to ignore the fact that thought itself is highly rhythmic – and that spontaneous thoughts are often the least original we have. The 'flash of inspiration', welcome as it is, has given spontaneity an undeservedly good name. First thought = worst thought, speaking personally.

PR 97:3, 2007

patterns converge on the same fractal statistic[3] that we find in natural dynamic systems – everything from quasar emissions to river discharge, traffic flow, sunspot activity and DNA sequences. It is something often referred to as 'pink noise'. This is neither 'white noise' (in acoustics, it's that *shhhh* sound where all frequencies are heard simultaneously, at equal power) where the relation between one note and the next is uncorrelated and completely random); nor is it correlated 'brown' or – more accurately – 'Brownian noise', where pitch of the next note is decided wholly on the position of the previous one, through the application of an inflexible rule. Music generated on a white noise algorithm is ugly in its unpredictability, and Brownian just as so in its predictability. But if we hit upon something in between, something 'pink', we find it beautiful: in other words, something that corresponds to our ideal balance of predictable regularity and surprise.

While analyses of static forms in nature – the outline of a landscape, for example – reveal correlated 'Brownian' patterns,[4] when it comes to natural dynamic processes we find pink noise dominating; it appears to be the characteristic signature of complex systems, i.e. those which display non-random variation. The changing content of our sensory experience seems to hover around the pink noise mark; this sensory music is as much a product of the nervous system as of nature – the *input* received at our physical extremities can be near-chaotic white noise, but our brains filter it down to pink, screening out the irrelevant noisy data, and leaving only those patterns of change which have become useful to our specific evolved intelligence. The wholly dynamic, time-based medium of music is dominated by this, and the pattern of regularity and variation in its pitch and volume (just like human speech, incidentally) matches perhaps more perfectly than any other kind of art the spectral density of our flickering perception of the world.

It seems reasonable to assume that our brains also perceive the dynamic system of the successful poem as similarly balanced. (The poem *itself* can be thought of as operating, in its way, like a miniature nervous system, screening the pink noise of our perception even further, leaving only a pattern of locally significant data.) The best poetry has nothing so

---

3   The l/f ratio of spectral density.
4   Perhaps an explanation why we find Brownian noise acceptable in static visual art, but not in dynamic time-based art; the static and visual aspect of poetry – its typographic arrangement on the page – is tellingly 'correlated' in its stanzaic and lineated symmetries, however.

easily measurable as note pitch and length, however, but I'd suggest that were we able to accurately measure its concrete and abstract speech, its light and dense lines, the pattern of its metrical agreement and disagreement, we would see something identical emerge: an honourable echo of nature, of its balance of correlated and uncorrelated, of randomness and self-similarity.[5] And, perhaps, in its most crucial equilibrium: that of

5   Were we *really* able to measure those things accurately, there would be nothing to stop us automating the process. While I believe that one day it will be entirely possible to write a great poem with a computer, we will probably have already 'gone biotech' by then, and begun the smart move from carbon to silicon – in which case it won't seem such a big deal to our bionic scions. (Indeed such an elusive poetic algorithm already seems to exist in our wet brains, and it doesn't seem miraculous or impossible to us: it probably should.) We are far closer to devising such a thing for music, though, and the fact that poetry and music are comparable systems seems to suggest that we only lack a proper description of our own compositional process. The perennial fear is that the work would shed its 'humanity' – but one only has to look at the way traditional music skills have been ported over to programming to see those fears are quite unfounded. On the contrary – programmers invest their music with as much humanity and human expression as any other language, and the laptop turns out to be as humanly responsive as any other instrument. (Paradoxically the necessity of *programming in* the humanity, has led to a bizarre expertise in the expressive exaggeration of human error: computer-based music is already in its Romantic phase.) The fear is just the standard wariness over new means of production: similar misgivings were initially voiced over cameras, typewriters, the pianoforte and the printing of books themselves. There is no good reason why computers should not soon be useful to our art. Generative music programming – essentially the art of judiciously modulating white noise aleatoric data with some brown noise rules to produce something delightfully 'pink' – is fairly close to providing some very decent music, and reminds us that Bach's genius was computational as well as inspirational. Poetry is a vastly more complex business only because its listable parameters are far, far more numerous, but *not* – who would seriously claim this – because it captures any more of the human spirit than does music. Current efforts at generative poetry are still aspiring to the merely daft, and most depend upon stochastic algorithms to produce surreal effects of 'the fatuous banana spliced my windmill' variety – which appear 'poetic' only because nonsensical linguistic input overstimulates our connecting faculties. Poets, needless to say, have had nothing to do with their programming. An algorithm for poetry would be incredibly complex, but not infinitely so; and its detachment from such overvalued and sentimental constructs as 'the individual voice' could be just the thing to propel us into a new era of Classicism, should we desire or require such a thing.

predictability and surprise, the familiar and the unfamiliar, the known and the unknown. Wholly familiar 'Brownian' poetry consists in the mere rehearsal of what the poet (and usually the reader) already know to be the case, and unfolds in a wholly predictable manner; it fails because it doesn't surprise. 'White' poetry is all unfamiliarity and novelty and discontinuity, and fails because it does nothing *but* surprise. (This sounds just dandy, until we consider that there is nothing so predictably dull as an infinite series of exceptions). If our aim really is epiphany, the poem must demonstrate a move from the known to the unknown, an uncorrelated leap from a correlated position; but it can only do so by actually *making* it – and therein lies the risk and seriousness of our word-game.

There is a musical balance to be achieved too. Poetry *naturally* refines the music of language to something pink – something correlated, modulated by something variable – and it's that mechanism I'll spend the rest of this essay discussing. Poetry achieves a balance of shifting vowel and echoed consonant, of airy music and stop-heavy music that is, perhaps more than any other physical property it exhibits, the true emblem of its natural art.

★

One of those hellish things you learn after ten years working in editing – I hardly dare confess this – is that you can hold a poem a yard away, and without having read a word, know there's a 99 per cent chance that you won't like it. Most often this is because any random two- or three-line passage appears to contain all the letters of the alphabet. (Centred text, copperplate fonts and falling bits of potpourri are also excellent pointers.) This means the poem is unlikely to have any music. The phenomenon of 'music' in poetry is often spoken about as if it were a mysterious quality; but if we mean 'music' as in 'music', rather than 'some ineffable thing which my poetic intuition can subjectively divine, but is beyond human articulation', it's actually very simply characterised. Except in some very particular cases, it means that the poem displays deliberate organisation and some form of symmetry or parallelism in its arrangement of sound. If a 'music' is ascribed to a poem, but cannot be described through pointing to some parallel phonic effect (or – stretching the definition to its limit – a patterned silence), the only music the listener has identified is that which resides naturally in the language itself.

The error is often made because this language-music is not inconsiderable. Even in everyday speech, given a choice of synonyms, we will express an unconscious preference for the more harmonious (i.e. the contextually lyric) sound when we need to make strong sense. This effect is naturally strengthened the more considered our speech, and speechwriters alliterate and assonate almost helplessly; written prose betrays a higher degree of lyric patterning again – and poetry, of course, even more so. (The self-conscious foregrounding of this patterning in prose is what – next to a lingering over description – most often leads to the equivocal diagnosis of 'poetic' writing.) But even a random series of words will appear to demonstrate a musical coherence simply by virtue of any one language being a closed phonemic system, and having a finite set of sounds it can combine.[6] Each language uses only a fraction of the possible sounds that human voice can produce; English does remarkably well – of the two hundred-odd phonemes in global use, it manages around fifty. We might pity the native Hawaiian speaker with their mere thirteen, but a poet would sensibly envy them. When you think about it, it must be an effort to speak a sentence in Hawaiian that is *not* lyrically coherent.

Nonetheless, even without salient sound effects like rhyme, assonance or alliteration to point to, we often have the strong sense that something is going on beside the mere intrinsic musicality of the language; and indeed there is.

In English poetry, the feeling that a piece of writing is 'musical' usually means that it quietly exhibits two kinds of phonetic bias. Between them they represent the repetition and variation, the similarity and difference (the motif the human brain craves in everything it perceives, if it is simultaneously to make both connections and distinctions) that we find in every aspect of poetic composition. I'll name them now, and expand on them later. The first is the deliberate variation of vowel sounds; the second is consonantal patterning.

Between them, these two tendencies have come to represent an

---

6 This is the 'musicality' we quickly divine in languages or dialects we have trouble understanding (but are slow to acknowledge in our own); left to focus on the sound, we can attend to their pure music – hence the apparently infinite suggestiveness of song-lyrics in those languages. Someone once asked me to comment on that cut-up collage stuff you get with your spam-mail, saying how beautiful and close to poetry some of it sounded. The trouble is that *any* old random garbage often strikes us as beautiful and poetic: this, however, pays a compliment to language itself, not to the poem. In such circumstances, having little in the way of conventional meaning to distract us, we can attend to the sound alone, and enjoy the distinctive gabble of the Anglophone.

unconscious 'lyric ideal' in English. Importantly they must be *no more* than tendencies. Generally speaking, if sound-patterning is too strong, too conspicuous, it will be perceived as contrived, and distract from the sense – open Edith Sitwell's *Collected Poems* at random, if you want to see what I mean – unless it performs some explicit mnemonic or structural function, like Anglo-Saxon alliteration or terminal rhyme. (These *are*, in a way, perceived as contrivances – but they are passed over as the age's agreed modes of poetic artifice, the conventions of the poem's expert making, their invisible fashions.) A normative shift towards vowel heterophony and consonantal homophony creates the unconscious experienced 'lyric ground', above which the consciously registered saliences of rhyme, assonance and alliteration can cleanly stand. Just as we see a global shift from denotative to connotative speech in the poem, so we see (concomitantly, bootstrapped from the phonosemantic system) a global shift from an inchoate language-music to an explicit poetry-music. All poets with half an ear default to the lyric ground more or less all the time; it is, in effect, the poet's working medium, the canvas, clay and stone from which they carve out the poem.

In the human voice, the vowel carries the bulk of the feeling in its complex tonal and quantitative discriminations, while the consonants which interrupt that breath makes the bulk of the sense. The consonant, in making the distinction between *blue* and *shoe* and *true*, gives the phonetic differentiation we need to have a sign-system capable of carrying distinct meanings; the envelopes with which it shapes the vowel allow for discrete words to be heard, in much the same way that physical borders allow us to perceive discrete objects. The material basis of that sign-system, though, is the voiced breath. Vowel fills the word with its fairly uniform stuff, while the consonant carves it into recognizable shapes. Consider, say, a mother's frustrated demand to her child, 'Put down the cup.' It's easy to separate out the four vowels | ʊ | aʊ | ɪ | ʌ | ('oo – ow –ih – uh') then imagine the first vowel pitched high to indicate urgency, the second dipping down an interval of a fifth or sixth to reinforce the impression of sane control, the third pitched identically to the first to reinforce the imperative, and the last rising another fifth – and increased in loudness – to convey the non-negotiability and frustration of the demand. The emotional sense would be clear from such a performed sequence of tones, if not the literal sense; but the consonants *pt dn th cp* alone will give us a fair stab at the semantic content, if not the tonal shape. (Note that with the consonants removed, speech suddenly becomes an extremely complex kind of singing.)

In the non-performative context of written language, however, things are trickier. Try all the different ways you can pitch 'I love you', if you want to demonstrate the hopelessly attenuated emotional palette of written speech; spoken, it's easy to draw out shades of meaning that are alternately questioning, pleading, heartfelt, insecure, angry, desperate, tender, insincere, placatory and so on, just by modifying the song of the vowels. In written language, the performative cues have to be given by interpreted sense; this is provided in a thousand different ways, but phonically, it's something delegated largely to the consonant. Because written speech doesn't represent the pitch- and length-patterns that give it its expressive range, it's easy for the vowel to become devalued – to the extent that some graphic systems have done without it altogether. Poetry, in declaring itself as emotional, urgent speech, and in signing its kinship with song, puts the vowel back centre-stage. How does it do this?

Because vowels have perceptible duration, they are easy to hear. You can test this by trying to repeat the vowel sounds in the previous sentence; you should be able to do so almost thoughtlessly, and just repeat the sentence as a form of de-consonated babytalk. *Because vowels have duration they are easy to hear:* ə ˈɔ | ˈaʊ ə | æ | ʊ ˈa ə | eɪ | æ | ˈɪ ɪ | ʊ | ɪ | – or something like it. Now try and do the same with the consonants. It's almost impossible without thinking about it very carefully. The vowel is the main durational component of the word; the consonant we often experience as temporally negligible. [...]

However it cheers me to think that in poetry we have long thought of ourselves as starting not to start with the *logos* but the *pneuma*, not with those Platonic consonantal forms, but with the ether that encircles and unites them – the inspiration, the afflatus, the breath; the breath being the infinite possibility into which consonant, not vowel, must be driven to make it have any sense in the currency of our speech. This strikes me as a far more serious kind of word-game. Poets from Tennyson to Antonio Machado have often lighted on 'wind' as the idealized inspirational source – shaping its one long vowel around every object it meets, embodying our paradoxical pursuit of unity through an utterly distinct articulation of the specific. And of course it brings weather, words, voices, scents from afar, from impossible elsewheres.

Singing works by 'unnaturally' elongating the vowel and so diminishing the prominence of the consonant. This can be seen in its treatment of end-rhymes; sung, the words *soon, room, cool, roof* are often perceived as close-to-full, and the longer the note, the closer they get. For lyricists, then, assonantal rhymes can work like full rhymes: when the Bobster sings 'Let me sleep in your meadows with the green grassy leaves / Let me walk down the highway with my brother in peace', we're relatively untroubled by the inaccuracy of the rhyme, however upset some of us are by his voice. And as you'd expect, in exaggerating the vowel, singing will often foreground the emotional sense at the expense of the denotative.[7] Instrumental music itself may be considered usefully as an unbroken vowel, a kind of pure tonal and quantitative speech whose purpose is to carry emotion alone – like the spoken vowel, only vastly more supple and articulate. But the absence of consonant in music means that we are left with something possessive of emotional articulacy, but with no differentiating ability, no way to construct a sign-system, and thus no denotative power. When Richard Strauss said, with little irony: 'I look forward to the day I can describe a teaspoon accurately in music,' everyone was justifiably sceptical; indeed the teaspoon has remained wholly elusive. In a good jazz ballad solo, especially in an instrument close in timbre to the voice, like a tenor saxophone, the displacement and pitch of the notes are so closely mapped to the rhythms and cadences of a plaintive and convincing conversational speech that you can easily imagine 'enconsonating' the notes to give a denotative sense. (Some 'vocalese' artists couldn't resist doing just that to a number of famous solos – with predictably farcical results.)[8] In a sense, however, poetry does precisely this: in making a normative shift towards privileging the vowel and so

7 This is what people mean when they say things like 'She could break your heart singing the phonebook.' More practically, most librettists will have had the miserable experience of hearing their best line rendered unintelligible by having it set for long notes in the upper register of the soprano voice – which has the vowel /i/ and no other; though composers have devised a million other ways to lose lines too. This is one reason the librettist-composer relationship should sensibly be considered a co-operative, and not collaborative one.

8 Something to think about, or not: since consonant is the tool of differentiation, of denotative meaning, a block of consonant (like the Torah) seems to propose a monosemic source, which is why the multiple reinterpretations suggested by Kabbalistic re-envoweling appeared to many as wholly heretical; a block of vowel (like music), on the other hand, seems to imply a polysemic source, which is why a single interpretation seems *equally* heretical – as well as hilariously reductive, and instantly redundant. As anyone who has suffered Eddie Jefferson's enconsonation of Coleman Hawkins' classic solo on 'Body and Soul' will testify with alacrity. ('Don't you know he was the king of the saxophone,' etc. No shit, man.)

restoring some of the quantitative length found in speech, it edges towards a kind of transitive music.

It is this exaggerated prominence given to the vowel that primarily distinguishes the characteristic noise of the poem from prose or conversational speech, though the effect is very subtle. In received ideals of 'beautiful' English lyric, we tend to find, upon close examination of the texts, that vowels are strongly emphasized through a pattern of their deliberate contrast and variation, so that each word retains its distinct spirit, and has the sense of standing in a clearly-stated and discrete spatial and temporal relation to those on either side.

[…]

Let me wind this up by proposing an analogy: consonant is to vowel as noun is to verb. Consonant is bounded form, non-durational, atemporal, like the static object; vowel is spatially free, durational, temporal, like the dynamic process. Consonant divides as instant and boundary divide; vowel unites as space and time unite. Somewhere in the unconscious, the echoed consonants imply similarities of form – and singular arrangements of them, differences; varied vowels imply spatial and temporal separation, and echoed vowels, space-time parallels, proximity, and similarities of interior spirit.

[…]

93

W.S. Merwin
Europe

After days untold the word
came You will see it
tomorrow you will
see what you have only heard of
ever since you were too small
to understand and that night
which I would scarcely remember
I lay looking up through
the throb of iron at sea
trying again to remember
how I believed it would look
and in the morning light
from the bow of the freighter
that I know must have gone by now
to the breaker's decades ago
then I could make out the shadow
on the horizon before us
that was the coast of Spain
and as we came close another
low shape passing before it
like a hand on a dial
a warship I recognised
from a model of it I had made
when I was a child
and beyond it
there was a road down the cliff
that I would descend some years later
knowing it when I reached it
there they were all together
it seemed for the first time

PR 96:2, 2006

94

Mariola with Angel Choir
Medbh McGuckian

In the shrill turquoise air
Of first century Palestine
The rough-hewn cross is already
Regenerating: lily crucifix.

Jesus's lips are a winestock:
His Z-bend, the ropelike winding
Of his legs, are provocations
To the senses. He is smiling

Almost as broadly as the pet
Swan on his foot rest – his keynote
Above all is assurance –
Bells and fragrances.

What strikes now is the sudden
Glory of his smile in its measured
Beauty, and the smiling
Of his censing angels, an array

Of thirty bust-length
Jubilant and psalmodic,
Great and trumpeting,
Colossal and tremendous angels:

Angel with Crown of Thorns,
(Meaning whether herbs or harmonies
Are capable of preventing
A demon from afflicting mankind),

PR 97:1, 2007

Angel with Hawk, Lure and Gauntlets,
Angel with Bird of Prey, playing
A game with a hood, the frowning
Angel of the Expulsion.

Some slim and lithe, others
Squat, one so fat as to seem
Incapable of flight – one mighty angel,
The Angel of the Millstone.

Weighty, ample figures,
Prodigious and surprising,
In their magnificent ranks
And zestful deviations.

In their hilaritas, their buoyant
Musicality, their multiplicity,
Their dazzling, swift and powerful
Intelligences sharpening language

With their final vocabularies:
Strong, resident angels,
Vigilant, secreted angels,
Imported to stand on colonettes

And crown the sacred kings of England;
Greeting the precocious dawn
Near the East window with its Northern
French geometry whereby one might

Be seduced by it, and seduction
Become rapture. (In summer especially,
The progressive illumination
During the dawn office of Lauds.)

The ninth order of angels, assuming
In their bustling jollity the wings
Of the morning: still alert to this church
And its clumsy prayer, rotated

To their nimble and peculiar
Fingertips, spectacular and outspread,
Facing away in their strange idiom,
The spinning of the angels called virtues.

95 *from* Lyric and Razo: Activism and the Poet
John Kinsella

An essay on activism and poetry is by necessity a personal one. For
me, environmentalism, for want of a better word, is what I do in
life and in writing. However, long ago I differentiated between
polemic and open-endedness, between rhetoric and, if one likes,
the lyric impulse. Rarely does one write a poem of pure anything;
but ultimately, though not exclusively, I try to keep the balance
towards the open-ended lyric rather than propagandist rhetoric.
Although I can get mighty pissed off and even write poems with
subtitles like 'a poem of abuse'; but I try to undo my own sincerity
and zeal with irony and/or figurative tugs of the carpet from
beneath the certainty of my 'feet'. A poem in which language is
not the prime generator is no poem at all for me. What's more,
such a poem is a hell of a lot less effective as activism. If the reader
has to work at the poem, s/he is more likely to think about the
issues being explored, struggled with. Poetry should be a struggle.
[...]
While many might argue that prose would be a more effective

tool for the activist – that is more to the point, and more direct – I would argue differently. However, prose might form an important prelude, even component, of poetry. Be it Dante's *La Vita Nuova*, or the *razos* written to accompany troubadour songs, explication is an active and integral part of poetry. Whether in the glosses of *The Rime of the Ancient Mariner*, or the prose 'responses' within the haibun, prose becomes a counterpoint. This prose doesn't have to 'explain' a poem – in fact, who really wants a poem explained? – but it can interact and hence enrich, and highlight or offset the poem. A bit like a frame around a painting, or the space around a sculpture. This essay, then, is an auto-*razo* to an activist poetics.

[...] As an anarchist, interaction with legals [...] does not appeal to me, but in the end they are the translators of language to fact in the structures with which one has to deal regarding this matter. 'The law' takes the kernel of the poem and writes the *razos* that come before it. As a connected action, I took the poems I had written about [an] issue, and circulated them. I had done the same thing after attending the Ludlow Tuart Forest protest a few years before.

Poetry is an effective way of taking the discussion out of 'interest areas' into a broader discussion. I would argue that the metonymic connection between the trees we exploit for paper, and our writing, is just cause for investigation of source and culpability on behalf of the writer. I gave a workshop a few years ago when two smart teenagers spent their time mocking environmentalism in writing because of this very reason. It's an obvious target, nothing really smart there, but I had to pay them credit for their consistency. The issue, the contradictions, weren't going to go away. Computers excepted (and they too bring their own myriad of environmental issues), paper is the tissue of the writer's body. I was down south last week, checking out plantation timber: native bushland surreptitiously cleared, the use of pesticides and herbicides – the golden dream is not always so golden. It needs vigilance, monitoring, and writing about. What we write with and on are part of the responsibility.

The problems of the plantation timber industry aside, the starting point is the preservation of native forests. Here is a poem written in protest to the logging of jarrah in native forests in Western Australia. It was written prior to the Arcadia protest, but with the same region and actions in mind. The first two lines are taken from the 'Love Sonnet' by Zora Cross (Australian poet who wrote largely during the First World War) of the same number:

XXXI

We must look around upon our children dear,
Living through them, this present and that past;
And this is never more evident
Than when walking through old-growth forest;
The toddler ambling ecstatically the filtered light,
Rough-barked jarrah towering and closely packed,
Birds endemic to that place only
Darting around the undergrowth; his pleasure
Palpable, loggers nowhere nearby,
Though yellow markings on trunks,
Pink ribbon fluttering down the valley,
A 'grammar' of his children's barren landscape;
Denecourt's wild walks take us nowhere here,
A lust for aluminium undoing the propaganda.

There are connections between the naturing of the poem and the naturing of de-natured lives: the European wild walk as entertainment and reconnection with 'lost primeval roots' is played with in relation to the colonisation of 'Australia'. This is a poem that celebrates place, and laments loss, but also tackles language as the generator that makes such colonisation possible and likely, as well as challenging it. Language and activism co-exist tautologically, capable of achieving the same ends, and also of being mere distractions. Activism as an act of mere habit is like uttering clichés without respecting and experiencing the richness of the clichés – their necessity for existence, their different inflections and implications with every use.

I chose this poem, in the context of this essay, for the last line: the jarrah is also cleared for mining bauxite, which is then turned into aluminium. Most of us make use of aluminium, including the locked-on activists: in their dragons, and in cooking their meals around the campfire. The inescapable irony in action becomes the undoing of the poem in language. 'Human kind / cannot bear very much reality.' How many of my essays have quoted this truism? The following poem was written sometime after visiting the Arcadia activist site, but with the future activism outlined above in mind. It is part of my version of Dante's *Paradiso*, in progress at the moment. The allusions are all to Dante's twenty-first canto: the contemplative, the golden ladder, predestination, and the usual condemnation of papal corruption. The ingredients are all there for a piece of activist verse that is also a nature lyric (after all, that's what I basically write), and a piece of metatext:

Canto of Arcadia (Saturn, 21)

She won't smile the smile of incineration.
They won't sing the song of disintegration.
Together sprung, noise music, see-through mirrors.

Locusts spin in flurries. They have begun to fly.
The bobtail out the back is fat. Crow feathers
are strewn over acres. Rings forming

in the bright sky. Their descent is known.
The ladder is propped up against the rainwater
tank – I have to ascend to clear the leaves

from the grille, but she would only have me descend:
precarious, I perch. My ears are giving me hell.
Two days ago we drove down to Arcadia.

Into Arcadia along forestry roads, rutted
by logging trucks filling the quota. The protest
camp with its wire and papier-mâché

quokka. Mainland quokkas ranging the jarrah forest.
Four hundred meter corridor – promised – barely
two hundred. The sacred stream, arterial, filled

and forded. In and out of dieback like humour.
Fifty-year regrowth cradling the undergrowth.
Marri trees less useful to Gunns – horror

company – left as Habitat. Marked H in rings.
Occult emblems glowing out of brown-greens.
Ensconced in the forest, fallacy is sucked

into machinery, police wagons. About the campfire
dreadlocked souls discuss lock-on methods. Concrete
and car bodies and piping and their own impact

on the forest. I am here now, the soul glow still
intense but tremulous. Camp dogs snap at flies –
that's memory, and taking the message out

is what's supposed to happen. To be arrested
is to arrest attention? To believe in something
is better than believing in nothing? Tree by tree.

She won't smile the smile of incineration.
They won't sing the song of disintegration.
Together sprung, noise music, see-through mirrors.

This poem leads a dual life as 'entertainment' to be read in a
volume of poetry, and as 'activism', preferably read aloud to both
activists and those one is protesting against, in order to provoke
discussion and debate over a specific issue. It fits in neither place
comfortably; neither do I want it to. It is a hybrid.

[...]

There's not much of a gap between love and activism and the
creation of a poem. Apart from protesting against a destruction,
the activist poem also attempts to provide moments of the
beauty / 'good' one is attempting to preserve. That even out of loss,
a future positive might be achieved. [...]

96

Alice Oswald
Two Moon Poems

1   In a Tidal Valley

flat stone sometimes lit sometimes not
one among many moodswung creatures
that have settled in this beautiful
Uncountry of an Estuary

swans pitching your wings
in the reedy layby of a vacancy
where the house of the sea
can be setup quickly and taken down in an hour

all you flooded and stranded weeds whose workplace
is both a barren mud-site and a speeded up garden
full of lake-offerings and slabs of light
which then unwills itself listen

all you crabs in the dark alleys of the wall
all you mudswarms ranging up and down
I notice you are very alert and worn out
skulking about and grabbing what you can

listen this is not the ordinary surface river
this is not river at all this is something
like a huge repeating mechanism
banging and banging the jetty

very hard to define, most close in kind
to the mighty angels of purgatory
who come solar-powered into darkness
using no other sails than their shining wings

yes this is the Moon this hurrying
muscular unsolid unstillness
this endless wavering in whose engine
I too am living

PR 97:3, 2007

2 Mud

this evening those very thin fence posts
struggled up out of the mud again
and immediately the meal began, there was
that flutter of white napkins of waders hurrying in

there was that bent old egret
prodding and poising his knife and fork
and so many mucous mudglands
so much soft throat sucking at my feet

I thought be careful this is deep mud this is
pure mouth it has such lip muscles
such a suction of wet kisses
the slightest contact clingfilms your hands

there goes that dunlin up to her chin in
the simmering dish of mush and
all night that seeping feeding sound
of moistness digesting smallness

and then I creep-slid out over the grey weed,
and all those slimy foodpods burst under me
I thought I know whose tongue I'm
treading on and under whose closed eye

every stone every shell every sock
every bone will be crammed in.
to my unease the meal went on and on
there were those queues of reeds

dipping their straws in the dead
there was that sly tide swiftly refining
I thought really I should have webbed feet
I should have white wings to walk here

& facsimile from *The Minotaur*
Harrison Birtwistle

97

Ludbrooke: His Old Approach
Alan Brownjohn

Ludbrooke remembers saying to a girl
Watch this space! Which girl he can't recollect,
Or the space in which he planned to reappear.
He seems to think it had been a time for action,
A time for trying out some new approach;
But his only action had been to bark *Watch this space!*
And smile, he hoped intriguingly, as he left her
– And was that enough to count as an 'approach'?
Then whether he said it sober or after drinking
He is unsure. He keeps this metaphorical
Cabinet of approaches for future use.
How is it they gather dust even in the darkness
Of metal drawers too cumbersome to pull out?

& *from* It Must Change
Marjorie Perloff

[…]

For many of us, [the] blurring of boundaries has been regarded as a
healthy sign, a marker of our new found *interdisciplinarity*. Perhaps. But,
whatever the 'inter' in the topics listed above, there is one discipline that
is conspicuously absent, and that discipline is what the Greeks called
Poetike, the discipline of Poetics. True, the South African Truth
Commission may be better understood when we examine its workings
as a form of theater, and the meaning of 'holiness' for the followers of
John Wycliff may well have a strong rhetorical component. But in these
and related cases, the 'literary,' if it matters at all, is always secondary; it
has at best an instrumental value. Accordingly, it would be more accu-
rate to call the predominant activity of contemporary 'literary' scholars
other-disciplinary rather than *inter*-disciplinary.

PR 97:3, 2007
PR 97:1, 2007

Why *is* the 'merely' literary so suspect today? There can be no easy answer to this question, but perhaps the first thing to acknowledge is that it is by no means a new one. Consider, for instance, the argument of Plato's *Ion*. This early dialogue, written sometime in the first decade of the fourth century BCE, is set in Athens: it presents Socrates in conversation with the rhapsode Ion, who has just returned from Epidarus, where he has won first prize at a festival in honor of Asclepius. A *rhapsode* was part performance artist, part literary critic; he gave public recitations, followed by critical commentaries upon them and drew large audiences. Ostensibly Ion, whose specialty was Homer, drew twenty thousand people at Epidaurus; he wore a golden crown and received handsome payment.

Socrates begins by positing that surely a *rhapsode* 'must comprehend the utterances of the poet [in question], for the *rhapsode* must become an interpreter of the poet's thought (*dianoia*) for those who listen.'[1] How is it, he wonders, that Ion is 'skilled in Homer, but not in Hesiod or the other poets'? After all, Socrates suggests, don't all the poets talk about war, about the relations of men, good and bad, the birth of gods and heroes, and so on? Ion has no answer: he only knows that Hesiod puts him to sleep whereas he adores Homer. To which Socrates responds:

> The riddle is not hard to solve, my friend. Now, it is plain to everyone that not from art and knowledge (*ouk techne kai episteme*) comes your power concerning Homer. If it were *techne* (art, method) that gave you power, then you could speak about all the other poets as well. (532c)

Indeed, Socrates concludes, it is not through art (*ouk en technes*) but through divine inspiration [*en-theos*], through being taken out of his senses (*ekplexis*) that the *rhapsode* can recite and comment on Homer (533, 35): he is, in fact, a second-order or lesser poet, no more than a middleman passing along the Homeric aura. Thus, in the rest of the dialogue, Socrates 'proves' that Ion knows less about charioteering than any charioteer and hence cannot properly talk about athletic contests in Homer, and that the same thing is true for the physician, the diviner, and the fisherman. Defensively, Ion finally responds that what he does know is 'The kind of

---

1 Plato, 'Ion', trans. Lane Cooper, *The Collected Dialogues of Plato*, ed. Edith Hamilton and Huntington Cairns (Princeton University Press, Bollingen Series LXXI, 1961), pp. 216–28. I refer, as is conventional, to the marginal sigla, here §530, of the standard Greek edition. *The Republic*, trans. Paul Shorey, is cited from the same Bollingen edition.

thing [...] that man would say, and a woman would say, and a slave and free man, a subject and a ruler – the suitable thing, for each' (540b). This is in fact the doctrine of *to prepon* ('fitness'), which will become central in Aristotle's *Poetics*. But here Socrates pooh-poohs the idea and concludes that there is no such thing as an art and science of poetry, no such thing, in other words, as literary criticism.

Logically speaking, this conclusion has always been difficult to counter. Whereas economists or physicists, geologists or climatologists, physicians and lawyers, must master a body of knowledge before they can even think of being licensed to practice, we literary scholars, it is tacitly assumed, have no definable expertise. Is it a question of having mastered the history of English literature from Beowulf to the present? Certainly, in the United States this is no longer a requirement: we are, after all, not British, and besides downplaying American literature, the EngLit requirement would not include Anglophone literature from Australia and Africa, from the Caribbean and Canada. The same argument applies in the case of French or German or Spanish literature.

Is our expertise, then, in literary theory? For a brief moment in the sixties and seventies, this seemed to be the case: 'everyone' had to know their Marx and Freud, their Benjamin and Adorno, their Foucault and Derrida, their Lacan and Kristeva. But increasingly, this Eurocentric theory has come to seem less than adequate in dealing with the growing body of minority, transnational and postcolonial literature, and so poststructuralist theory is being replaced by critical race studies and related models, but so eclectic have the categories become that in most colleges and universities there is now no theory requirement at all.

The third traditional role of literary studies – evaluation – is currently dismissed as largely anachronistic. Value is generally understood as a cultural product: what we value depends on our race, class, gender, and ethnicity, our prior educational experience, our age, and so on. There are no universally 'great' works, no individual geniuses. True, Shakespeare continues, somewhat grudgingly, to be taught and studied everywhere, but I have heard prominent scholars say this is not because the author William Shakespeare wrote such unique and wonderful plays, plays to which we feel everyone should be exposed, but because Shakespeare is now a code word for a giant culture industry and historical complex: a carrier of socio-political meanings too influential to ignore.

Given these aporias of literary study, perhaps, administrators are beginning to argue, English departments should concentrate on the study of composition and rhetoric, disciplines that really do teach students things they need to know, and on language learning, so important in business, professional life, and especially for those in government or with government contracts. Indeed, as you have all heard, the current administration has made a great push to strengthen the role of the 'less-frequently taught' languages – Arabic, Farsi, Chinese, and so on – in the curriculum.

Still, I wonder how many of us, no matter how culturally and politically oriented our own particular research may be, would be satisfied with the elimination of literary study from the curriculum? Again, Plato provides us with an understanding of the conundrum. It is the Plato of the *Republic* who argues that the future Guardians of the State should not be exposed to poetry, precisely because the poetic is too appealing, too seductive, too dangerous, too prone to the telling of powerful 'lies' about gods and mortals. [...]

But how and why does the art called poetry exert such a magic spell? If it brings us no closer to the true or the good (the exemplary case of the latter is the Nazi love of Goethe and Beethoven), how can it be judged powerful enough to be dangerous, to transform the lives of those it touches? Again, why do so many people want to *be* poets, novelists, artists, composers, even as others, like many of us here tonight, want to be *rhapsodes*?

[...]

A specter is haunting the academy, the specter of literature. Just this year, 2006, Terry Eagleton, perhaps best known for such theory primers as *Literary Theory: An Introduction* (1983) and *The Ideology of the Aesthetic* (1990), has published a book called *How to Read a Poem*. Eagleton's opening chapter, 'The Functions of Criticism,' begins as follows:

> I first thought of writing this book when I realized that hardly any of the students of literature I encountered these days practiced what I myself had been trained to regard as literary criticism. Like thatching or clog dancing, literary criticism seems to be something of a dying art.[2]

It is not, Eagleton goes on to say, that students don't read texts closely. 'Close reading is not the issue. The question is not how tenaciously you cling to the text, but what you are in search of when you do so.' Students today, he worries, are only taught 'content analysis'. [...]

---

2   Terry Eagleton, *How to Read a Poem* (Blackwell, 2007), p. 1.

I think this is right on the mark. I have heard graduate students discuss the vagaries of romantic self-consciousness in Shelley's 'Ode to the West Wind' who cannot tell you what an ode is, what apostrophe is, or why (much less how) this one is written in terza rima. But whose fault is this? Not that of theory, for consider – and I concur – the excellent theorists, from Roman Jakobson and William Empson to Hélène Cixous and Julia Kristeva, who have written close critical commentary on particular poems. Rather, Eagleton posits, the culprit is 'a specific way of life'. 'What threatens to scupper verbal sensitivity,' according to Eagleton, 'is the depthless, commodified, instantly legible world of advanced capitalism, with its unscrupulous way with signs, computerized communication and glossy packaging of "experience".' Indeed, 'what is at peril on our planet is *"experience itself"*.'

[...]

Who, then, is being duped here, and how? You may recall that in 2004 the National Endowment for the Arts issued a report called *Reading at Risk* that concluded ominously, from a survey of respondents who were asked how many 'literary' books (novels, poems, and plays) they had read in the preceding year, that the current cultural 'crisis' is such that 'literary reading as a leisure activity will virtually disappear in a half century.'[3] But what *is* 'literary reading' and is such reading confined to books? [...] Is reading fiction, never mind *what* fiction, always preferable to reading an essay like [...] one from *Smoking Gun* on line? And what about the values of book production? When Penguin, one of the most distinguished publishers, brought out the Pevear translation of *Anna Karenina* in 2001, its cover depicted the nude knees of a woman, with a bouquet of flowers held by her right hand, between the knees. This was the edition picked up by the Oprah Book Club, the edition that sold nine hundred thousand copies. *Anna Karenina*, anyone?

[...]

Contemplating such questions, those of us who teach literature may come to see that we have a lot more *expertise* than we think we have. It is time to trust the literary instinct that brought us to this field in the first place and to recognize that, rather than lusting after those other disciplines that seem so exotic primarily because we don't really practice them, what we need is more theoretical, historical, and critical training in our own discipline. *Rhapsodes*, it turns out, can and should serve a real

3 Dana Gioia (ed.), *Reading at Risk: A Survey of Literary Reading in America* (National Endowment for the Arts, 2004).

function in our oral, print and digital culture. Supply and demand, or should I say, surveying the Beckett field of 2006, demand and supply: the time is fast coming, I believe, when this basic law must and will operate in our favor.

Presidential Address, MLA; December 2006.

98

One Secret Thing
Sharon Olds

One secret thing happened
at the end of my mother's life, when I was
alone with her. I knew it should happen –
I knew someone was there, in there,
something less unlike my mother than
anything else on earth. And the jar
was there on the table, the space around it
pulled back from it, like the awestruck handmade
air around the crèche, and her open
mouth, was parched. It was late. The lid
eased off. I watched my finger draw through
the jelly, its egg-sex essence, the four
corners of the room were not creatures, were not
the four winds of the earth, if I did not
do this, what was I – I rubbed the cowlick of
petrolatum on the skin around where the
final measures of what was almost not
breath swayed, and her throat made a guttural
stream-bed sound, like pebbly relief. But each
lip was stuck by chap to its row

PR 98:1, 2008

of teeth, stuck fast. And then I worked
for my motherhood, my humanhood, I
slid my forefinger slowly back and
forth, along the scab-line and underlying
canines and incisors, upper lip and then
lower lip, until, like a basted
seam, softly ripped, what had been
joined was asunder, I ran the salve in-
side the folds, along the gums,
common mercy. The secret was
how deeply I did not want to touch
inside her, and how much the act
was an act of escape, my last chance
to free myself.

99 Song for Natalie 'Tusja' Beridze
Don Paterson

O Natalie, O TBA, O Tusja: I had long assumed the terrorists'
balaclava that you sport on the cover of *Annulé* –
    which was, for too long, the only image of you I possessed –
was there to conceal some ugliness or deformity
    or perhaps merely spoke (and here, I hoped against hope) of a
young woman struggling
    with a crippling shyness. How richly this latter theory has
been confirmed by my Googling!

O who is this dark angel with her unruly Slavic eyebrows ranged like two duelling pistols, lightly sweating in the pale light of the TTF screen?

O behold her shaded, infolded concentration, her heartbreakingly beautiful face so clearly betraying the true focus of one not merely content – as, no doubt, were others at the Manöver Elektronische Festival in Wien –

to hit *play* while making some fraudulent correction to a volume slider

but instead deep in the manipulation of some complex real-time software such as Ableton Live, MAX/MSP or Supercollider.

O Natalie, how can I pay tribute to your infinitely versatile blend of Nancarrow, Mille Plateaux, Venetian Snares, Xenakis, Boards of Canada and Nobukazu Takemura

to say nothing of those radiant pads – so strongly reminiscent of the mid-century bitonal pastoral of Charles Koechlin in their harmonic bravura –

or your fine vocals, which, while admittedly limited in range and force, are nonetheless so much more affecting than the affected Arctic whisperings of those interchangeably dreary

Stinas and Hannes and Björks, being in fact far closer in spirit to a kind of glitch-hop Blossom Dearie?

I have also deduced from your staggeringly ingenious employment of some pretty basic wavetables

that unlike many of your East European counterparts, all your VST plug-ins, while not perhaps the best available

probably all have a legitimate upgrade path – indeed I imagine your entire DAW as pure as the driven snow, and not in any way buggy or virusy

which makes me love you more, demonstrating as it does an excess of virtue given your country's well-known talent for software piracy.

Though I should confess that at times I find your habit of maxxing
   the range with those bat-scaring ring-modulated sine-bursts
and the more distressing psychoacoustic properties of phase
inversion in the sub-bass frequencies somewhat taxing
   you are nonetheless as beautiful as the mighty Boards
themselves in your shameless organicizing of the code,
   as if you had mined those saws and squares and ramps straight
from the Georgian motherlode.

O Natalie – I forgive you everything, even your catastrophic
adaptation of those lines from 'Dylan's' already shite
   Do Not Go Gentle Into That Good Night
in the otherwise magnificent 'Sleepwalkers', and when you
open up those low-
   pass filters in what sounds like a Minimoog emulation they
seem to open in my heart also.

O Natalie: know that I do not, repeat, do *not* imagine you
with a reconditioned laptop bought with a small grant from the
local arts cooperative in the cramped back bedroom of an
ex-Communist apartment block in Tbilisi or Kutaisi
   but at the time of writing your biographical details are
extremely hazy;
   however, I feel sure that by the time this poem sees the light
of day Wire magazine will have honoured you with a far more
extensive profile than you last merited when mention of that
wonderful Pharrell remix
   was sandwiched between longer pieces on the notorious
Kyoto-based noise guitarist Idiot O'Clock, and a woman called
Sonic Pleasure who plays the housebricks.

However this little I have gleaned: firstly, that you are
married to Thomas Brinkmann, whose records are boring – an
opinion I held long before love carried me away –
   and secondly, that TBA
is not an acronym, as I had first assumed, but Georgian for
'lake' – in which case it probably has a silent 't', like 'Tbilisi', and
so is pronounced *baa*

which serendipitously rhymes a bit with my only other word
of Georgian, being your term for 'mother' which is 'dada', or
possibly 'father' which is 'mama'.

I doubt we will ever meet, unless this somehow reaches you
on the wind;
we will never sit with a glass of tea in your local wood-lined
café while I close-question you on how you programmed that
unbelievably great snare on 'Wind',
of such brickwalled yet elastic snap it sounded exactly like a
12" plastic ruler bent back and released with great violence on
the soft gong
of a large white arse, if not one white for long.

But Natalie – Tusja, if I may – I will not pretend I hold much
hope for us, although I have, I confess, worked up my little
apologia:
I am not like those other middle-agey I-
DM enthusiasts: I have none of their hangdog pathos, my geekery is
the dirty secret that it should be
and what I lack in hair, muscle-tone and rugged good looks I make
up for with a dry and ready wit... but I know that time and space
conspire against me.

At least, my dear, let me wish you the specific best:
may you be blessed
with the wonderful instrument you deserve, fitted – at the
time of writing – with a 2 Ghz dual-core Intel chip and enough
double-pumped DDR2 RAM for the most CPU-intensive
processes;
then no longer will all those gorgeous acoustic spaces

be accessible only via an offline procedure involving a
freeware convolution reverb and an imperfectly recorded
impulse response of the Concertgebouw made illegally with a
hastily-erected stereo pair and an exploded crisp bag
for I would have all your plug-ins run in real-time, in the
blameless zero-latency heaven of the 32-bit floating-point
environment, with no buffer-glitch or freeze or dropout or lag;

I would also grant you a golden midi controller, of such
responsiveness, smoothness of automation, travel and increment
    that you would think it a transparent intercessor, a mere
copula, and feel machine and animal suddenly blent.

    This I wish you as I leave Inverkeithing and Fife
    listening to *Trepa N* for the two hundred and thirty-fourth
time in my life
    with every hair on my right arm rising in non-fascistic one-
armed salutation
    towards Natalie, my Tba, my Tusja, and all the mountain
lakes of her small nation.

100

Vanitas
David Harsent

i

The death's-head bell has a tongue like a barber's strop
capped with a dangle of shot... meanwhile

she takes the flower she was bound to cut
and places it in the vase, displacing a single drop

of water onto the satin cloth, and stoops to set
a sand-clock on the other side. It's troubling to see the weal

that tracks from her cheek to her throat and out of sight
by the ruche of her blouse; the hang of her lower lip,

fattened by weeping; the way the light
brings a touch of blue to her cheekbone, the first of night.

The garden is crowding the window. From where I sit,
I can watch the silhouettes of nightbirds fall

on the upper panes, grow still a moment, then peel
off and away, as if they had rested briefly in the glaze;

but the woman, without asking, brings a light
the better to see herself in the darkening glass

her face amid a smudge of wings and trees
as she stands looking out but also looking back

to me in my chair, near-breathless as I can get,
silent, saying nothing with my eyes.

This is a lesson, I think, in how to feel:
the bloom, the woman, her wound, that the chair is set

slightly to one side, that my hands now fall
slack to my lap... and, of course, love in the guise

of a skull licked clean, the dome chock-full
of darkness, of errant music, of thoughts of me.

ii

Imagine a shred of song drawn through a blown egg, think
of a whisper held in an empty house, of a promise made

in a moment of weakness, of who you have to thank
as the eye-sockets flicker and fill, as the lips repair,

the voice thin but distinct: *You see in me
the last of the feckless romancers: his smile, the smile*

of the beside companion, the smile-in-air
of the trickster, the smile of betrayer betrayed,

of the just-abandoned or else the soon-to-be,
of the hangman, the hanged man, the dog-faced boy,

the hobbledehoy, the jack-in-the-box, the shill,
of tyrant and martyr coming together in joy...

The woman starts the clock; a petal falls;
darkness settles to perfect night; the bell

carries a note too deep or else too shrill
to break the silence. Best to be watchful now, best to be still

what happens next is anybody's guess:
the window a mirror perhaps, the room a wilderness.

Index of Authors

Acknowledgements

For permission to reprint copyright material, the following acknowledgements are made:

JOHN AGARD, 'Remember the Ship'. Reprinted by permission of the author. MONIZA ALVI, 'Eine Kleine Nachtmusik', from *Split World: Poems 1990–2005* (Bloodaxe Books, 2005). SIMON ARMITAGE, 'Chainsaw versus Pampas Grass' from *The Universal Home Doctor*, by Simon Armitage. © Simon Armitage. Reproduced by permission of Faber and Faber Ltd. JOHN ASHBERY, 'Avant de Quitter Ces Lieux' appeared in *Hotel Lautréamont* (Carcanet) and was subsequently published in *Notes from the Air: Selected Later Poems* (Carcanet). Copyright © 1992, 2007 by John Ashbery. All rights reserved. Used by permission of Georges Borchardt, Inc. and Carcanet Press Ltd. for the author. W.H. AUDEN, 'A New Year Greeting', from *Epistle to a Godson*, by W.H. Auden © The Estate of W.H. Auden. Reproduced by permission of Faber and Faber Ltd. PAUL AUSTER, 'After Jacques Dupin', from *Fits and Starts*. Reprinted by permission of the author. JOHN BAYLEY, from 'English Equivocation'. *English Equivocation* by John Bayley © 1986. Reprinted by the kind permission of Professor John Bayley. HILAIRE BELLOC, 'Desert' by Hilaire Belloc from *The Poetry Review* (© Hilaire Belloc, 1949) is reproduced by permission of PFD (www.pfd.co.uk) on behalf of The Estate of Hilaire Belloc. JOHN BERGER, from 'I Would Softly Tell My Love', from *Hold Everything Dear* (Verso, 2007). Reprinted by permission of Verso. JAMES BERRY, 'Bluefoot Traveller', from *Hot Earth Cold Earth* (Bloodaxe Books, 1995). LAURENCE BINYON, from 'The English Lyric'. Reprinted by permission of The Society of Authors as the Literary Representative of the Estate of Laurence Binyon. HARRISON BIRTWISTLE, 'Facsimile from The Minotaur'. Reprinted by permission of the author. EDMUND BLUNDEN, 'A Day in December'. Reprinted by permission. EAVAN BOLAND, 'What We Lost'. Reprinted by permission of the author and Carcanet Press Ltd. JOSEPH BRODSKY, 'Sextet' from *Collected Poems in English*, edited by Ann Kjellberg (Carcanet Press Ltd, 2001). 'Sextet' from *Collected Poems in English* by

Donald Hall'. © Copyright of the Estate of T.S. Eliot. Reproduced by permission of Faber and Faber Ltd. GAVIN EWART, 'The Peter Porter Poem of '83'. Reprinted by kind permission of Margo Ewart. HARRY FAINLIGHT, ['The Moon Shows Through']. Reprinted by permission of the Estate of Harry Fainlight. RUTH FAINLIGHT, 'The Same'. Reprinted by permission of the author. PAUL FARLEY, 'Big Safe Themes'. Reprinted by permission of the author. ELAINE FEINSTEIN, 'Another Anniversary'. Reprinted by permission of the author and Carcanet Press Ltd. JAMES FENTON, 'The Manifesto against Manifestoes'. Reprinted by permission of the author. LAWRENCE FERLINGHETTI, 'The Old Italians Dying'. Reprinted by permission of SLL/Sterling Lord Literistic, Inc. Copyright by Lawrence Ferlinghetti. ROBERT FROST, 'The Gift Outright' from *The Poetry of Robert Frost* edited by Edward Connery Lathem, published by Jonathan Cape. Reprinted by permission of the Random House Group Ltd. JOHN FULLER, 'England' from *Collected Poems by John Fuller*, published by Chatto & Windus. Reprinted by permission of The Random House Group Ltd. ROY FULLER, 'False Image'. Reprinted by permission of the Estate of Roy Fuller. DAVID GASCOYNE, 'Variations on a Phrase', from *Selected Poems* (Enitharmon Press). Reprinted by permission of Enitharmon Press. ALLEN GINSBERG, 'Bayonne entering NYC'. © 2006, The Allen Ginsberg Trust, all rights reserved. ROBERT GRAVES, 'The Chink', and from 'Chaucer's Man (On John Masefield)', from *Complete Poems In One Volume*, edited by Patrick Quinn (Carcanet Press Limited, 1995). THOM GUNN, 'The Painter as an Old Man'. Reprinted by permission of the Estate of Thom Gunn. JOHN HAFFENDEN, interviewing W.S. Graham, from 'I Would Say I Was a Happy Man'. Reprinted by permission of the author. IAN HAMILTON, from 'Ian Hamilton in conversation with Gregory Le Stage'. Reprinted by permission of Aitken Alexander Associates Ltd. IAN HAMILTON FINLAY, 'Evening/Sail', reprinted by permission of the Estate of Ian Hamilton Finlay. Tony Harrison, 'The Ode Not Taken' © Tony Harrison. Reproduced by permission of Faber and Faber Ltd. DAVID HARSENT, 'Vanitas'. Reprinted by permission of the author. RUPERT HART-DAVIS, CHARLES MONTEITH, DIANA ATHILL, COLIN FRANKLIN, ERICA MARX, 'Why Publish Poetry?'. Reprinted by permission. SEAMUS HEANEY, 'Man and Boy, from *Seeing Things*, by Seamus Heaney. © Seamus Heaney. Reproduced by permission of Faber and Faber Ltd. W.N. HERBERT, 'Cabaret McGonagall'. Reprinted by permission of the author. ZBIGNIEW HERBERT, 'Breviary', translated by George Gomori and Clive Wilmer. Reprinted by permission of the translators. GEOFFREY HILL, extracts from *Speech! Speech!* (Penguin, 2001) © Geoffrey Hill reproduced by permission of Penguin Books Ltd. PHILIP HOBSBAUM, from 'Larkin's England'. Reprinted with permission of Rosemary Hobsbaum c/o Dr David Sutton, Reading University Library. RICHARD HOGGART, from 'The Journey of Sidney Keyes'. Reprinted by permission of the Estate of Richard Hoggart. FRANCES HOROVITZ, 'Buzzard' from *Collected Poems* (Bloodaxe Books, 1985). TED HUGHES, 'Four Ages (*Metamorphoses*, Book I)' from *Tales from Ovid*, by Ted Hughes. © The Estate of Ted Hughes. Reproduced by permission of Faber and Faber Ltd. 'Four Ages' by Ted Hughes from *After Ovid: New Metamorphoses* edited by Michael Hofmann and James Lasdun. Anthology copyright © 1994 by Michael Hofmann and James Lasdun. Reprinted by permission of Farrar, Straus and Giroux, LLC. MICK IMLAH, from 'Twenty Ways of Saying Happy Birthday'. Reprinted by permission of the Estate of Mick Imlah. KATHLEEN JAMIE, 'In Praise of Aphrodite', from *Mr and Mrs Scotland are Dead* (Bloodaxe Books, 2002). ALAN JENKINS, 'Orpheus' from *A Shorter Life* by Alan Jenkins, published by Chatto & Windus. Reprinted by permission of the Random House Group Ltd. ELIZABETH JENNINGS, 'Goings', from *New Collected Poems*, by Elizabeth Jennings (Carcanet Press Ltd, 2002). JACKIE KAY, 'Darling', from *Darling: New & Selected Poems* (Bloodaxe Books, 2007). MIMI KHALVATI, 'Ghazal'. Reprinted by permission of the author and Carcanet Press Ltd. JOHN KINSELLA, from 'Lyric and Razo: Activism and the Poet'. Reprinted by permission of the author. PHILIP LARKIN, 'MCMXIV', from *The Whitsun Weddings*, by Philip Larkin, and 'Horror Poet, from *Required Writing: Miscellaneous Pieces, 1955–82*, by Philip Larkin. © The Estate of Philip Larkin. Reproduced by permission of Faber and Faber Ltd. 'Horror Poet' from *Required Writing* by Philip Larkin. Copyright © 1983 by Philip Larkin. 'MCMXIV' from *Collected Poems* by Philip Larkin. Copyright © 1988, 2003 by the Estate of Philip Larkin. Reprinted by permission of Farrar, Straus and Giroux, LLC. JOHN LEHMANN, from 'Relief and Admiration (on George Barker)'. Reprinted by permission of David Higham Associates, on behalf of the Estate of the author. PRIMO LEVI, 'Unfinished Business', from *Collected Poems*, by Primo Levi. © The Estate of Primo Levi. Reproduced by permission of Faber and Faber Ltd. 'Unfinished Business' from *Collected Poems* by Primo Levi, translated by Ruth Feldman and Brian Swann. English translation copyright © 1988 by Ruth Feldman and Brian Swann. Reprinted by permission of Faber and Faber, Inc. an affiliate of Farrar, Straus and Giroux, LLC. GWYNETH LEWIS, 'The Hedge', from *Chaotic Angels: Poems in English* (Bloodaxe Books, 2005). MICHAEL LONGLEY, 'A Poppy' from *Collected Poems* by Michael Longley, published by Jonathan Cape. Reprinted by permission of the Random House Group Ltd. JAMES LOVELOCK, 'Address to the Global Forum of Spiritual & Parliamentary Leaders on Human Survival'. Reprinted by permission of the author. EDWARD LUCIE-SMITH, from 'Thoughts After Advent'. Copyright © Edward Lucie-Smith. Reproduced by permission of the author c/o Rogers, Coleridge & White Ltd., 20 Powis Mews, London, W11 1JN. NORMAN MACCAIG, 'Introduction and a Selection' and 'Sounds of the Day'. Reprinted by permission of the Estate of Norman MacCaig. HUGH MACDIARMID, from 'Scottish Literature Today', and 'By Wauchopeside', from *Collected Poems* (Carcanet Press Ltd, 1993, 1994). GEORGE MACKAY BROWN, 'Beachcomber'. Reprinted by permission of The Estate of George Mackay Brown. LOUIS MACNEICE, from 'Broken Windows or Thinking Aloud', from *Selected Prose of Louis MacNeice*, edited by Alan Heuser (Oxford University Press, 1990). Reprinted by permission of the Estate of Louis MacNeice. SARAH MAGUIRE, from 'Adrienne Rich in Conversation with Sarah Maguire'. Reprinted by permission of the author. DEREK MAHON, 'Day Trip to Donegal'. Reprinted by kind permission of the author and The Gallery Press, Loughcrew, Oldcastle, County Meath, Ireland from *Collected Poems* (1999). F.T. MARINETTI, from 'Le Futurisme', translated by F.S. Flint. Reprinted by permission of the Estate of F.S. Flint. E.A. MARKHAM, from 'Truly, Deeply, Sonorously'. Reprinted by kind permission of the Estate of E. A. Markham. GLYN MAXWELL, from 'Letters to Edward Thomas'. Reprinted by permission of the author. PETER MCDONALD, from 'From Ulster with Love'. Reprinted by permission of the author. MEDBH MCGUCKIAN, 'Mariola with Angel Choir'. Reprinted by permission of the author. W.S. MERWIN, 'Europe'. Reprinted by permission of The Wylie Agency on behalf of the author. CZESŁAW MIŁOSZ, 'Prudence', translated by the author and Leonard Nathan. © 1995, Czesław Miłosz. All rights reserved. HARRIET MONROE, from 'Modern American Poetry'. Reprinted by permission of the Estate of Harriet Monroe. EDWIN MORGAN, 'For the "International Poetry Incarnation", Royal Albert Hall, 11 June 1965'. Reprinted by permission of the author and Carcanet Press Ltd. ANDREW MOTION, from 'Skating: Memories of Childhood'. Reprinted by permission of the author. PAUL MULDOON, 'Why Brownlee Left', from *Poems 1968–1998*, by Paul Muldoon. © Paul Muldoon. Reproduced by permission of Faber and Faber Ltd. LES MURRAY, 'The Holy Show'. Reprinted by permission of the author and Carcanet Press Ltd. HENRY NEWBOLT, from 'Robert Bridges, The Classical Poet'. Reprinted by permission of the Estate of Henry Newbolt. SEAN O'BRIEN, 'Authentically Excruciating' and 'Fantasia on a

Mrinalini. Reprinted by permission of Visva-Bharati. R.S. THOMAS, 'All Soul's Night'. © Kunjana Thomas, 2001. Reprinted by the permission of the Estate of R.S. Thomas. ANTHONY THWAITE, 'Memories of Rothwell House'. Reprinted by permission of the author. SYLVIA TOWNSEND WARNER, 'The Raven', from *New Collected Poems*, edited by Claire Harman (Fyfield Books, Carcanet Press Ltd, 2008). DEREK WALCOTT, from 'The Poet in the Theatre'; the Poetry Book Society's Ronald Duncan Lecture at the Purcell Room, South Bank Centre, on 29 September 1990. Reprinted with permission of the Poetry Book Society. C.K. WILLIAMS, 'Grief', from *Collected Poems* (Bloodaxe Books, 2006). 'Grief' from *The Vigil* by C.K. Williams. Copyright © 1997 by C.K. Williams. Reprinted by permission of Farrar, Straus and Giroux, LLC. HUGO WILLIAMS, 'Egg and Spoon'. Reprinted by permission of the author. JAMES WOOD, from 'Terry Eagleton in Conversation with James Wood'. Reprinted by permission of the author.

The editor would like to thank James Brookes, Paulette Burke and Rebecka Mustajarvi for their editorial assistance.

Every effort has been made to trace copyright holders. The Poetry Society apologises if any material has been included without appropriate acknowledgement and would be glad to correct any errors or omissions in future editions.